CONVERSATIONS WITH McCARTNEY

Paul Du Noyer was a music journalist for more than 30 years, whose interviewees ranged from Madonna to Pavarotti, David Bowie to Mick Jagger and The Beatles, not least Paul McCartney and Ringo Starr. Born in Liverpool, Paul was educated at the London School of Economics. He has written the definitive musical histories of both Liverpool and London.

CONVERSATIONS WITH McCARTNEY

Paul Du Noyer

HODDER &
STOUGHTON

First published in Great Britain in 2015 by
Hodder & Stoughton
An Hachette UK company

First published in paperback in 2016

2

A CIP catalogue record for this title is available from the British Library

Paperback ISBN 978 1 473 60904 4

Typeset in Bembo by Palimpsest Book Production Limited,
Falkirk, Stirlingshire

Printed and bound by Clays Ltd, St Ives plc

Hodder & Stoughton policy is to use papers that are natural, renewable and recyclable products and made from wood grown in sustainable forests. The logging and manufacturing processes are expected to conform to the environmental regulations of the country of origin.

Hodder & Stoughton Ltd
Carmelite House
50 Victoria Embankment
London EC4Y 0DZ

www.hodder.co.uk

For my parents

Contents

Introduction ix

PART ONE

1 Things He Said Today 3
2 Rocker with a Lolly Ice 13
3 How to Become a Beatle 26
4 The Toppermost 43
5 It Started to Be Art 57
6 My Dark Hour 73
7 Rage Against the Machine 82
8 The Astronaut and the Moon 91
9 Starting From Scratch 100
10 Soaring 108
11 Wings Folded 117
12 Of Frogs and Firemen 127
13 That's a Great Idea, Eddie! 138
14 British Light Music 148
15 John 158

PART TWO

16	Unfinished Business	171
17	Apollo C. Vermouth	185
18	A Pot of Gold	196
19	This Magic Experiment	206
20	Beyond the Smile	217
21	Living is Easy with Nice Clothes	230
22	Heaven and Earth	237
23	Punks and Rivals	249
24	If I Were Not Upon the Stage	255
25	Another Wide Prairie	266
26	More Cowbell	275
27	Do It Now	286
28	Fallibility	292
29	Linda	305
30	Love	319
	Finale: Fifty Favourites	326
	Acknowledgements	337
	Index	339
	List of Illustrations	351

Introduction

I don't actually want to be a living legend. I came in this to get out of having a job. And to pull birds. And I pulled quite a few birds, and got out of having a job, so you know, that's where I am still.

Paul McCartney

The nearest I have come to dying, so far, was an asthma attack in childhood. I found myself in a Liverpool hospital with an oxygen mask clamped to my face and radio headphones on my ears. The station was broadcasting the Beatles' new record *Abbey Road* in its entirety. That is why, when people call the group's music 'life-affirming', I understand them in a very literal way. At that moment, I suddenly realised how much I loved them, and how much I wanted to live.

That was in 1969. Whereupon, of course, the bastards split up.

I forgave them, naturally, and followed all their solo careers with rapt attention. I grew up and became a music journalist, with the good luck to interview Paul McCartney on many occasions. John Lennon died before I ever had a chance to meet him, which is my biggest professional regret. But Paul and I seemed to hit it off.

That is how this book came about. I have drawn together our scattered conversations from each of those encounters, and reordered them into a single narrative. From it emerges, I hope, the story of McCartney the musician, told in his own words with a few of mine as well. His long career has produced a stupendous body of work that rewards listeners at every turn.

His position is unparalleled, whether we measure it in commercial success, artistic achievement, or his influence on others. In terms of posterity, his reputation will ultimately be unassailable. I'd also contend that McCartney's music, sometimes dismissed by critics as safe and bland, is more often questing and downright strange.

Since he joined John Lennon's band the Quarrymen in 1957, Paul has scarcely paused for breath. He'll write a timeless love song with the same ease that other people draw breath. He'll play rock and roll with more raw sex and aggression than you tend to encounter outside of penal institutions. The Queen of England thinks he's marvellous, but even the edgiest avant-garde types admit that his music can take a walk on the weird side. From kiddie-pop to classical, there is hardly a genre that he hasn't tried; probably only Picasso could rival Paul McCartney's claim to stylistic breadth.

It's actually very hard to have a hit record. To keep on having them is practically impossible. For all his peaks and troughs, McCartney's career rivals that of any contender we might nominate. The crumbs from his table would be the pride of lesser songwriters. The glory of show business is that it gives the people what they want. The glory of art is that it gives us what we never knew we wanted. And the glory of Paul McCartney is that he does both.

Have the results been consistently wonderful? Not at all. But when his star is in the ascendant there is no composer in the whole of popular music to match this man's ability to write the songs that make the whole world sing.

The Beatles attained a state of pop perfection very early on. After that, they did what seemed incredible, by revealing with each new record a new and completely different type of perfection. It couldn't last forever and it didn't. But Paul, like John Lennon, was expected to perform the impossible again and again, or else be held to the cruellest of accounts.

Paul, it was allowed, had a craftsman's facility that could glide from manic to manicured. But his soul, it was said, was still in show business. While his achievements as a Beatle made him a hip figurehead of the new rock culture they had helped to create, his heart could not abandon the occasional nursery rhyme or treat for the mums and dads.

A shameless crowd-pleaser, then? The stereotype has a nugget of truth, insofar as he never saw a reason to limit his musical palette. But it does him a grave disservice in suggesting that he was a lesser artist by virtue of his versatility. If you were feeling poetical you could say McCartney's work is like an oak tree: the trunk is strong and broad but its branches spread and twist in fantastical patterns.

He wisely shies away from this analogy, but Picasso's transcendence of category, his sure grasp of traditional skills with an appetite for the new and untried, are things McCartney admires. And by now there is also the sheer enormity of his output, a tribute to both his energy and longevity. McCartney's music has not developed in any one direction over time. Instead it resembles a kind of unwinding spiral, achieving an ever-wider circumference.

Born on 18 June 1942, Paul McCartney emerged before the days of rock and roll; he was formed in a world that has utterly vanished now, and which was hastened on its way by the Beatles themselves. He came of age in the aftermath of the Second World War, one of the biggest disruptions in human history. All minds were now fixed on a *modern* world, and the less it resembled the past, the better. Nothing could be learned by looking backward. Or so it felt at the time.

Paul could be every inch the teenage rebel that his generation specialised in producing. But he was never, in his heart, an iconoclast. That's a contradiction that has persisted throughout his music, and it's the source of some critics' contempt for what he did. But it's really one key to his greatness. He's among the last of that dwindling number who were not fundamentally shaped by rock, because they already had some musical understanding before it reached their ears.

~

But this book is not all about the Beatles. I once mentioned to McCartney how writers tend to compress the decades of his life after 1970 into a desultory postscript. Paul replied:

> Now you mention it, you can see it. I've met enough journalists, having to get articles that are winners, to know the game. 'He was a Beatle.' That's basically the game. Any book on John Lennon they do the same. They condense the Yoko period: 'Oh yeah, peace chants, they wore funny hats and sunglasses, and he was militant, wasn't he?' It compresses fairly easily.
>
> But I like it in a way – it's the same about music that I've written in that period – because I think it's undiscovered. It's really been blanked: 'No, he didn't write anything since the Beatles.'
>
> Once you start to look . . . I mean, commercially there definitely are things that outsold anything the Beatles did, like 'Mull of Kintyre'. But critically I don't think people would consider that. Although an awful lot of people liked it, so who am I?

It's not that he's embarrassed by the Beatles, even if their legacy dogged his early solo years. In all my interviews I found he'd bring them up more often than I did:

> I used to say to my kids, 'You're the only ones who never ask me about the Beatles!' I used to wish their friends would come round and say, 'What was it like being in the Beatles?' 'Well, let

> me tell you . . .' And the kids would all go out the room: 'Oh bloody hell . . .'
>
> That's how kids are, they don't want to hear about that shit, but their friends would. So I'd chunter on [*cheerful windbag*]: 'Oh! It's funny you should say that!' An hour later . . .

The trap is that the Beatles make us skimp the great music he's made in his forty-five solo years. In this book I want to correct that imbalance. Paul said to me that his career will one day be seen in its totality. I'd like to think that day has arrived.

The richness and diversity of McCartney's solo work, from that infamous chorus of frogs to his most esoteric electronica, needs to be recognised. The beauty of his back catalogue is in its endless variations and surprises. The devil may be in the detail, but in McCartney's case we find our angels there as well.

His own repertoire runs into many hundreds of songs. We all know that he wrote 'Penny Lane' and 'Hey Jude'. We should acknowledge that after that came lesser-known beauties that will, in the end, outlive us all. McCartney's post-Beatle material is a curiously undervalued treasure trove of pop history. He agrees:

> That's my theory, that in years to come, people may actually look at *all* my work rather than the context of it following the Beatles. That's the danger, as it came from 'Here There and Everywhere', 'Yesterday', 'Fool on the Hill', to 'Bip Bop' [from Wings' *Wild Life*], which is such an inconsequential little song. I must say, I've always hated that song.
>
> I think there will be an element of that in time to come. And with John's work too. They'll look at it in greater detail and think, Ah, I see what he was getting at. Because it's not obvious, that's the good thing. It's a bit more subtle than some of the stuff we've done, which was out-and-out commercial. But I think it'll look more and more normal as time goes on.

Though I've rearranged the sequences, the earliest interview in this book dates from 1979, when I was sent to a backstage press conference before a Paul McCartney Liverpool concert. It was a dream assignment, and the moment I realised I had stumbled into the right career. If the book is not so much a biography as a portrait, it's at least a portrait taken from life. With a couple of cited exceptions, every McCartney quote you'll read here is first-hand.

I met Paul regularly when I was a journalist on magazines such as *NME*, *Q*, *MOJO* and *The Word*. I also helped him on editorial projects including tour brochures, press kits and album liner notes. Our focus was always on the music, though not in a narrow or technical way; in talking of his songs he'd share many memories, and describe the personal joys and sorrows he had felt along the way. There are certainly gaps in the narrative that follows, because we always had particular topics to cover. But he talked freely about every stage of his career.

Part One of this book is roughly chronological, and Part Two is more thematic. In real life his conversation is liable to roam back and forth, and I have 'remixed' our interviews to improve continuity. In all, across those thirty years and more, he vividly described for me the whole business of being Paul McCartney.

It helped that I was from Liverpool. We both began our lives in Anfield, the district of terraced streets around the famous football ground; then we moved out to identical houses on opposite sides of the city. Twelve years apart, we'd attended similar schools. We would sometimes digress and discuss bus routes, docks and department stores in absurd detail.

But in his own mind he never became the superstar he became in everyone else's. He hates to look remote, or grand, and he always took pains to make our interviews *feel* like conversations.

I don't pretend to be his friend, but our encounters were friendly. I saw at close range the crushing demands on his time and attention. He bore it all with remarkable patience, including my incessant questions. I came away with the idea that Paul McCartney is a decent guy, who happens to be a genius.

PART ONE

CHAPTER I

Things He Said Today

Interviewing McCartney

It's impossible at first to forget you are 'talking to Paul McCartney'. During our interviews my mind would flood with memories of growing up, listening to his music, knowing him only as some semi-mythical phantom. Any lifelong Beatle fan would feel the same, and it takes a while to master this star-struck awe. Since then I've observed the tense excitement of other people who found themselves in his presence for the first time.

The man himself will handle it with practised ease and winning self-effacement. It's a skill that everyone has noticed in Paul McCartney – variously interpreted as plain good manners or, less favourably, the manipulative charm of a PR schemer. I think he does have a good understanding of how he appears to the outside world, but he is not obsessed by questions of image. Most probably, the years of experience have taught him how to turn his natural affability into an everyday *modus operandi*.

Nor are musicians immune to the weight of all that history. I've interviewed all Paul's band members since 1989 and each confessed an occasional sense of inner disbelief. Guitarists describe the on-stage thrill of playing the very riffs they'd wrestled with as raw beginners. Co-vocalists recall the astonishment of trading harmonies with a voice from the first records they ever owned. Drummers talk of summoning up the courage to lock into a rhythm with the most celebrated bass player of all time. In the end, they're professionals and they cope, but who can fault them for those heart-stopping moments?

I believe my own heart stopped, on the day in my childhood when Paul McCartney of the Beatles drove past me in his Mini car, in a country lane near Liverpool. We were out in search of footballers' houses, to pester them for autographs. But a real Beatle? Taking a spin around the turnip fields of Lancashire? This was stardom on a planetary level: 'Did you just see what I saw?' And when I first saw Paul perform, with Wings at the Liverpool Empire, I think I was one of thousands in the crowd who marvelled as much at being in the same room as him, as at the music itself. Such are the feelings of all fans, everywhere the world.

Then there were the times when I was McCartney's whole audience. Awaiting my interview slot I'd sit at rehearsals and find myself a few feet away, the sole abstracted object of his gaze while he found the piano chords to 'Fool on the Hill', or thundered through 'All Shook Up', as if I were an entire stadium of souls in one body. Around the room were his regular team, so oddly unconcerned, unravelling cables, shifting instrument cases, finding quiet corners to make phone calls. I was the only one with the leisure to watch and marvel.

The interviews in this book were mostly done at two locations: either his London office, MPL, or his Sussex studio, the Mill. The former is a tall and narrow townhouse overlooking Soho Square. During our conversations, by the wide window of his upstairs room, Paul's eye might wander across the leafy lawns where office-workers like to lunch. MPL's interior style is quietly art deco. Its walls are hung with modern paintings, or framed photos by Linda McCartney, and pride of place goes to her famous shot of Paul and John, laughing and grasping each other's hands at a *Sgt. Pepper* party in 1967.

The Mill, officially called Hog Hill, is a few hours' drive from London in calm countryside near the south coast. Its ancient precincts now house rehearsal space and a recording studio. Propped in one corner is the double-bass played by Elvis Presley's sideman Bill Black, a true totem of rock-and-roll history and bought by Linda as a birthday present. I never dared touch it – nor the storied Höfner bass so often by my chair – but Paul was wont to give the instrument a reassuring pluck when he walked past.

His daily work schedule is quite structured and we were rarely interrupted, except for tea and chocolate biscuits. 'Or have a cappuccino,' he might say at MPL. 'Don't forget, la' [the Scouser's pally contraction of 'lad'], you're in Soho now.'

From the earliest days of the Beatles he was noted for diplomacy, especially when set against the abrasive Lennon. On stage he talked the most to audiences, even if John was seen as the leader. And in foreign countries he makes the effort to speak a little of their own language. But diplomats are mistrusted for their guile, as much as they may be praised for tact or sensitivity to the feelings of others.

Yet I've never found him the calculating PR man that detractors allege. Take, for instance, his unwisely dull response to John Lennon's murder in 1980 – 'It's a drag, isn't it?' – when a magisterial statement, carefully prepared, was so badly needed. He was, at that moment, sincerely numbed by shock and grief, but the quote caught fire. His handling of the Beatles' split, described in another chapter, was likewise a case of blunders off the cuff, hardly a masterpiece of spin.

He's more comfortable than most stars, though, in the set-piece interview. McCartney's played the media game for much longer than any writer that comes to meet him. He was schmoozing the *NME* (when it was still the *New Musical Express*) whole decades before its current staff were born. He is familiar with the music magazines and TV shows in any given territory. Like Queen Elizabeth II, who has received every prime minister since Winston Churchill, he has seen them come and seen them go.

'There's always gonna be someone who'll detract from what you do,' he says:

> When we [The Beatles] first came into it there was a guy at the *Daily Mirror* called Donald Zec, and his whole gig was being mean. If you got an interview with him, there was a danger he was gonna turn it on you. But everyone else was really quite nice. You'd sit down and [*eagerly*]: 'Oh yeah. I'll tell you about my album.'
>
> But it's become *more* like that now. A lot of people have figured, 'That's a good idea, let's bitch at everyone, let's make it all up.' Cos they certainly do that. It's fairly crazy. If you tried to make any sense out of it you'd go round the twist yourself.

He remains a willing interviewee, at least when he has a reason to do it. A characteristic session might start with Paul whistling, and slapping a brisk rhythm on his legs, while I prepared my first question. That's far from typical of stars in general, who tend to wait with martyred resignation or bristling suspicion.

'OK, whaddya wanna know, la'?' would be his first line.

When he was pushing the *Anthology* documentary, album and book project, the Beatles' official retrospective on their career, he had to curb his own enthusiasm in deference to the other surviving members:

> That's what it was going to look like. We were gonna do a press conference as the Beatles. So if I did too much, it could steal from it. My normal thing is anyone who comes along: 'Oh sure, Norway!' you know? Then when it's the press conference it's, 'Well, we've heard all that *he* has to say.' It's just my natural

reaction if I'm plugging something, to see anyone who wants to see me. I decided I should probably cool it a bit.

After his big tour in 1990 he admitted to feeling nervous at facing the world's press again. But he was soon back in his element – and it was almost *too* easy: 'I looked forward to hard questions, cos I got bored with all the others. You suddenly realise, "I know every bloody question they're going to ask me." You got your confidence up. You're just talking to people again, instead of "revered journalists".'

Paul's high tolerance of interviews extends to the interviewers themselves. He's unusual among celebrities in the extent to which he asks journalists about themselves, and few can resist such flattery. Even before the 'selfie' became common currency it was standard for Paul to pose alongside his starry-eyed inquisitor for a photographic memento. Personal touches are PR gold. During one filmed interview, after he'd picked up a mandolin and played me his new song 'Dance Tonight', written for his baby daughter Beatrice, he leant across and gave me his plectrum. At such moments the inner fan will push aside the professional hack.

More generally, I had the impression he responded well when I seemed well-briefed on his career – sometimes, as he'd laughingly acknowledge, more so than he was himself. And he likes to be spoken to in the same informal way that he applies to others. Like anyone else, he dislikes the feeling of being cross-examined. Our conversations were always structured to be interviews, but never as interrogations.

McCartney is a confident speaker, who knows how to control his interviews without seeming to dominate. He is articulate and fairly concise in his replies, but when he's relaxed, or looking to gently steer away from something disagreeable, he can be chattily discursive. It isn't always easy to interrupt him – not only because of his power, but also because his every thought is usually of interest to someone.

He is, after all, a living voice from history, and his asides can be valuable. 'Ha!' he says. 'That's one thing I do. Go off at tangents.' But long experience of being interviewed has helped him see his spoken thoughts as if they were already written down.

His default accent is a mild Scouse, probably strengthened when speaking to a fellow Liverpudlian. He has twice been married to Americans and spends a great deal of time in that country, but there is little of the mid-Atlantic in his speech, which remains essentially that of a 1950s English grammar-school boy. He was not raised in the backstreets and his family were aspirational. He has confessed to a lingering guilt at mocking his mother's attempt to correct his Northern pronunciation.

The young Beatles, except for Ringo, were suburbanites whose sing-song accents lacked the guttural harshness of Liverpool's docklands. His speech is still musical in a more literal way, tripping into snatches of melody or some vivid imitation of an instrument, in a manner that defies the printed transcription. He is never content to merely describe some music; he must in fact *perform* it, there and then.

Likewise, he doesn't just *report* somebody else's words: he prefers a theatrical impersonation. He'll never pass up the smallest opportunity to play a comedy Scotsman, a stolid Lancastrian or a crafty Cockney. He deploys, sometimes, a vaguely camp lisp, especially to mock some example of old-time show business. It's no surprise to hear that back in childhood, he and his younger brother Mike adored LPs by the actor and comedian Peter Sellers.

We all have our verbal tics, and Paul's most noticeable habit is an overuse of modifiers and qualifiers. It's something he has noticed when I present him with transcripts of our interviews. It stems, I think, from his impulse to play down statements that might sound vain or intimidating. Thus, 'the Beatles were a great *little* band' or 'I've been *fairly* successful' or 'you find you've become *a bit* well-known'. It sounds pleasantly modest in person, but looks coy in print.

More generally he delights in language. When the chance of a pun or a wordplay presents itself, he seldom resists. Naturally that taste for the verbal frolic will seep into his songwriting, as he explained while discussing a couple of 2005 tracks, 'How Kind of You' and 'English Tea':

> I love language. I'm interested in the way English is spoken by British people. At school I did Spanish, Latin, German, and I liked English. My dad was big into crosswords. So I like language.
>
> I started to notice that posh English people not only have a different accent, they have a different vocabulary. I know some posher, older English people and they're lovely but they say things in a different way. I might say, 'That was nice of you. I wasn't feeling too good.' They might say, 'How kind of you to think of me when I was out of sorts.' As a student of that, through the years, I love it. I'm playing with the language.
>
> I just heard 'Walrus' today, actually, and it's all related. It goes back to *Alice in Wonderland*, croquet, with the flamingos, all very deep, formative stuff. 'Lines of hollyhocks and roses listen most attentively.' It's Lewis Carroll.

Paul has been called upon to recount his life story on countless occasions since 1962. He's well-practised in the art, even if the anecdotes grow more selective, and the narrative more polished, through years of repetition.

His memory is not so neatly chronological as interviewers tend to want. His brain may present events of the past as a haphazard collection of snapshots. To make life easier, he will practically outsource his own recollections, and I was often relied upon to prompt him with some career detail or other.

Once, over lunch with Paul and the writer Mark Lewisohn – the world's pre-eminent custodian of Beatle history – it struck me that we scribes were serving Paul as a kind of external hard drive.

(I also recall that this was an MPL Christmas lunch, and Paul was gamely wearing a paper hat from the cracker he had pulled with my wife.)

In one interview I was trying to verify the sequence of the Beatles' rooftop show in 1969. Filmed on top of their Apple office building in Savile Row, London, for the *Let It Be* movie, they played 'Get Back' and, unwittingly, made their final bow to the outside world. At the time, I suggested, he wouldn't have known this would be their last performance in public? 'No . . .' He paused. 'Was it, by the way? I don't know, man. We never check all that shit. I'm still pretty flaky about it, as you can see. It's an interesting thing. It's handy having all these analysts around. Those of us who *do it* get reminded of what it was.'

Even so, the world swirls with written histories of the Beatles and his own life that McCartney cannot see any truth in. He's especially sceptical when people describe his partnership with John Lennon – an essentially private affair that nobody on the outside can properly understand. How can those people be such experts, he reasons, when they weren't even in the room?

But even superstars are human, and ageing wears away the sharper edges of recall. Whenever I've returned with Paul to a subject we discussed years before, he's advised me to take the earliest version as best. I was fortunate to conduct our longest sequence of interviews as far back as 1989 – a few years before the *Anthology* project in 1995, by which time he was freely admitting the problem of complete accuracy:

> We finally did an interview with the three of us, in the same room, at George's house. And we couldn't remember anything

in common. It's great, it's real people, it's how life really is. You live this dream that there's a definitive version. There isn't.

It came to a head with this story we always tell about one of our drivers – I've probably told it to you – he came to Paris cos he said he could speak French. And he was a bit of a fake. So Ringo was going, 'He got to Paris and it was [*gruff Cockney*] "Er, *gendarme*? Come 'ere." The gendarme comes over, and we're starting to doubt his wisdom already. "Can I park *ici*?" We go, Hello, *I* could have done that.'

Then one of us had a sore throat, we wanted honey and lemon. When the driver ordered it up he said, 'Leave this to me: Gar-kon? Gar-kon, come 'ere'. He looks him in the eyes, flaps his wings and goes Bzzzzz . . .

Ringo's telling this story for the *Anthology* and he starts off, 'We're in Paris with this chauffeur and he's come over cos he can speak French, and George had a sore throat.'

The camera pans over to George to get his reaction. George goes, 'No, I thought *Paul* had the sore throat.'

It pans over to me: 'I'm telling you, *John* had the sore throat.' And I've worked out since, that if Ringo thinks it was George, it couldn't be Ringo. If George thought it was me but it wasn't me, then if I thought it was John, then it was John.

And he needed *citron et miel*. That's how I found out what honey was. It's hysterical. There's no such thing as a definitive thing and you realise it's true of all history.

And Ringo on meeting Elvis. [The Beatles visited Presley at his house in Los Angeles in 1965.] I said, 'Well, he met us at the door, I remember that bit vividly.' Ringo says, 'No. I remember him not standing up all night.'

Not standing up? He was playing pool. He met us at the door. We had completely different memories. Give it another couple of years, a couple more brain cells go *blink* – and there's no bloody story left.

An assistant came into the room to suggest today's session should end. 'What time is it?' Paul asked. 'Ten past nine? We'd better go home, hadn't we? Our families are going to miss us. We'd better leave it there now. I've had a long day's hard.'

Happily there were many other days. Let's now hear the things he said. We begin, of course, in Liverpool.

CHAPTER 2

Rocker with a Lolly Ice

McCartney on Liverpool, childhood and musical epiphanies

When Paul McCartney was born in 1942, rock as we know it did not exist. Even its closest antecedents, rhythm & blues and country, were barely heard of in England. So I asked him about his earliest memories of the music he heard as a child.

Satirising the cliché that introduces most Beatle biographies, Paul leaned towards my tape recorder and launched into the voice of a portentous American announcer: 'Nineteen forty-two! Liverpool! Hitler's bombers were wracking havoc . . . Uh, *wreaking* havoc? Ah well . . .'

The Liverpool docklands were indeed ravaged by enemy air-raids and Paul grew up in a war-shattered city. But at least there was always music. He and his brother Mike, born two years later in 1944, were raised in a series of small suburban houses by their parents Jim and Mary McCartney. Jim was a keen musician who found his eventual career in the Liverpool cotton trade; Mary was a midwife. The family were close, but in 1956, when Paul was just fourteen, his mother succumbed to breast cancer and the menfolk were left to soldier on. The extended family rallied around and music was central to their sense of consolation and kinship:

> The first things were the BBC radio, cos we didn't have a record player. My dad liked to make crystal radios. Just after

the war you used to see these crystal radios that everyone made. And they bought a nice big family radio, which us kids used to sit on the floor and listen to. And he'd made up – again, war surplus – a pair of headphones for me and my brother. I remember this old brown electrical wire. He led it up the bedroom, so if we had to go to bed, and there was something on the radio, he'd let us listen for a quarter of an hour or so.

The big things on radio were *Family Favourites*, for people stationed abroad, a big request programme. It was like the hit parade, almost, one big place where you got all the popular records. I remember 'I'll be Home' by Pat Boone [in 1956] being mega. I went off Pat Boone soon after, but that's one record I still like, a great soldier's record: 'I'll be home, my darling . . .'

The next one was telly. Most people got television sets for 1953 and the Coronation. All your parents would say, 'There's nothing good on this television, all terrible stuff, ruins the art of conversation.' Some people still say that. And probably rightly. But we used to say, 'Oh, everyone's got 'em, Dad.' So when the Coronation came along in 1953 literally the whole street got 'em and you'd see the aerials going up.

Home town references would pepper our conversations. One day, in a break from filming a video, he joined me in his dressing room to draft a foreword for my book about the city's music scene, *Liverpool: Wondrous Place*.

'D'you want a bit of chocolate?' He rummaged through the snack bowls. 'I'm having an energy rush . . . Mmm, it's like condensed milk.'

(Condensed milk, from tins, was a childhood treat in Liverpool. Sweet and creamy, it was even poured over bread to make the delicacy called 'conny-onny butties'.)

'Condensed milk.' Paul went into a reverie. 'I used to think, if I ever get rich, I'll buy a tin of condensed milk and have it all the time.'

To get the foreword rolling, I asked him again where his musical journey had begun, and what part his upbringing on the banks of the River Mersey had played in that story:

> The big factor about Liverpool was it being a port. There was always sailors coming in with the blues records from New Orleans, from America. Different ethnic things, you could get African music, calypsos via the Caribbean community, which I think was the oldest in England. So with all these influences, from the radio at home, the sailors, the immigrants, it was a huge melting pot of music. And I think we took what we liked from all that.
>
> The first things were memories of my dad at home, playing the piano. He was a cotton salesman, and he'd learned to play the piano by ear when he was a kid. He'd been in a band called Jimmy Mac's Jazz Band. By the time us kids were growing up, I would lie on the carpet and listen to him play things like 'Stairway to Paradise', by Paul Whiteman, or one I loved called 'Lullaby of the Leaves', and he made a couple up himself.
>
> He would just noodle around on the piano and it was lovely. He had a mate at the Cotton Exchange, another salesman called Freddy Rimmer, who'd come around and play sometimes, so there was quite a musical atmosphere in the house. There was always a piano, because of my dad.
>
> The thing was, every New Year, there was always a do, a big family do. There would be someone on piano, and most of the time that was my dad.
>
> He always said to me, 'Learn to play the piano and you'll get invited to a lot of parties.' That was the rule in his day, when there wasn't much radio or TV. Certainly no record players. So he'd play old favourites and I remember everyone joining in, getting him drinks, all the old aunties, the women, sitting around the edge of the room, joining in. They knew all the words and melodies to these old songs. And they'd go on for hours, getting

progressively more tipsy. But it was a fabulous musical atmosphere.

In Jimmy Mac's Jazz Band, my dad had his brother Jack on trombone and a mate of theirs on banjo, and he used to tell funny stories of their gigging days. He said, 'We used to have to change the name every time we went back anywhere, because they didn't always want us. If we changed the name they might not remember us.'

They went once as the Masked Players: it had got so desperate they had to wear masks! They bought these cheap Woolworths' masks and went back to the Co-op or somewhere, to play. This was in the 1920s when he had this little band, kind of a hot period for music generally, with the Charleston and all that. And he said, 'You know, during the evening, the glue started to melt on these masks and ended up dripping down our faces.'

Then you'd go to other people's houses, play their collections. I remember my Auntie Gin having 'Tumbling Tumbleweeds' [by Slim Whitman]. And then a couple of early Elvis records. I'd try 'em all. I put my cousin Kath's 78s through the clothes mangle. Just to see if they'd go through. They cracked, and she was well pissed off. My brother and I got a big telling-off for that.

In Liverpool it was very home-made. My dad was a spotlight operator, so they used to see all the music hall come through Liverpool and he knew the songs. Between the two houses, he'd take home the programmes that people left lying around. My Auntie Gin and Auntie Milly would iron them, he'd take them back and sell 'em to the second house! Meanwhile teaching them the songs that he'd just heard, by the artists who came through town.

And of course they had these photographic memories, so they remembered it all and would sing it at parties.

These family parties helped make Paul what he became. They explain his aptitude for entertaining a crowd of all ages and tastes. We can imagine him honing those famous social skills, charming the older ladies with a cute line here, engaging everyone with a winning grin there. And, crucially, becoming his dad's apprentice at the front-parlour piano.

His father's job, at a cotton broker's, was a vestige of Liverpool's long seafaring connections to the United States, and of its infamous role in the slave trade – Jim McCartney's office was near the old Confederate embassy. Jazz bands like Jimmy Mac's reflected a local taste for all things American. Post-war, in the dockside streets where Ringo Starr was raised, young Cunard sailors amazed their peers with imported zoot suits and steel-stringed guitars.

The McCartney clan was large but close-knit, and Paul attended their get-togethers all over Liverpool. His own teenage home, in suburban Allerton, belongs nowadays to the National Trust, and in the corner sits a piano like Jim McCartney's; Paul has kept the original, and still uses it to compose the occasional tune. He told me more for the album sleeve notes to 2012's *Kisses on the Bottom*:

> Us kids would arrive at the New Year's do. The carpets would get rolled back. The women would sit around on chairs with their little drinks of rum-and-black and gin-and-it, or Babycham.
>
> The way I figure it, my parents' generation were just recovering from World War Two. In Liverpool they'd all been bombed. So they were now set to have a good time. *Determined* to have a good time. And they latched on to these very positive songs. No matter how poor you were, most people managed to get a piano. The one we had in our house, my dad later told me he'd bought off Brian Epstein's dad, in NEMS [North End Music Stores, the chain of shops owned by the Epstein family]. People wanted positive songs to lose the memory of the war. And I grew up in that.

Ironically, the Beatles played their own small part in killing off such traditions. I have a tape recording of my own family in Liverpool at Christmas, 1963. Every adult can sing, to at least a competent amateur standard, and each one does sing – sentimental Irish stuff, pre-war music hall, whatever. But the children do not sing; we are encouraged to try the year's fab pop hit by our local heroes, a song called 'She Loves You'. It doesn't work. The stand-alone ballad has been replaced with beat music, on records. The front-parlour singsong was dying. Our generation would let the legacy drop.

Paul's first exposure to rock and roll came in 1956. 'So we had telly, and one night it was talking about [*in posh BBC voice*]: "The scene of devastation, teddy boys, rockers, have trashed cinemas in London. And this is what's causing all the fuss: *One-two-three o'clock, four o'clock rock . . .*"'

That was, of course, the opening of 'Rock Around the Clock' by Bill Haley & His Comets. The song was featured in the movie *Blackboard Jungle*, and screenings in Britain prompted teen riots.

'And for the first time ever I got this electric tingle down my spine. *That's for me!*'

On 20 February 1957, when Paul was fourteen, Bill Haley came to town in person:

> I loved that. I saved up a lot of pocket money – it was probably something like twenty-four shillings, which in pocket money terms, when you got about two shillings a week, was quite a few weeks. I went on my own, couldn't find any schoolmates who could afford it or were prepared to save up. It was in the Odeon cinema in Liverpool, just behind the Empire.
>
> The only disappointment was the whole first half was Vic Lewis and his Orchestra, really *not* what I had come to spend all this money on.

In the interval the lights went up, I bought a lolly ice. I think I had short trousers. I almost remember having my school cap with me. But I just had to see this thing.

Then the lights go down and from behind the curtains, again you heard 'One-two-three o'clock, four o'clock rock,' that electricity again. And – bingo! – then they opened. There they were, great. I'm a big fan, particularly of the guitar player, what was he called? Something like Franco Zeffirelli . . . a name I really used to know . . . Rudy Pompilli! [Probably Franny Beecher; Pompilli played sax.] We loved guitar players. So that was the first of it coming over.

The first thing coming through the *airwaves* that shocked me was David Jacobs' show. He played 'What'd I Say' [Ray Charles's US Top 10 hit in 1959]. It was insane, because he even played both sides: it ends with [*confused party shouts, then Jacobs' smooth BBC tones*], 'And now, on the other side . . .' It starts up again! So that did it for me. I immediately wrote down 'Ray Charles, What'd I Say' and went to the record shop the next day.

By that time, though, inspired by British singer Lonnie Donegan and the home-grown skiffle craze he instigated, Paul was already playing guitar: 'Lonnie Donegan was a big influence, cos we actually then got the feeling that we could be part of it. We could actually *do* something.'

When McCartney was growing up, Liverpool was a prominent seaport with some repute for boxers and comedians, and notorious for teeming Victorian slums, but it had no clear identity. Via the Beatles, its catarrhal 'Scouse' accent – named after sailors' slang for a meat stew – became celebrated. The city's new renown was reinforced by its football teams, whose impassioned supporters sang *en masse* and won a reputation for salty wit.

Scousers belonged to a sort of unwalled city state with its own take on life, by turns sentimental, subversive and surreal. In 1989 Paul was telling me about a newly released song, 'Put it There':

> 'Put it there' is what my dad used to say: 'Put it there, if it weighs a ton.' He had loads of mad expressions, my dad. He was a great guy, and like a lot of these Liverpool guys, you never think about it until years later, when you're grown up and it's 'What did he *mean*?' He used to say, we were living on a little estate in Speke – God, does that seem like a million miles away from now, Speke, to meganess . . .
>
> What was I saying? Oh yeah, we'd be talking about some kid on the estate and he'd say, 'You know the one, his dad's got a little black penknife.' Yeah OK [*whistles to suggest loopiness*], mad, mad person.' But they were full of that, as you know. You'd say, 'But *why*, Dad? Why do we have to do that?' He'd say, 'Because there's no hairs on a seagull's chest.'
>
> I love all that. It's why I like surrealism so much.

When the Beatles first won national attention, being from Liverpool was their second biggest trademark – after those extraordinary haircuts. In 1963, their very accents seemed to epitomise a new young Britain, cheeky and sharp, unencumbered by hierarchy or deference.

Besides which, the group's shared Scouseness was a means to shore up their internal solidarity. It was a defence they'd already perfected in the alien environment of post-war Hamburg, the scene of their tough musical apprenticeship before becoming famous. Throughout their time together, the Beatles were surrounded by a kind of Liverpool Praetorian Guard. Their mentor Brian Epstein was a local man, as were the loyal lieutenants Neil Aspinall and Mal Evans. Foremost in their entourage was a cadre of other Liverpudlians such as Derek Taylor, Terry Doran, Tony Bramwell, Tony Barrow, Peter Brown and Alistair Taylor.

When Paul was twenty-one years of age, the Beatles' fame became stratospheric, and normal life was no longer feasible. Fame may not change the star, but it certainly changes everyone else's behaviour towards the star. McCartney's touchstone of reality is therefore those early years, in family and in Liverpool. Scousers are impatient of pretension, and Paul always speaks of his trips back home as a valuable way of keeping himself psychologically grounded.

There is a theory that many famous people remain frozen in the moment they became famous. It's not the case that Paul McCartney failed to develop, either emotionally or intellectually, but I do think a part of him has never left a certain long-lost Liverpool, where ghost trams rumble over roads now covered by shopping malls, beer comes in brown bottles and moustachioed men in peaked caps represent the full majesty of the Corporation:

> I've done great for some scruff from Speke. Cos that's all I am, man. *You* can understand that. Well, you're not a scruff, I don't think *I* was much of a scruff. We were quite well off, really. We didn't have a telly, we didn't have a car, that kind of stuff, but it was great.
>
> And I must say, in truth, that I've never met anyone better than those people. And I've met a few, including the Prime Minister of this fair country [at that time Margaret Thatcher], and a few other fair countries. Not *any* of them has come near to some of those people that I'm from. I've tried to meet people who were better, and groovier and had better opinions, but I never really met any. I've met people who were more far-out. But in the end, some of those basic things like 'Oh, you won't find yer happiness there, luv,' turned out to be true, you know?

McCartney's greatest homage in song to his home town is 1967's 'Penny Lane', inspired by the suburban bus terminus whose routes thread throughout the city; Penny Lane was on the front of my bus to school, though I lived on the other side of Liverpool. It recalls his boyhood wanderings – a sort of literary boulevardier in short trousers – perfecting the observational bent that became a characteristic strand in his writing.

'I used to go down to get my bus, actually, cos the bus was always full, I had to go about ten stops back. It was like a thousand kids at the school, so come four o'clock, that stop would be crowded and I used to go down the Pier Head, which was the beginning of the terminus. I'd walk through the town, clocking everything.'

He thinks he might have been moved to write 'Penny Lane' on hearing John's draft of 'Strawberry Fields Forever', which hymns a leafy retreat not far away. As early as 1965 he had fixed on the street's name as a potential song title, having heard John use it in his first draft of 'In My Life', which took the form of a nostalgic Liverpool travelogue.

Memories of Liverpool might keep him grounded, but they also offer him a support when he branches out from pop music. His 1966 soundtrack for *The Family Way* takes the working-class brass bands of Northern England for its starting point. His first full-scale attempt at classical composition was the *Liverpool Oratorio*, an autobiography in all but name. The most abstract work he has ever released is *Liverpool Sound Collage*, a fractured and spacey affair with cut-up elements from a sonic field trip to the city's streets.

In his polemical single 'Give Ireland Back to the Irish', Paul sings of 'a man who looks like me', in reference to his ancestry and Liverpool's historic role as England's most Celtic city. Its population had been dramatically swollen by emigrants from across the Irish Sea, as well as from nearby Wales. This side of McCartney's heritage was the starting point of his *Standing Stone* symphony, and he remains entranced by it:

I like all that because my roots are there. Being Liverpool-Irish goes back to that side of things. I like the history. I grew up in Liverpool with a fairly blinkered view of things.

My education, which I was lucky to get, started to show me stuff, but not a lot. Geography was mainly [*droning voice*]: 'The gross national product of Peru is ten thousand megatons of coal.' They close it down. There was nobody until my English teacher [the inspirational Alan Durband] started to show me fun bits of literature and that to me is the whole secret of everything.

I've been on that trail ever since. It's actually rather cool. You go to Ireland now and you realise, 'Wow, the Celtic saints, the language and the music.' You see where it's all come from, instead of 'Oh, he's a daft old guy with a penny whistle.' It's a much more valuable heritage than I was led to believe. It was probably my fault, but I don't think they taught us the good bits.

It's 25 July 2013, a horribly hot afternoon in Liverpool's grandest music venue, the Philharmonic Hall. Wearing a dark suit with a white shirt and a light tie, Paul is on stage for the annual graduation ceremony of LIPA – the Liverpool Institute for Performing Arts – a thriving academy that he co-founded in 1996. It's housed about a hundred yards away in what used to be his school, the Liverpool Institute. In fact, LIPA has now expanded to swallow up the former art college next door, alma mater to a wayward student named John Lennon.

Looking fit and chipper, McCartney had just turned seventy-one and played a gig in Canada only two nights earlier. Despite the heat he stays for the whole three-hour ceremony, listening to the speeches with respectful attention, then standing to receive the day's 263 graduates, in their gowns and precarious mortar boards. He greets each one with a handshake, a kiss or a hug, has a few private words and steers them into position for the photographer. It may be a conveyor belt but every single recipient is made to feel unique.

Finally he makes his own speech, offering encouragement to those now entering the uncertain world of work. And with his brother Mike looking on, he recalls how as boys they were brought here each year for the school speech day – another pupil had been George Harrison. He remembers looking out from this stage to see his mother and father in the audience. He could not know what the future held, any more than the students here this afternoon. But he reassures them that they are entering a sort of family, just like the family of more than a hundred people on his recent tour.

Family and Liverpool are recurrent words in any conversation with McCartney: the two ideas are practically fused. It's the same for many natives of this defiant, controversial and big-hearted city. All Liverpudlians feel related, especially when they're somewhere else. You can leave Liverpool, but it never quite leaves you. It never left Paul McCartney.

Giving birth to the Beatles made Liverpool a magnet for the fans who cross continents to walk those massive docksides, sup beer in its subterranean bars and visit John and Paul's primly restored suburban homes. Magical Mystery buses ferry them from one place of pilgrimage to another. Buskers wail outside the Cavern; hotels and souvenir shops pipe that timeless catalogue night and day.

McCartney comes home often enough, and has championed Liverpool for so long, that he is now the city's favourite son. Scousers no longer complain that the Beatles abandoned them for the bright lights of 'that London'.

Ringo Starr once said to me that the Beatles did not move to London – they moved to the world. Which is true in a sense, although Paul made London his main home from 1963 onwards.

The city of their childhood helped to shape their characters and to some extent their art, but there was little chance of the group building a global career there.

As recording artists signed to EMI, the label's Abbey Road studio was their perfect habitat, where they had world-class expertise on hand to help them. The press and TV media, upon which they depended, were likewise dominated by the nation's capital city. London, in short, was the heart of the British music business.

More than that, the young Beatles were bright, energetic men who had absorbed what Liverpool had to offer them. Their ambitions were huge and they required constant stimulation. They raised their game dramatically in London, because it offered all manner of novel influences. But in time they outgrew London too, and sought out new ideas, everywhere from Haight-Ashbury in San Francisco to the Ganges.

Liverpool endowed them with the most Beatle-ish quality of all – a democratic perspective that was humorous and humane. But they needed more. Liverpool remained for them a spiritual anchor, not a physical ball and chain. When you leave your home for a voyage of discovery like the Beatles' career, there is no going back.

CHAPTER 3

How to Become a Beatle

We were little kids, you know? We were youngsters

I was filming an interview with Paul in 2007. After a few stalled takes, he turned to me and in a picturesque phrase said, 'We'll get it right now. We'll move majestically to the end, like the steam train bringing Mr Epstein into Lime Street Station to tell us we had a record deal.' (Brian Epstein, the Beatles' manager, had struggled for months to interest the London record companies, until EMI's Parlophone label stepped in.)

After their split in 1970 it was hard for McCartney to speak freely about the Beatles; it was either too painful, and sometimes sub judice, or else an obstacle to building his solo identity. In later years, however, his conversation opened up. A typical tangent occurred when we discussed a vintage song he'd recorded in 2012, 'Home (When Shadows Fall)':

'That's one I remember from my dad's era. I used to do an instrumental version of it, just before the Beatles. I liked the chords, so I used to play a guitar instrumental, when me and John were just getting it together.'

It's interesting he should say that, because, as we've noted, the Beatles were alive and listening in the days before rock and roll. As much as Elvis Presley, old songs gave these young friends a common musical ground:

Yes, songs from that era, we'd actually grown up with. It's funny, in films like *Nowhere Boy* [the 2009 biopic of Lennon's early years], you'll get this thing where John's mum is teaching him rock-and-roll or buying rock-and-roll records. But two of John's favourite songs, when I met him, were 'Close your eyes, put your head on my shoulder . . .' which is very much a Thirties/Forties song. And the other one was 'Little White Lies': 'Doo-doo diddle-oo, the lies that you told me . . .' When I met John those were the kind of songs that we'd been listening to. ['Close Your Eyes', written by Bernice Petkere, is a 1933 song. 'Little White Lies', by Walter Donaldson, is from 1930.]

That attracted me to him. I thought, yeah, I love that song. And he'd say, 'I love *this* one, or that one.' They did have quite an influence.

As we know, the four lads' transition from music fans to actual musicians was the consequence of American rock and roll – and specifically its folksy local variant, skiffle. For Paul and his peers, the figurehead of skiffle was a wiry, nasal-voiced troubadour named Lonnie Donegan:

He was British, but a trad jazz guy who played banjo and doubled on guitar, and these guys were all into blues. They commercialised the blues: 'Rock Island Line' [Donegan's first Top 10 single in 1956]. He had this huge hit in America, which was unheard of. So he became a giant in Britain. And he was guitar-oriented instead of piano, so that sprung up millions of skiffle groups, everybody everywhere.

This became the craze that year – get a guitar, you only had to know a couple of chords, because it was blues. Somebody had to get a washboard to do the rhythm, metal ones preferred, glass wasn't quite as good a sound. It was fun cos you'd go to your mum, or an old auntie: Got any washboards? 'Oh yer Auntie Ethel used to have one of them, it's in the shed.' And a tea-chest bass. So it was very cheap. These days in America I've seen kids playing with cardboard instruments, rap groups with a pedal and a cardboard bass drum, and guitars made out of cardboard. It makes a noise, not very musical, but it's enough for them to sing to and rap over.

It's like that, with not much money around. When those things catch hold they spread like wildfire. Everyone in the street can do it: 'Yeah, I've got a tea chest!' So that's what happened all over England but particularly in Liverpool. It appealed to everybody. There were millions of them.

A couple of talent contests came to town. Jim Dale, he of *Barnum* [the Broadway musical] and all that, he was like a young pop star, older than us, but they just knew how to get into show business. That was the difference between them and us. They lived in London, they knew people at the 2i's [a Soho coffee bar and cradle of the British rock scene]. So Jim took a talent contest out. I had mates at school who went on it; that was showbiz, you went along to see your mates. They came second, I think. Cass and the Cassanovas.

Once that happened we started to have guitars and we didn't look back. Once you had a guitar you were in show business. Virtually.

As none of us had any money, it was a great little earner to be a semi-pro band. We could pick up a couple of quid a week, just enough to take your girlfriend to the pictures or something. That was a big incentive.

I then got into the Quarrymen, through my friend Ivan Vaughan, who was a mate of John's. They asked me to join, after I'd seen John. And we got into the scene. We didn't realise, but there were millions of groups. Wherever we showed up there'd be a group or two, the sort of Roy Orbison groups, the Shadows groups. There were skiffle contests that you tried to win, and talent contests.

> After skiffle, when rock and roll came on the scene and we heard Elvis, Gene Vincent, Fats Domino and Little Richard, Jerry Lee Lewis, the game was up. You felt a kinship. Even though all those people were American, and I'm just some little Liverpool kid, it's like, Yeah, we all *get* it. That was it. All hell broke loose. We just had to do it for a career. And the rest is sort of history.
>
> In Liverpool it gradually developed into a music scene – a group scene – and became a very rich scene. There were millions of groups. And as we got better, we all got pretty good repertoire, and it grew from there.

The Quarrymen, formed in 1956 by Lennon with other boys at Quarry Bank School, were early disciples of the skiffle craze. The recruitment of Paul in July 1957 – after the Quarrymen were playing at a garden fête in Woolton and Paul had impressed John with his off-the-cuff rendition of Eddie Cochran's hit 'Twenty Flight Rock' – dramatically improved their musicality and the scale of their ambitions. And through Paul came his younger schoolmate George Harrison, a year later.

At some points, musical analysis will only take you so far. The random combination of these three teenagers proved to be the seed of something extraordinary. Their vocal harmonising, for one thing, was unexpectedly marvellous. None of them received formal training, though Paul had done a stint in the choir of a local church, St Barnabas; he could skip, within a heartbeat, from a wild falsetto scream to a softly rounded ballad style that blended perfectly with John's drier, more nasal delivery, even before they'd dreamt of writing new material together.

After the other members drifted back to civilian life, this core trio evolved into the Beatles, adding John's art-school friend Stuart Sutcliffe on bass and then the drummer Pete Best. They steadily assumed leadership of the Liverpool beat scene. But as yet, like all British rockers, their whole understanding of rock came from across the Atlantic:

It was basically the ones who had hits in Britain. Elvis was top of the list, he was the ultimate groove. We didn't know he was taking it off blues, we thought it was him. We just heard Elvis singing 'Love Me Tender', didn't know anyone else had ever done it. [Its tune dates back to the American Civil War.] Or 'That's Alright Mama', or 'Hound Dog'. It just added to his legend: How does he think of these things!

And he was a great-looking guy with the sideburns. We fell in love with him. Not in any sexual way, just pure . . . religious more than sexual.

He was brilliant. Until he went in the army, and then he was goosed. He used to call everyone 'Sir' after that – mind you, he used to call everyone 'Sir' before that, it was just Southern – but he came out of the army and it felt servile. He went into films and I never got off on him again. But that first period is etched in my mind. I love all the records before the army.

Then you started to hear Little Richard, who I loved, just cos he was so outrageous, this high voice, screaming, with a raw edge to it. I'd always been a bit of a mimic; some kids at school can do the voice, I could always do a few comedians, and Little Richard I got off as a party piece. For the end of term at school, we took our guitars in and did 'Long Tall Sally' on the desk, in G, so that became part of my repertoire, the screaming bit.

Later he was to say, 'I taught Paul everything he knows, all right Paul? Whooo-oo! I taught him.' Which isn't quite true, but I certainly did base all that stuff on him.

Then you got Fats Domino, who was monstrous, a totally different kind of black thing, down here, you know [*indicates his chest*]: 'You broke mah heart', and New Orleans. You learn what it is later. Elvis was Southern. They're nearly all Southern, actually, but at first we never realised, it was all just American.

McCartney is one of those naturally musical people who can get a tune out of anything, even a table of wine glasses. At thirteen he was grappling with a trumpet that his father bought for him. A few years later the family acquired a drum kit for Paul's younger brother Mike, but it was the older boy who took to it. Soon he had learned to play drums very competently and would do so throughout his career.

Before Paul learned guitar he could bash out numbers on his dad's piano, though he swiftly ditched a course of lessons. With his left and right hands exploring the possibilities, he soon knew more about musical range than the average strummers of his neighbourhood skiffle bands. In 1957, when he so impressed John Lennon with his rendition of 'Twenty Flight Rock' at Woolton village fête that summer, Paul didn't even *own* a guitar. A friend had lent him one to practise on.

Soon after that he traded in the trumpet for a guitar of his own. Until it was restrung, of course, he had the left-hander's obstacle to overcome. And typically, he turned this to his advantage. Literally coming at the instrument from a different direction, he was obliged to understand the music upside down, back to front, inside out. Nothing went to waste.

Do you still have your first amp?

> Yeah, I think I bought it from Curry's, the electrical shop; as you were going through to get your records you'd see vacuum cleaners, washing machines and amps. Nobody could afford electric guitars, that was a couple of years later. They were very expensive, so what you would buy was a pick-up and an amp, and you'd put a pick-up on your acoustic. And I got this green amp called an El Pico.
>
> Great, took it home, but it was really built for a bygone era. The input would say mike and gramophone, but we used to put the guitar in it. It was probably the cheapest I could find. Not being a cheapskate, but my family didn't have much. It was

enough, anyway, and I've still got it. It's brilliant, now it's like a fuzz monster; anything you put in overloads the shit out of it, it's great, a good sustain.

Who else was important?

Jerry Lee Lewis, huge. We loved Jerry Lee, cos he seemed like the ultimate country performer. I liked 'Whole Lotta Shakin'', we also liked 'You Win Again', a couple like that, the slow country B-sides.

We'd collect a lot of those records, and for our repertoire we started doing the B-sides. We figured if we did chart stuff, everyone else could do it. Often, if it was a mimicry job they could do it better than us, just by rehearsing longer. So it was better to try and get around the back door and learn a B-side, because they wouldn't bother with the B-sides.

This was getting into the Beatles now. We started off with 'I Remember You' [by Frank Ifield], the pop stuff, but you'd go to a place and another band would have it in their act, and it was such a piss-off, them saying, 'We're coming on before you, we're gonna do "I Remember You".' No man, you can't, it's our big number! We got fed up with the fact they had our repertoire. Or we had theirs.

So we looked for this other avenue. That's how I got 'Till There Was You', a Peggy Lee record. I just liked the tune. I didn't really understand when it said on the label 'From *The Music Man*'. Later I understood it was from the musical that has '76 Trombones' in it. I just learned it up. I like Peggy Lee a lot.

We started to look for the B-sides, like 'Cracking Up' by Bo Diddley, 'Havana Moon' by Chuck Berry. And James Ray, 'If You Gotta Make a Fool of Somebody' – nobody knew that, and you should have seen the looks on their faces when we came up as a rock band doing a waltz. Musicians would stop: 'What's that, man?'

In Hamburg [where the early Beatles played several seasons

in the clubs, pre-fame] we got fed up of repeating ten numbers all the time. We tried to make it so we could play all day, sometimes seven or eight-hour shifts, but we didn't want to repeat. That became the big trick. So we'd make tunes up, or we'd do silly versions of 'Tequila' and stuff – 'dn-dn-de-de-knickers!' – just so we could have a laugh. But we learned all these numbers, and when we came back to England we had a wide repertoire.

And Buddy Holly?

Buddy Holly, yeah. 'That'll Be The Day' was the killer with him. The good thing was anyone who wore glasses, like John, could hold their head up high when Buddy came out. Till then you wouldn't be seen dead in glasses. John used to go round bumping into lampposts. But when Buddy came out it was 'Sure! Pop them on.'

The big attraction as well with Buddy was that he wrote his own stuff. Whereas Elvis didn't. Jerry Lee did, a lot of it, but Buddy seemed to write all his own stuff and it was three chords. For people looking at this idea of writing our own stuff, which we were starting to do, the three-chord idea was great, cos we didn't know more than four or five.

We got into Buddy and his songs were easy to learn: 'Rave On', 'Think It Over', 'Listen To Me', 'Words of Love', 'I'm Gonna Love You Too', 'That'll Be The Day', 'Oh Boy!', 'Peggy Sue', 'Maybe Baby', we knew all of them. We did them at a talent contest in Manchester, only three of us and John didn't have a guitar . . . That's right, he borrowed one, don't think he gave it back either. But that's another story.

Great days, cos obviously the excitement is mixed with your teenage-ness, which is exciting anyway. Going to Manchester for a talent contest, the nerves of it, and then the relief, and then the piss-off once you lost. We lost every bloody talent contest we ever went in. Never came anywhere.

Always got beaten by some terrible loser. Nearly always the woman on the spoons. It was in Liverpool, cos they'd all get tanked up and by about eleven-thirty when the judging went on they're all going, 'Go on Edna!' *Chk-k-kkk*. Bloody good she was too. She always creamed us, this old lady. I think she used to follow us round, the bastard. 'Where are the Beatles trying this week? I'll beat 'em. I've got the measure of them.'

The bass was not McCartney's chosen vehicle; he'd instinctively imagined himself as a guitar-slinger in the classic rock-and-roll style, with a sideline in piano. But in Hamburg with the Beatles he'd sometimes deputise for their original bass guitarist Stuart Sutcliffe, who was right-handed. Eventually, and reluctantly, Paul became the band's regular bass player-cum-pianist.

When did you first get the violin bass?

In Hamburg. I'd gone out to Hamburg with a Rosetti Lucky 7, which is a crappy guitar but it looked quite good, a red guitar. But when you looked a bit closer it was really glued together and it fell apart quite quickly. I think someone broke it over me one drunken evening – we had an early Who – it was obvious we couldn't save it. So that was it. And I got on piano then, I couldn't not have anything.

Oh, I tried to piece that guitar together, I didn't have it plugged in for a while, but I thought this is silly, hardly any strings on it, not plugged in. There's gonna be someone who's gonna notice. So I turned my back on the audience and started playing piano, which I knew a little bit. That was where I started the whole piano thing. That was good for a while.

Stuart Sutcliffe was in the group then. And contrary to rumour that I was pushing him out, cos I really wanted to be on bass, it isn't true. It's the opposite: nobody ever wanted to be on bass. Guitar was the happening thing.

Stuart was going to stay in Hamburg, cos he'd fallen in love with this girl Astrid [Kirchherr], who was part of a little set who called themselves the Exi's, existentialists. They were very cool in black, tight trousers, little high-heeled boots. She was blonde, she had a short Peter Pan pageboy haircut, she looked dead cool. We'd never seen a chick like it. She dressed like a boy, a very slim little boy, so it was all, Fuckin' hell, look at her!

I think we all fancied her but she fancied Stuart, who'd been the one guy who'd never been able to pull anything in our band. We'd always pulled before poor old Stu, but he got these great shades and he struck a James Dean pose, got his hair going groovy like James Dean, so she went mad for him. And their group used to really like Stuart. I think it went: Stuart, John, George, me, Pete Best. That was their order of preference. They took some great photos of us.

And Jürgen [Vollmer], who was one of the guys, he was the guy whose haircut we copied to get the Beatle haircut. Till then we had it back, a Tony Curtis as we used to call them. It all seems so cute now, 'A great Tony Curtis you got there!'

Stuart was leaving the band and he wanted to stay in Hamburg, so we had to have a bass player. He lent me his bass, so I got off the piano and came up on the front line again. But I actually play it upside down. I kind of wangle my way around that. I always have to be inventive, because I was having to play things upside down. The guitar breaks, you'd have to go on to piano, try and think up something. So when Stuart was going to stay I thought, it's obvious, I'm gonna be bass player now. I got elected, or lumbered, as the case may be.

In Hamburg there was a place we used to go, this guitar shop, and there was this bass [the Höfner Violin] that was quite cheap. I couldn't afford a Fender. Fenders even then seemed to be about a hundred quid. All I could afford was about thirty quid.

It sounds funny, when people are doing my 'mean image': Oh yeah, typical. But it's not mean, it's being scared to spend money. With my dad we were always teetering on the edge of not having much. So for about thirty quid I found this bass.

And to me it seemed, because I was left-handed, it looked less daft because it was symmetrical. Didn't look as bad as a cutaway which was the wrong way.

So I got into that. That became my main bass. I got a couple through the years. The one I have now [1989] is one of the ones from the last Beatles tour, before I got the Rickenbacker. The great surprise was that even though it was little and cheap and cheerful, it had an amazing deep sound, and I'm still chuffed that I use it regularly.

And it's very light, that's the great buzz about it. Any bass you pick up these days, like I've got a five-string Wal, and it's like picking up a chair. But this little Höfner, you just string it up, it's like it's not there. So you can walk around and move around, and it actually alters your playing. You play a lot faster, very easily. Recently I saw the *Let It Be* on-the-roof thing, and I just noticed how light it looked to play this bass. I've got right back into it.

So I bought that back there in Hamburg. And set off on the road to stardom.

It was at the Cavern club in Liverpool, of course, that the Beatles built the core of their support. The dank warehouse cellar had been converted for jazz, but in 1961 it bowed before the 'Merseybeat' onslaught of local guitar groups. Sadly for me, I was too young to catch any of the Beatles' 275 shows there, but I went just before its demolition in 1973, to breathe that unwholesome yet historic atmosphere. Since then, the Cavern has been successfully rebuilt in replica, and for a 2006 book about the venue, McCartney faxed me some thoughts about that period:

My first memories were of us trying to get booked there, but in the early days the Cavern only booked jazz and blues artists and frowned upon upstart rock and rollers like ourselves. We fibbed about our repertoire and managed to get a date there, where we proceeded to announce songs like 'Long Tall Sally' as being written by Blind Lemon Jefferson and 'Blue Suede Shoes', the famous creation of the legendary blues artist Leadbelly! When the owners of the Cavern realised what we were doing, they sent up little notes to the stage complaining, but by then it was too late and we had managed to infiltrate.

We were so persistent that we eventually became regulars at the sweaty little cellar. Sometimes the condensation on the ceiling from the people crowded in there would drip onto our equipment, causing the amps to fuse and the power to go off. We then improvised, singing a cappella, anything we could think of that the audience would be able to join in with. We came to know regulars like Bob Wooler, the great DJ, Paddy Delaney, the legendary bouncer, and Ray McFall, the enthusiastic owner.

My second worst memory was arriving at the Cavern for one of the famous lunchtime sessions and realising I had forgotten my Höfner bass and as I was left-handed nobody could lend me one, so I quickly drove half an hour to my house, picked up the bass, but arrived back in time for the end of the Beatles' set, having been replaced by a bass player from one of the other groups. I seem to remember it was Johnny Gustafson of the Big Three.

It was the breeding ground for what would become the Beatles' early repertoire and I will always think of the place with great affection for the days spent with my pals in its sweaty, damp atmosphere with the audience chewing on cheese rolls, swigging Coca-Cola and sending up little bits of paper to the stage with requests for songs such as 'Shop Around' and 'Searchin' to be played for crowd members calling themselves things like the Cement Mixers and so on.

Meanwhile up in the daylight, the four young kings of the Cavern were enjoying their last months of relative freedom. Brian Epstein, the twenty-seven-year-old manager of a nearby record shop called NEMS, had seen the Beatles at the Cavern in 1961 and vowed to make them famous. In 2004, Paul recalled for me that long-lost era when the Beatles could still go hitchhiking:

> I was with George, that last summer before it all started. George and I were trying to get down to Devon. We started off in Chester, went through the Mersey Tunnel, we heard that you couldn't get lifts on the Liverpool side but once you went through, all the lorries that were going south went that way. So we walked until we found a grass verge to sit on and started thumbing.
>
> John and I did it once to get to Paris. We decided we need a gimmick – imagine these little minds ticking over – so we had bowler hats with our leather jackets and haversacks or suitcases. Two guys with bowler hats and black leather jackets! The lorry drivers would think, Well, I'd better give *them* a lift to see what the story is here. We got to Paris on that one and had a great time.
>
> George and I did it, minus the bowler hats, and we used to hitch to Harlech in Wales for a little holiday. We'd hook up with the local band, sit in the café until someone would talk to us, playing the jukebox:
>
> [*Welsh accent*] 'Hello there.'
>
> 'Yeah, we're from Liverpool, like. The capital of Wales.'
>
> 'Ooh! Are you, boyo?'
>
> 'Yeah, we're like big town people, cosmopolitan.'
>
> And another time with George, going down to Paignton [in Devon, 1959], we had nowhere to sleep. So we slept on the beach, which sounded like a great idea until the middle of the night when you realised that the sand is cold and hard. We tried to pull some girl from the Salvation Army. This is going back. But I think I'd better draw a curtain over that episode.

All four Beatles served their romantic apprenticeships in the normal run of teen romances growing up in Liverpool; it doubtless offered some material for their early love songs. And their stock of sexual experience was certainly increased by exposure to the red-light rawness of Hamburg. John was the first to marry, after his art-school girlfriend Cynthia fell pregnant with their son Julian in 1962.

Around this time, Ringo also met his future wife, a Liverpool hairdresser named Maureen Cox, while two years later George would hook up with the future Mrs Harrison, the model Patti Boyd, when she played a cameo in the movie *A Hard Day's Night*.

Finally signed to Parlophone in May 1962, and having installed their local pal Ringo Starr in place of previous drummer Pete Best, the Beatles made their debut LP: 'When we came to record,' says Paul, 'George Martin would say, "What do you know?" What do you want? He used to turn down half of my ballads but it was probably just as well, things like 'Falling in Love Again', the Marlene Dietrich song from *The Blue Angel*. He wanted pop and mainstream ballads.' For the 1995 *Anthology* project, Paul listened back to some of those tyro attempts from February 1963:

> In the early days when it broke down we'd have mini-arguments in the studio. There's one really cool bit, I think we're doing 'I Saw Her Standing There', and I'm trying to struggle without a plectrum, a 'pleck' as we used to call them. It's very hard without, cos you can get a *donga-donga-donga* double hit on the pleck. It's pretty hard *now*, but then, when I was not as practised [*fast, intense*] *de-de-de-de*! The whole song is like, 'God, get me out of here!' After the third verse you're going, I wish I'd done [*placidly*] *dum, de-dum, de-dum*. But it just goes relentlessly all the way.

So I break down. I'm suddenly, Oh shit! We were doing a reasonable take, too. And John goes, 'What! What's wrong?' So I'm saying, 'I haven't got me pleck with me!' and John's saying, 'Well where is it, soft arse?' That was a common term of endearment at the time. Or soft head? Soft arse, I think was the big swear word of the time. Then you hear Neil – Neil Aspinall, the head of Apple, who was our roadie, five quid a night – he comes up to me, 'Well Paul, I did tell you . . .'

I'm going, 'I'm not soft arse. It's in me suitcase at the hotel.' And it reminded me of when we used to come down, be staying for a few days in the hotel at Russell Square, the President Hotel. We were little kids, you know? We were youngsters.

Even with a record deal to their name, these youngsters still had to charm that august institution the BBC. With limited competition from Radio Luxembourg, the national broadcaster was the only important outlet for rock, and by no means always enthusiastic – its pop arm, Radio 1, was still five years in the distance. During the series of interviews we did in 1989, Paul picked up the narrative of that courtship:

At the BBC they held auditions. And they didn't generally like us, it wasn't what they were looking for. If it looked like being very Beeb, you'd try and throw in some of your more middle-of-the-road numbers, more than obscure R&B.

You had to audition, very showbiz, very holiday camp. Arrive there in the morning and be told what time they wanted you, wait around, done up in costume, really go for the bloody thing, and it would be some terrible old village hall or something: 'All right, next!' Just go on with some Buddy Holly or something. And then go home very disappointed.

In the end we forced those BBC auditions so much, and once we'd clawed our way into that position, we always managed to turn a few girls' heads. Like *Saturday Club* at the Playhouse, down by Charing Cross arches. [Paul went back

> to the Playhouse Theatre a few weeks after this interview to rehearse his new band for the 1989 tour.]
>
> *Saturday Club* was an institution, like *Top of the Pops*. Saturday morning I used to love, cos it would be my one big lie-in of the week. I'd wake up and there'd be this great pop programme where you could listen to some cool new sounds, Brian Matthew [the BBC radio presenter] doing his stuff. So when we came to do it, it was like the big time. And they used to like us cos we were kind of wacky. John would come up with some of his stuff, on air, live. We threw stuff in, we always worked at it quite hard.

Another of the Beatles' new responsibilities was to woo the national press. Characteristically, Paul would find this less onerous than the others have tended to claim it was:

> I think it was a good idea, actually. We were interested, we'd only been to Liverpool. We hadn't been to London, so when you got to walk around Fleet Street, this was like going on holiday. I loved it, I think we were all quite into it, go the pub, have a couple of bevvies, nothing too crazy, breeze around these guys' offices. You'd see them on their home territory, got a better idea of who they were.

The Beatles were becoming THE BEATLES. Pretty soon, this group would never have to seek attention, or audition, or find themselves short of a plectrum. The reason is that – in 1963 – everything went slightly mad. Their debut single, 'Love Me Do', had dented the charts; its follow-up, 'Please Please Me', was a smash hit. After that the band began to look infallible: 'From Me to You', 'She Loves You', 'I Want to Hold Your Hand'. By late summer, in Britain at least, nobody who had picked up a newspaper, or glanced at TV, could possibly be unaware of this group's existence. Mayhem attended their every public sighting. From enchanted teens to sceptical politicians, everyone was becoming infected.

And in February 1964, the Beatles flew to the USA. Primed by radio stations across the very homeland of rock and roll, young fans turned out in their thousands to welcome them at New York's JFK airport. And two days later, when they played on Ed Sullivan's TV show, even the young fans' parents had to blink in astonishment.

The world, in short, was falling under a spell. And perhaps it has never quite woken up.

CHAPTER 4

The Toppermost

Paul, I love you, great, gosh, fab, gear, groove.
Here, I've enclosed some Jelly Babies

Beatlemania looked like an overnight sensation. But the view from inside the bubble was different. As Paul sees it: 'What happened with the Beatles' career is that it just built. Whenever people said, "God, how do you cope with all that fame?", my theory is that it just built steadily. You got little clubs in Liverpool, Hamburg, ballrooms in London, theatres, stage shows, TV, it just kept going up.'

One day in 2004 our talk turned to his earliest memories of national success, just before that game-changing arrival in America. If the Beatles' impact was at first measured in screaming crowds and chart positions, the next stage was acceptance by the Establishment. Characteristically, Paul was up for it.

Like Elvis before them, the Beatles emerged from the delinquent netherworld of rock to be embraced by the entertainment mainstream. Yet, within a few years more, they helped create an entire rock culture that would leave all the chirpy comedians and seaside variety shows far behind:

> The big thing was it was showbiz. I know we've talked about this before, but the Beatles was a cool period, because the rock-and-roll industry was yet to happen. It was a little thing much loved by its addicts, but the whole idea of a business was yet

to happen. So we were incorporated into show business. We'd do these shows like *Morecambe & Wise*, and you would be on bills with people like Ken Dodd.

It was fun for us, cos you would get to see them rehearsing. Dickie Henderson doing 'One More for the Road' and falling off his stool, Frankie Howerd, people like that. So to us, who loved all these comedians and liked a bit of a laugh, it was a refreshing change from playing the clubs. It wasn't just, you go in, you see another group playing, do your act and go home, couple of quid. It was exciting.

That was the world you were in. These people used to do Summer Seasons and a lot of *our* people, like Cilla and Cliff and the Shadows, people in our world, went on to do that. *We* didn't, but we'd rub up against it. We'd go down to Bournemouth and Tommy Cooper would be there in the bar, buying you a drink – *jus' like that* – and it was exactly how you'd imagine it to be.

I must say I loved all that. I found it very exciting to be actually near Tommy Cooper, and I remember it with great fondness. I never get blasé about those things.

We'd just be doing the Sunday night that they weren't playing. Doing their night off. So they were often around because they had to stay there the whole summer, and you'd run into them. You'd play *our* audience, who'd come on the Sunday night, and you'd run into maybe the Shadows in Blackpool, and so you got to know these people.

Among the Beatles' seaside jaunts in summer 1963 was a week of shows in Weston-super-Mare. They're best remembered for a cod-historical photo sequence on the beach:

With those Victorian bathing costumes. Which got everywhere. There was always some photographer saying, 'I've got an idea for a photo!' What is it? 'Well it's Victorian bathing costumes!' Oh all right, go on then. Or it's butchers' babies, dolls and meat.

So we'd just do it all and some of it got through and some of it didn't.

The memories of Weston-super-Mare are great because it was time off, nothing to do except a little show in the evening. Cushy number. So we'd be sunbathing. We'd never heard of sunblock: my auntie used to use oil and vinegar. Vinaigrette, basically. She smelt to high heaven but got a good tan.

We would just sit out in the garden. I remember this place we were staying, just us, the Beatles and Brian Epstein, and next door – a lot of this would be lost, except on older readers – Terry, of *Terry and June* . . .

Terry Scott [a stalwart of British TV sitcoms].

Yeah. He must have been in a show. So he was over the wall from us, and we could hear him. We were impressed. These people were the stars and we weren't, we were just some little gigging act. A lot of fond memories, going down to the beach and so on. But that was the nearest we got to playing Summer Seasons.

I remember playing on a bill with the Kinks, and it was just when 'You Really Got Me' had come out. Man! To be there, then, was like being there when Hendrix appeared. Very exciting. And that is still a killer number. I remember us all ducking, trying to get out front and not let the audience see us, to watch the gig.

Those were great memories.

In 1989 we talked about some Beatle lifestyle topics – food, drink, cigarettes – and it was Ringo that Paul remembered most. In this respect the depiction of their drummer in *A Hard Day's Night*, as a sort of comical little mascot, was misleading. The last to join the line-up, Ringo was older than the others and rather more worldly. Apart from his extensive stints with other bands, he had real experience of the world of work, having served on River Mersey boats and held a factory apprenticeship. The others had barely known anything but school or college. In pubs, for example, they took their cue from him:

> It started off as bourbon-and-7 Up. Which Ringo drank, being the sophisti-cat amongst us. He always was. If there was anything American, like Lark cigarettes, Ringo knew it all. He had a big car. He might have been a GI, Ringo, the way he lived. He had a Ford Zephyr Zodiac. Unbelievable, while we all had these little piddly cars.
>
> Ringo was older, he'd worked Butlin's. He'd grown a beard. He had a suit. It was all very sophisticated, and he used to drink Jack Daniel's or bourbon. I'd never heard of bourbon. So I said, 'I'll have one of those too.' Bourbon-and-lemonade was the drink, and that turned into Scotch-and-Coke. Probably when we couldn't get bourbon. I think I heard Ringo order it: 'If you haven't got bourbon, I'll have Scotch.'
>
> He was a grown-up, Ringo. Always been like a grown-up. I suspect when he was about three he was a grown-up. Scotch-and-Coke. That became the rock-and-roll drink.

You all smoked cigarettes, didn't you?

> Peter Stuyvesant was the first one. Again, because they were American, looked so cool. 'Oh, didn't you know? He was the fella who discovered New York.' Is that right? 'Yeah.' Appear suave and sophisticated. 'You want one?'
>
> And you'd pop 'em up, you know that little pop-up? Instead of Player's where you had to push it and open it and do all that. These, you let them fall down to the hole then threw 'em out of it. All very American.
>
> Ringo was the guy who, when he was smoking with a girl, he'd light two. All of that charm. He was a charming bastard.

He used to smoke Peter Stuyvesant and that went through to Rothmans. I got into Senior Service and finally gave up after the flu at some point. When you had to smoke that one to get back into ciggie smoking after the flu, tastes like cotton wool. It's horrible, it's the worst cigarette, and I thought, this is really terrible.

I've done that a few times in my life, got back into smoking after a cold has laid you out for a couple of days. And I just thought, No, this is stupid. I was luckily able to give it up. It never really bothered me.

What did a Beatle eat?

Steak and chips, if you could get it. I still like egg and chips, it's one of my favourites. Chips and bread and butter – chip butty! Omelette. If you were abroad omelette was about all you could get. Grilled cheese sandwich, all very plain.

Ringo hated onions and we hated gherkins. I always imagine there's a classic Beatle picture where you don't use us – like the one where they've got Beatle boots outside the hotel door. It's like, There they are, you can tell it's the Beatles. For me, I've got a similar image in the restaurants. Plates were clean, we'd eat all the chips and everything, except for these little gherkins – two on everyone's plate. 'Eeeew,' like *Spinal Tap*. 'What's *this* supposed to be?'

The nearest we'd ever got to that was pickled onions. When you talk to people in Britain about pickles, it's not like what Linda means. She means gherkins, dill pickles, all the American delicatessen stuff. We still think of pickled onions. 'With a nice bit of brown sauce.'

Wherever a Beatles tour came to town, the great and the good would scramble to bask in that reflected glory. Thus there was a punishing round of dignitaries to be met and civic honours to receive:

We got blasé about it after a while. Because you sort of realise, Well, what is it, the freedom of a city? What does this mean? Can you rob the banks? No, it doesn't really mean anything. It's just a kind of honour. So it's good to get. You get the 'Key to Indianapolis'. It's all a big ceremony really. It was a picture with the Lord Mayor. And meet his daughters.

You used to have to do something to keep yourself amused because it was so mind-numbingly boring. 'Hi. Oh you're . . . Oh, great to meet you.' No, it *isn't* great to meet them, not every day. Sometimes, if you're lucky it might be great, but normally it isn't.

I got this little trick: I used to fake a squint just to keep myself amused. [*Crosses eyes, offers hand earnestly.*] 'Hello. Nice to see you. Hello.' And the others used to like it if they'd spot it. It's great. You expect them to go away saying, 'You get close up, he's got a funny thing with his eye . . .' Ah well. We had to keep amused, one way or another.

Tell me about the Jelly Baby business.

Oh God, yeah. Anything that was kind of cute caught on. We did like Jelly Babies. I think one of the newspapers said, 'What's your favourite sweet?' One of those 'Lifelines' as they called it. *NME* did it. Pet hate, pet love, favourite food, favourite sweets, favourite girls' hairstyle. It was always long blonde hair we liked. And Jelly Babies – I think we all probably put it in.

So they started arriving with every letter: 'Dear Paul, I love you, great, gosh, fab, gear, groove. Here, I've enclosed some Jelly Babies.' That was all right, you'd give them away to your mates. But then they started throwing them on to the stage, and they're very sticky, those Jelly Babies.

The worst was the Washington concert [11 February 1964]. You couldn't move. You stuck like superglue to the stage. We started to tell them, Look, we don't like 'em any more. Could you tell all your readers we now hate Jelly Babies? Mind you,

Bassett's shares went up. [Bassett's were the sweets' manufacturers.] They did, literally. It was such a craze that one year we got letters from Bassett's. 'Here's some more if you want!'

Maybe it appealed to girls' maternal instinct. I've only just thought that. It really could have done, young girls used to latch on to all that. It was fun until they started throwing them on the stage. And they'd cop you in the eye, too. Someone like George could get really pissed off. It was like the gobbing craze later [during punk rock]. Only not as revolting.

I wondered about the apparent mayhem of Beatlemania: the screaming and fainting, the police escorts. Paul's largely sunny recollections contrast with George Harrison's darker take on it all, or the lurid accounts that John Lennon was wont to give:

If you're going to a place, you don't want to fail. The sign of success is applause, or razzamatazz, or how many people turn out to see you. So all of that is fun. We recently did some promotion in Paris and Spain and they gave us a police escort. But it was dead handy. You try getting through Paris traffic, it's impossible. It was very exciting then. I still think it's exciting. You just don't want to get stuck in a traffic jam and have a big scene happen. It was a security thing.

It was good for us, you got to the airport quick, a great luxury. I need it for everyday life, to get me through London when there's a rail strike: 'Doo-doo, Paul's coming through, stand back!'

People said, 'Don't you get frightened, you know, all that hysteria?' I don't think we ever got frightened. We used to say it's just the same as guys going to football matches. This is like the girls' equivalent. They'd throw things and they'd scream for their team. It just makes a different noise with girls. It's like the junior hockey finals at Wembley. Have you ever heard that noise? My kids went one year. It's all nine to twelve, young girls. It's not [*gruff roar*], it's *Wheeee*! A real little high noise. Used to remind me of Hitchcock's *The Birds* or something.

It was all right because we knew some of them individually. We'd grown up with these kids and whenever you'd see them in little knots by the stage door, they'd all be OK. They wouldn't be crazed. The worst of the craziness was like in Paris once, someone pulled out a pair of scissors and tried to cut your hair off, and you know what people are like about your haircut. You've got it going right, you don't need anything off it, thanks. I didn't even like the barbers to touch it. Got quite annoyed at that.

The hysteria was nowhere near that. It was a benevolent hysteria. It was just like applause. And once or twice it was handy: if you were out of tune or not singing too good, it didn't matter. Whereas when everyone sat there and listened, you really had to sing in tune. We nearly always played fairly good at recordings and live.

The hysteria was OK. You get chased around and in and out the cars. I didn't mind as long as it was part of what we did at work. But if it ever intruded into your private life, that was when we got annoyed. You like the idea of being able to switch off and say, 'No, I'm not *him* tonight. I'm just me now. You've got to give me time as me.'

That was annoying sometimes, but not half as much as you'd think. Generally I think we just took it as a sign of approval: They like us!

⁓

It's clear that the band's internal bantering helped them cope with it all. Once, researching a piece about the *Let It Be* LP, I wondered if Paul was bothered by the treatment of its title track. It is after all one of Paul's more deeply felt compositions, with a mystical vision of his deceased mother as its central image. Before he starts to sing, however, John pipes up in a shrill satirical Northern voice: 'Hark the angels come!' Afterwards, the song is abruptly succeeded by the vulgar knockabout (its subject is a famous whore of Liverpool's sailor-town) 'Maggie Mae'. Hardly a respectful way to bookend 'Let It Be'?

'Nah,' he laughs, lightly. 'That was just the occupational hazard of being in the Beatles . . .'

> We could take the piss out of each other. I know what you mean, but we always did that. On the Royal Command Performance I had to sing 'Till There Was You' or something, in front of all these people. It's easy to do a rock-and-roll song; it was never easy to do the 'Yesterday's or 'Till There Was You's. You were so exposed. And George goes, 'Opportunity Knocks for . . .'
>
> It was always a piss-take, but it was part of the Beatles. I do one in 'Get Back', sort of 'go home' when he's doing his big solo, a fucking great solo. Taking the piss. George did it in 'For You Blue': 'Elmore James got nothing on this cat . . .' It was sort of saying, What a lousy guitarist, what a lousy song, what a lousy piano solo. But I think it was all pretty affectionate. It was just how we kept each other's feet on the ground. There would always be someone to take the piss. So it didn't bother me, no. It was just . . . part of the parcel.

Wherever possible I liked to ask Paul about Brian Epstein, their manager, whose importance to the Beatles was surely immense.

'One of my theories about why Brian Epstein was very good for the band,' he told me in 1989, 'was that he was an aspiring actor, who'd been to RADA and kind of failed. He'd gone back to work for his dad's record shop and that's where he discovered us. But when we eventually came down to London, whereas *we* would have just gone down the club – that's all we really had an entry to – Brian would give you entry to a more showbiz crowd, which was very stimulating:

So you'd meet people like the guy who did *M*A*S*H**, Larry Gelbart. And Vincent Price, people like that. It was very good for us. It broadened our outlook. And John would be meeting art people, and he'd been to art school. If you've been to art school, no matter whether you ended up as a binman, you've always got 'One day I'll be a great painter' or something. It separated us from the rest of the groups.

I don't know if it was just Brian, but that was one of the valuable things, to meet people like the producer of *Hard Day's Night* [Walter Shenson]. Or the photographer Robert Freeman. They were offbeat people, a little step above anything we'd ever met.

I've got this memory and I swear it's true, but unfortunately it's getting a bit long ago, and these things are like 'No, we couldn't have done that.' But the Beatles met Nureyev in Madrid. [They met ballet dancer Rudolf Nureyev in July 1965.]

Brian brought him around, it was late at night, and we were 'tired as newts' [drunk], bored out of our skulls, wondering what to do for a laugh. We met him with our swimming costumes on our heads. 'It's very nice to meet you.' Outrageous. Not in a tough way, but still a little surreal. Nureyev. With yer cozzies on yer heads. 'Pleased to meet you!'

I asked him to recollect some outstanding gigs. He suggested the first *NME* poll-winners' concert [at the Empire Pool in Wembley on 21 April 1963]. 'I got amazingly nervous before it on the Wembley Town Hall steps, where we met up. I got my first major attack of nerves and thought, I may well give up this business. But then, of course, did the gig, felt terrific and didn't. And that was great.'

Then there was the Royal Command Performance at the Prince of Wales Theatre, London, on 4 November 1963:

The 'rattle your jewellery', which was fabulous. I remember being in the car on the way there and we just made up these things. We never planned that much. We did the singing, we knew what songs we'd rehearsed. And I knew John would say something here and I'd say something there. And he just come up with that.

['*For our last number* ('Twist and Shout') *I'd like to ask your help. Would the people in the cheaper seats clap your hands? And the rest of you, if you'll just rattle your jewellery.*']

He used to do this 'clap your hands' sort of spastic, a bit un-PC now. But he come up with that rattle your jewellery and it was like, 'Oh yes! Classic line.' I mean, none of us had heard it before, he'd never used it. Fucking great. So we almost heard it for the first time there and then.

It was a really good gig and looking back on those tapes, we were really pretty pro, live. I like watching George's solos, the way he does them nonchalant. Professionalism. So that was a great one for the public.

A little later came Shea Stadium, that historic show at the now-demolished sports ground in Queens, New York City, on 15 August 1965. The Beatles returned there in 1966, and the two gigs set a template for all the gigantic live rock events of later years:

I was amazed that there didn't seem like there was one English name on any of the hangers. They were all the baseball team's: Kowinski! Slowoski! Slamoom! Kabeem! Kaboom! 'Er, is there a Watson in the house?' Ha! It was very American, immigrant families. Kopperboppolis! It was all that.

So we put on the gear and suddenly we were in the tunnel and ready to go out – into we didn't know what – and then as we emerged it was a long way to the stage. Normally we just came from the wings, and you were on, or even from behind a curtain. But with this we had to make an entrance across the pitch, and there was all these New York cops, and so you see this long leggy stride we're all doing, occasionally running, in an effort to get across the pitch.

And then, of course, the deafening din of the flock of seagulls, like a million seagulls, the American audience screaming. We got on and the legendary PA was the baseball system, so it was worse than anything we'd ever played through. We were on this little stage, it was a bit windy, and all these people were screaming. We couldn't hear what we were doing, so it was very difficult to pitch. You couldn't hear if your guitar was still in tune after that long walk. Normally you'd have a little chance behind the curtain to go *dum-dum dum-dum*, OK, yeah. But this was . . . even if you put it right up to your ear you couldn't hear anything. So we just launched into it.

And John doing the keyboard in 'I'm Down' with his elbow. I think we went a bit hysterical that night. We couldn't believe where we were and what was going on. We couldn't hear a bloody thing and we thought, this isn't very good, but it's going down great. The hysteria started to kick in. If you watch the film, he's just doing this [*running elbow along*], as a solo! There's tears streaming down his face, just hysterical laughter. And the audience just screaming and trying to get on the pitch and fighting with the police. It was like a scene out of some film. But we were in it.

So there it was and suddenly it was over. They collected us in a van and we were driven out. It was a very bizarre happening. And later back in England, we actually re-voiced the whole thing because the microphones couldn't hear anything, and what you could hear was terrible. I must say to our credit, looking at it now, I think we did a good job cos it kind of looks live. We were in a studio in Wembley for at least two days redoing the vocals and guitars, everything that had to be redone.

It was such a fantastic memory, very exciting to do, but also complete madness. It was like being in a washing machine. Ha! You couldn't hear anything and you didn't know what was going on but you knew you had to get through it.

Of the 1966 show he recalls: 'Backstage there was a buzz, New York bands like the Young Rascals coming round, the Lovin' Spoonful, the local guys, who we were fans of. That was the nice thing about the Sixties, we all loved each other's records. We were all starting out on this career, and we admired each other, so us meeting John Sebastian was "Oh!" [*impressed*]. Cos I'd done 'Good Day Sunshine', based on his – what was his sunny song?

Daydream?

'Yeah, "What a day for a daydream". That really epitomised the summer to us and caused me to write 'Good Day Sunshine'. So it was great to meet someone like him and those bands. It was a real cool thing going on backstage.'

And, just for fun, there were still the media folks to wind up:

> There'd be American interviewers. God, we had some laughs with those guys. We never realised until much later, their reputations were *huge*. You're talking about Walter Winchell, people like that. All I'd ever heard of him was the voice-over on *The Untouchables*. So he's like mega and we didn't know. We'd do interviews with these guys on live telly, the big interview of the week: 'And I'm sitting here with Paul of the Beatles. Tell me, Paul, do you have an opinion on the Vietnam war?'
>
> 'No.' [*Very long silence . . .*]
>
> And on live telly that's fairly . . . You'd see the guy's sweat break out: 'Uh . . . Wacky! Well let's go to another question.' We were naughty boys sometimes.

Since their debut LP, *Please Please Me,* the naughty boys had proved their brilliance too, with five more hit albums in just over two years. Alongside a parade of chart-topping singles, the Beatles showed astonishing commitment to the album format, investing each one with vastly more care and effort than pop groups were expected to do. Previously, a hit single with a bundle of cover versions was deemed sufficient; the whole record might be no more than a hurried imitation of the act's standard live set. But now came *With the Beatles*, which did not include any of their singles at all. Its follow-up, *A Hard Day's Night*, was entirely written by Lennon and McCartney.

These were unprecedented feats for a mainstream act. Before the end of 1965 they added *Beatles For Sale*, *Help!* and *Rubber Soul*. For all the unforgiving demands of their tour schedules, and two feature movies besides, the Beatles' attention to songwriting and recording seemed, if anything, to deepen by the month. Nobody on earth could improve on a winning streak like that, could they?

Could they?

CHAPTER 5

It Started to Be Art

Oh I get it, you don't want to be cute any more

Bob Dylan to Paul McCartney, 1967

It's natural that rock and roll amazed a Fifties teenager like Paul McCartney. Right from the start, this music represented things far bigger than itself. For those who loved it, rock was intoxication: it was youth, freedom, rebellion and sensuality. In a post-war world with nothing better to offer, this noise was practically the meaning of life itself.

And for the many who hated that noise, it was barbaric; rock vaguely presaged something fatally rotten in western civilisation. More sophisticated critics found the new sound merely boring, doomed by its musical limitations to be a short-lived fad.

But nobody, pro or anti, spoke of it as *art*. Culture in the highest sense took place elsewhere – in the academies and conservatoires, the galleries and concert halls. Perhaps jazz music, embraced by a section of the intelligentsia, was on its own road to respectability. Modern jazz did not lack complexity. And like its related genres, the blues and spirituals, it was dignified by its relationship to the noblest cause of the time, the gradual acceptance of racial equality.

Rock, as yet, showed no such redeeming virtues. It was primitive. Much of it was mercenary. A few acknowledged it could be more than just a joyous din – that the best rock playing demanded high expertise, and the best rock songwriting had a literacy and wit that might rival Broadway. But rock culture? Nobody in the 1950s used the words 'rock' and 'culture' in the same sentence.

It was of course the Beatles – and Bob Dylan – who caused the great sea change. By the mid-1960s high-browed observers, writing in grown-up newspapers, were starting to pay attention and offer some cautious respect. Of the four Beatles, Paul McCartney was the most susceptible to this unexpected new source of flattery.

He was never big on what he calls 'analysis' of the music. But he was a grammar-school boy at heart, with a due regard for what his teachers would have considered 'proper art'. Rather more than John and George, both recipients of the same middle-class education, Paul was open to the prestige of higher culture. He loved to rock but he found something to cherish in nearly any sort of music, however traditional or square. He was inquisitive, and used his Beatle status to explore what London could offer. He'd visit the theatre, collect paintings, discuss the avant-garde with people who knew how to spell it.

In the albums *Revolver* and *Sgt. Pepper*, in singles such as 'Paperback Writer' and 'Penny Lane', McCartney carried his new learning lightly. Whatever ideas and influences he was taking on board, his trade was still pop music – the most popular pop, in fact, that there had ever been – and he was true to his calling.

Anyone who'd paid attention could see there was a strangeness creeping into the Beatles' work – an LP called *Rubber Soul*? A riddle of a song called 'Norwegian Wood'? That was in 1965. By 1966, it was clear that something fundamental was changing. Up until then, the band's success was made manifest by surging crowds at airports, and by each new territory that fell under their sway. But they suddenly abandoned all that, opting instead for the electronic cloisters of Abbey Road, often for months on end.

The year 1966 is often seen as great turning point for music. You and the Beach Boys, Bob Dylan, the Byrds, all checking each other out, making great leaps forward. Do you remember that?

I'm not very good on specific years. But I believe you, it was '66.

That summer you were recording Revolver.

The main thing is, people were getting high. It was the shift from drink to pot. It wasn't much more serious than that. There'd always been pills on the fringe of it all. So it became more of a beatnik scene, like jazz. But Dylan really was the big influence on that. He was coming out of New York poetry, and we were crossing over into each other.

[As Paul tells it, Dylan would greet his guests by inviting them to 'have a joint, man. I don't drink too much but I'll smoke a joint.']

You can't really put it down to anything else, unfortunately. It would be nice to have a clean little cover story, but we haven't. It was actually an alternative to booze. Scotch seemed a bit rough: the old barley is fairly debilitating once you've had a few. Pot was more gentle and thought-provoking.

That's what made the big turn in people's minds. 'Oh, you don't drink *Scotch*, do you?' You'd feel ashamed. It was a move away from accepted values and you thought it out yourself. It was more, Well, I don't think that's too good for me, I think wine might be better, or a bit of pot.

Donovan's got a funny story of me at his house in London before we went to India, and I show up with 'Ollamatingee [*a burbled string of random syllables*], blowin' his mind in a car . . .' And that turned out to be 'Eleanor Rigby'. As I was doing it the doorbell to his flat rang and there's a policeman. And those were the days of smelly substances, wafting . . . Hello, can I help you? The young policeman says, 'Is that your Lamborghini outside, parked with the wheels on the pavement, and the doors open, and the radio on?' And I said, Yeah. He goes: 'Would you like me to park it for you?' Ha!

It's different times now. There's been so much water under the bridge, people you've seen die from drugs. Now when you're talking about drugs you're talking crack, you're talking coke. So everyone's very anti-drugs, and quite rightly. But then it was a much less terminal thing.

A tray arrived with tea and chocolate digestives – gentler stimulants, for sure. Paul waved a 'Help yourself' hand across the table.

For much of the British public, startling LPs like *Revolver* and *Sgt. Pepper* were – at around two pounds each – simply too expensive to risk. Whole families might live on the average weekly wage of less than twenty pounds. In 1966 and 1967 it was a sequence of singles that alerted the nation to mysterious rearrangements in Lennon and McCartney's mental furniture.

Paul has counted 'Paperback Writer' as being among his best lyrics – it was certainly the first Beatle single to move beyond the scenarios of romance or personal emotion found in all its predecessors. Recorded in April 1966, the track catches that mid-decade transition from the 'beat groups', designed for provincial dance-halls, to the 'rock bands' that would soon be subduing whole stadiums. From the same session came the single's even heavier B-side, John's magnificent 'Rain', lurching forward like a sleepwalking giant.

In August, announcing *Revolver* itself, came a single whose sides were both mainly Paul's. 'Yellow Submarine' was probably no more than a children's song designed for Ringo's vocal range, but to early initiates of psychedelia it was ripe for other readings. Its flipside, 'Eleanor Rigby', was both a conventionally beautiful tune, brilliantly arranged, and also a dark meditation on corners of existence unknown to chart pop. However you heard either song, we were already a long way from 'I Want to Hold Your Hand'.

The first single of 1967 was the epic pairing of Paul's 'Penny Lane' with John's 'Strawberry Fields Forever'. Their juxtaposition was a poignant demonstration of McCartney and Lennon's respective strengths, and of their contrasting mental states at that time. Shell-shocked by the first four years of Beatlemania, John had withdrawn into a cocoon of private misery, living in Home Counties isolation amid the slow decay of his marriage to Cynthia. Whereas Paul was actually more chipper than ever – the most eligible bachelor in 'Swinging London', fired with a creative energy that placed him for the first time in effective charge of the Beatles' work. 'Penny Lane' was an overture to psychedelia's high summer, and it gave rise to a jolly Britpop genre all by itself.

I put it to Paul that from a listener's point of view, it suddenly seemed there were no more boundaries around music:

> Yeah. I remember going to see Dylan when he was at the Mayfair Hotel. He'd be in the back room, there'd be me, Brian Jones, Keith Richards, a couple of guys in the next room. I remember going in, after about an hour or so. It would be your turn to see him, like a homage visit.
>
> We used to visit people a lot like that. Went to see [philosopher] Bertrand Russell. Just ask, Can I come round and see you? I'm interested. 'Well certainly.' He lived in First Street in Chelsea, I knew some American guy assisting him, and we'd talk about Vietnam. Great, I was chuffed.
>
> But Dylan, when I got in, I played him a bit of the *Sgt. Pepper* album. He said, 'Oh I get it, you don't want to be cute any more.' And that kind of summed it up. The cute period had ended. We'd been artists with a cute edge, because that was what

was required. We'd really preferred to not do the cute thing. But it was a radical departure to say to *Top of the Pops*, 'No, we're gonna wear something really tough. We're gonna shake your house down.' We didn't want to do that just yet.

It started to be art, that was what happened. Dylan brought poetry into the lyrics, so you found John doing 'You've Got to Hide Your Love Away' – '*hey!*' A very Dylan impression. We were highly influenced by him and he was quite influenced by us. He'd heard 'I Want to Hold Your Hand' because it was number one in the States. After the middle eight it said, 'I can't hide, I can't hide, I can't hide' and he thought it was, 'I get high, I get high, I get high.' He said, 'I love that one, man.' He was well into that. I had to say, 'No, actually, it's I can't hide.'

We were cross-pollinating each other. He'd bring out a long record, so we knew it'd be OK to do 'Hey Jude' long. 'What d'you mean, man? "Like a Rolling Stone" is six minutes thirty. Why can't we have one seven minutes?' You started breaking boundaries, questioning previous values.

It went across the board, from the straight 'We go to the pub and have a Scotch' – became, you didn't go to the pub, you stayed in and maybe had dinner with people, and wine. A more gentle, civilised scene. It changed from showbiz to art and became very exciting with the cross-fertilisation. You'd get in with gallery owners. It was a great, exciting period for me.

Paul's adoption of, and by, the Sixties avant-garde became an interview staple of his. He was keen to emphasise it in the 1989 tour magazine, and would explore the topic more deeply in a 1997 book *Many Years From Now*, written by Barry Miles.

In the mid-Sixties Paul lived at his girlfriend Jane Asher's home, with her parents and brother Peter, and Miles (known always by his surname) was a close friend. When the couple moved to a new home in Cavendish Avenue, St John's Wood, around the corner from Abbey Road, Paul found himself the only Beatle still living in central London. Miles and the Ashers had drawn Paul into circles new to him, from 'straight' theatre to London's underground hippy culture.

In 1989, though, Paul was still torn between his impulse to broadcast that open-minded period, and a reluctance to score points off the late John Lennon. Posterity had decided that Lennon was the artistic adventurer and McCartney the play-it-safe, mainstream song-and-dance man. It's remained a perception he yearns to overturn.

As far back as his schooldays, Paul had admired the artier side of beatnik life. As baby Beatles, he and John were attracted by the style of Parisian students and that clique of Hamburg friends who – to their eager Liverpool eyes – embodied existential chic. Paul was already familiar with Liverpool's own avant-garde, led by the painter/poet Adrian Henri. Paul's own brother Mike was also on that scene, eventually forming the cabaret troupe Scaffold with the poet Roger McGough and John Gorman, taking surrealist satire into the pop charts:

> The funny thing is, John's ended up as the avant-garde guy, because he did all that with Yoko. Well actually, quite a few years before he'd even considered it, when he was living out in the suburbs by the golf club with Cynthia, I was getting in with people like Miles. I used to be at his house a lot, just him and his wife, because he was so interesting, very well-read. He'd turn you on to William Burroughs. I'd done a bit of literature at school but never anything modern. Steinbeck I'd read, but Burroughs and far-out shit . . .
>
> This I find interesting because it's something I didn't put around at the time. I helped start *International Times* [the underground newspaper] with Miles, I helped start the Indica bookshop and gallery where John met Yoko. Was big buddies with [art dealer] Robert Fraser and very into Magritte. So I had a rich avant-garde period which was such a buzz. I was living on my own in London

[he moved from the Asher household to St John's Wood in April 1965], and the other guys were married in the suburbs. They were very square in my mind, and they'd come into my pad where there'd be people hanging out, weird sculptures and stuff and I'd be piecing together little films.

I remember John came in: 'Great, what's this shit you're doing?' He was turned on by it all. In fact when he made that album *Two Virgins*, cos he was hopeless technically, I had to set up a couple of Brenell tape recorders and showed him this whole system that I used. That's where the 'Tomorrow Never Knows' loops came from. I used to sit at home like a mad professor, make all these loops and carry them in a little plastic bag.

Being John, the difference between him and me, he'd make the record of it. He'd get so excited: 'Fuckin' hell, gotta do it!' Whereas, being me, I'd experiment with it, but just bring it to our mainstream records. My thing was, always, not to shout about it. It still is, to a degree.

Indeed. John won his experimental reputation through tracks like 'I Am the Walrus' and 'Revolution 9'; George Harrison made adventurous solo albums in his Beatle years, the east-west fusion of *Wonderwall Music* and the self-explanatory *Electronic Sound*. But Paul's most daring effort, 1967's 'Carnival of Light', was considered too extreme for public consumption and remains unreleased. Commissioned for an early 'rave' by hippy venue the Roundhouse, he calls it 'the longest ad-lib psychedelic crazy track that we ever did. The only piece of music we ever did that was unstructured.' McCartney put the track together during sessions for 'Penny Lane' – a demonstration of his range as impressive as the fact that he'd recorded 'Yesterday' and 'I'm Down' on the same day.

'It was heady,' he says of the world he gathered about him in 1966. 'Miles led me into [poet Allen] Ginsberg, Cornelius Cardew [the experimental composer] . . . Very artistic. Like showing my movies to [Italian film director] Antonioni. And watching movies with Andy Warhol, round at my house. My place was almost the centre of the social scene at one point, because I was on my own. There was nobody to hang anyone up. "Hey Paul, what's happening man?" Well, we're just hanging out, got a few mates over. "Who's there? Mind if I come over?"

> It was like a salon, almost. Brian Jones, John, Mick, Marianne, always round there. Some magic moments. Robert Fraser was this gallery owner – the guy who got busted with the Stones. A great guy, he died a few years ago of AIDS. I bought a couple of Magritte paintings through Robert, when they were dirt-cheap. We didn't think he was going to be famous one day. He was just one that we all liked – the skies, the doves and the bowler hats.
>
> Robert's greatest conceptual thing is like a scene out of a movie for me. It was one of these long hot summers in St John's Wood. We were all in the back garden, sitting amongst the daisies with guitars or something, and he didn't want to break in on our scene. When we got back in he'd gone. But he'd left a painting as we came through the back door, just on the table. A Magritte painting, with an apple. That's where we got the Apple insignia.
>
> And all it said across the painting was, 'Au revoir'. This beautiful painting [*Le Jeu de Mourre*], that he knew I'd want, he just popped it there and split. Leaving it like a calling card: very pure and conceptual.
>
> I had a big period of all that, growing a beard and stuff. It's something I always mean to pick up at some point. Not the beard! Or maybe the beard. Take a sabbatical.
>
> I used to go to concerts like Stockhausen. That was me, all that shit in the Beatles. I'd play it to them: 'Listen to this, man!'

I went to this guy Luciano Berio, who's now an electronic classical kind of guy. *Pepper* came out of that. I'm not trying to say it was all me, but I do think John's avant-gardeness, later, was really to give himself a go of what he'd seen me having. He didn't dare do it in suburbia, because the vibe was wrong. He had to come to my house and sneak vicarious thrills.

That's my thing, really. I'd once said to John – I was talking about Stockhausen, Berio, Cage and these far-out composers – 'I should do an album called *Paul McCartney Goes Too Far.*' He said, 'That's a great idea, man, you should do it.' Of course I never did.

So Magritte I got interested in early on. What I loved was he was apparently a very normal guy. It all went on here [*points to his head*], no outward semblance of this surrealism. He used to paint from nine till one o'clock, break for lunch, very civilised Belgian gentleman. Two o'clock till five, finish painting. Very ordered, very normal. I loved the idea of this straight guy coming out with these far-out images.

I went to Paris with Robert Fraser, who was gay. Causing many catcalls from my friends: 'Hey! We know yer!' Piss off. I'm quite secure in my sexuality, lads. But it was, 'You can't go to Paris with him, man. Staying in the same hotel?' Anyway it was great, we went to see a friend of his who was a gallery owner, Alexandre Iolas.

After dinner he said,'Would you like to look at the Magrittes?' Just me, him and Robert and he's leafing through all these millions of Magrittes. 'I'll have a hundred!' But you can't do that. So I sorted out three of them, about three thousand pounds each, which is ridiculous to what they're worth now. But it was a buzz, just buying art.

Paul's informed taste and his position of influence made him a great fixer behind the scenes. One of his gifts to the rising rock culture was to secure a career-defining appearance for the little-known Jimi Hendrix at the Monterey Pop Festival:

John Phillips, 'Papa John' of the Mamas and the Papas, came over and said, 'We're doing a festival.' I was the guy who lived in London, so they could get to me easily. I invited everyone in. 'We're doing this festival in Monterey, and can you guys – the Beatles – play it?' I said I don't think so. I'll ask everyone but we're recording. I think we were doing *Pepper.* Also we weren't on the road, we'd stopped. So I said, 'We can't do it, but I know who could . . .'

For many people the peak of the Beatles' decade was *Sgt. Pepper's Lonely Hearts Club Band*, released in June 1967. More than any of the group's other albums, it's a record that Paul seems to dominate, despite some of John's greatest songs.

Sgt. Pepper was this whole idea: we were fed up of being 'The Beatles'. Everything we did had to be 'The Beatles'. We were trapped in 'What kind of songs does *John* do? What does *George* do? *Paul* does the ballads.' It was so bloody predictable. I said, 'Why don't we look at the whole thing?' Because of these artsy mates, with all these crazy, heady ideas. 'Why don't we pretend that we're another band?' Make up a name for it, make up alter egos, so we can make a whole album from the point of view of this other band.

So whenever a decision came up it was, 'What's *John* gonna do? Well, what would the John in *Sgt. Pepper's* do?' And it allowed you . . . what would the far-out side of you do? Rather than the marketing man's dream.

You could get away from those constrictions of the record company. 'I'd like a Marlon Brando picture!' And that's what the cover was. I asked everyone, Give us a list of your ten top heroes. John, of course, got far-out, as usual. He put Hitler and Jesus in. That was vetoed. Hitler particularly. It's not who was *his* favourite character but 'We've got to invent egos for these guys, who do they like?' I put Einstein, Aldous Huxley, just various people that we'd read something of. Steinbeck.

Then it got into funny ones. Cos you can't go long in a group like that without it getting to be Billy Liddell, an old footballer. [Actually it was Albert Stubbins, another Liverpool player.] Dixie Dean [of Liverpool's local rivals Everton]. And George came in with Sri Babaji, cos he was heavily into that, and this great idea that Babaji is one of the top Indian gurus, who keeps reincarnating. Fine, you know? Get a picture of Babaji, he's in . . .

Then I'd fight with EMI and we had to write letters to Marlon Brando, all the people. And I said, Just ask, write a nice letter. They said, 'We'll get sued!' I said, No you won't, just write them. I said to Sir Joseph Lockwood [EMI's chairman], 'Now Joe, come on,' cos I had a good relationship with him. 'It'll be all right.' So they wrote letters and everybody replied saying 'Yeah, fine, I don't mind, put me on a Beatles cover, it'll be cool!' Except one of the Bowery Boys [Leo Gorcey] who didn't want to do it, he wanted a fee. So we said, fuck him, and we left him off. One of them got on [Huntz Hall], one of them didn't.

'Day in the Life' was mainly John's song. I wrote the lyrics with him and we developed the song together, and when it got to that orchestral sweeping bit, we wanted something to happen there. Because the lyrics had gone, 'I'd love to turn you on . . .' Kind of looked at each other as we wrote those lyrics: 'Dare we do this? Yep. Sergeant Pepper. Hee hee! It's not us any more, we'll blame it on him.'

It freed us to make more daring decisions than you'd normally make. The costumes, all this alter-ego business . . . I said we should go to Berman's and Nathan's, the big theatrical costumier. When you're going to do one of those shows the director will say 'Meet me at Berman's.' I saw one of the *Z-Cars* guys there when we went.

[It's characteristic of Paul, who was then at the zenith of

global fame, that he remained starstruck by an actor from a TV police series.]

You can get a shape off a seventeenth-century frock coat and say, 'This feels good, but because this is *Sgt. Pepper*, make it up in wild turquoise.'

They have tailors there who make clothes for film productions. So it was as if we were in a movie. We each got a costume made up, George in that lurid green, me in turquoise . . . orange and yellow, I can't remember. Then we did all the flowers and that. We got Peter Blake involved, the artist, I went along to his house with Robert Fraser.

Originally the idea was that this group was being given a presentation by a Lord Mayor, on a kind of grassy knoll with like a floral clock, which is very typical of Cleethorpes and Lancashire and all the parks. It was going to be that, and might have said, 'Congratulations Beatles' or something. And we were going to be receiving a silver cup from this guy. I drew it all out, little sketches.

Peter Blake started developing them. [He collaborated with his then-wife Jann Haworth.] He said instead of the Lord Mayor and a floral clock, couldn't we have all these heroes that we'd written these lists of. Originally I'd just wanted them to be pictures of people around us, and he developed that into a better idea. So we got it to be that big crowd behind.

And it *wasn't* marijuana plants. They weren't. The florist just brought them in, but it got around that they were pot plants. They weren't. They were 'pot-plants' [i.e. plants grown in pots] not pot plants. It was just a big crazy session. We walked in and grabbed a few silly instruments, like a cor anglais, a clarinet.

And that was it, just a fantasy thing. A total 'What might we do if we were other people?' And it all came together into this huge psychedelic explosion. What it all meant together was more than the sum of these little ideas.

Robert was a big help, he was probably the best artistic eye I've known. Great judgement. And he wouldn't let us . . . In the centrefold of *Sgt. Pepper* we wanted to do an illustration by the Fool, who were a group of Dutch artists. They made clothes, actually, they made great keks [Liverpool slang for trousers] out of patchwork, velvet brocade, you could look at it for hours – mainly because everyone was stoned – quite a nice way to spend an evening.

We came up with this illustration, saying, 'Oh, it's really far-out. We're in the clouds, and everything.' But Robert said, 'It really isn't good art, you know?' We said, 'Piss off, it's our album, what do you know?' And he really insisted. I can tell now he was right but we had quite an argument.

He said, 'No, you've got to have these four big pictures, it's the only way. You've got a busy cover. You've turned your backs there, you've got all the lyrics, all these inserts. You've got to have four big, powerful images.' 'No, we want another fiddly little acid-y drawing.' So he was very helpful.

I wanted to tell you about 'Day in the Life'. We had to have a noise here. Because of all this Cage and Stockhausen [avant-garde music] stuff, I thought, OK, I'd try this idea on John. Let's take fifteen bars, and we'll do one of these avant-garde ideas. We'll say to all the musicians, You've got to start at your lowest note on your instrument, which is like a physical limitation – if it was a guitar it'd be E – and go to your highest note. It's all written down in orchestration.

That was the plan and you'd got to do it over fifteen bars. But the avant-garde thing was that you can go at any speed you want. It's like Brian Eno, a little set of instructions, written on a piece of paper. I had to go round and explain it all to them. They were fairly puzzled by this. Once they heard the noise it made and once I verified that this was the game, they were all right.

And it was funny, because the string players stayed together, like a herd of sheep. If you notice, they all go up together. The trumpet players, the brass artists, are the bigger piss artists, they don't care, they're the boys, they are. 'Oh yeah, man. Hey, I'm up for this!'

We just recorded it three or four times and made this almighty sound, like a noise you never heard before. And that came out of that rich period for me, where I was on my own, hanging out. It was very productive for me personally. You felt very proud of yourself.

Not everybody clambered aboard the Love Train. By 1967 the Beatles mop-top image was long gone. And the media's infatuation had begun to sour. Even Paul, the keen PR man, became more guarded.

'A bit later in life,' he acknowledges, 'they [the press] got snarly and bitter and twisted, and you never wanted to go down to their place. And probably our side of it got a bit big-time as well:

So it became a stand-off position. And all this serious analysis, I think, started heavily with *Pepper*.

That was where I noticed it. Up till then everything was pretty friendly, but *Pepper* was like a challenge to them, cos they all had pop columns and we were throwing *art* at them. People like Judith Simons, who was the *Daily Express* woman, an older lady who always had a fag on, real journalist with a notebook: 'Would you say you were the answer to Cliff Richard?' When *Pepper* came along they had to get swottier people in. You suddenly found a lot of university people in the pop columns, which until then you hadn't had. [*With snooty disdain*]: 'Who wants to be a *pop* columnist?'

In fact a new beast, the rock press, was being born. Back at the news desks, however, old-school reporters were unimpressed:

The newspapers weren't very nice to us: 'What's happened to the Beatles?' But it was great because we knew we were making

> this kind of legendary album. So we could go, 'Ha, ha, wait till they hear this.' They were saying the Beatles are finished, dried up. If you look at press cuttings from just a few months before *Pepper* it was quite good, actually. We didn't say anything. We were very liberated.

After August 1966 the Beatles no longer played live concerts, preferring the sanctuary of the studio. A year later their beloved manager Brian Epstein died of an overdose; the band were with a new mentor that day, the Maharishi Mahesh Yogi. We'll talk later on about the Beatles movies – suffice to say that 1967's offering, *Magical Mystery Tour*, did not capture hearts like its predecessors *A Hard Day's Night* and *Help!*

It's true, as Paul says, that the Beatles were breaking free of many limitations. But would they be happier without them? As the saying goes, Be careful what you wish for.

CHAPTER 6

My Dark Hour

Let It Be *and the beginning of the end*

In 1968, even the least attentive listener might detect a disjointed quality in the Beatles' new LP. 'The White Album' (its real title was *The Beatles*) gives an impression of three or four solo agendas with only occasional moments of true group solidarity. Still, there was much to marvel at and nobody was complaining.

Soon though, the Beatles' personal lives and musical ambitions grew too diverse for comfort. Paul married Linda Eastman and John married Yoko. Everyone was dabbling in side projects. Not even the founding of their business Apple Corps, both a label and an experiment in artistic patronage, could hold them together. The *Abbey Road* album, in 1969, sounded wonderfully cohesive, but it belied the brotherly discord at the quartet's heart.

The Beatles' break-up was the most painful episode of Paul's professional life. We covered this period in at least three lengthy interviews between 1989 and 2003. He spoke about it with a mix of unguarded passion and forensic care for the legal pitfalls. The Beatles' ex-manager Allen Klein was still alive at the time – he died in 2009 – and Paul painted him as the unambiguous villain of the piece. As always, he seemed torn between the desire to put across his side of the story, and a wariness of attacking his old friends.

Latterday singles were largely Paul's creations – 'Hello,

Goodbye', 'Lady Madonna', 'Hey Jude', 'Get Back' – augmented by Lennon's 'Ballad of John and Yoko' and Harrison's sublime 'Something'. They mostly topped the charts, just as 'Can't Buy Me Love' had done, or 'I Feel Fine', 'Ticket To Ride' and 'Day Tripper'. But the Fab Four were becoming four Fabs. Then came their fractious last film *Let It Be*, and its ragged partner album. By the time of their release, in May 1970, Paul had just announced he was no longer in the Beatles.

'When *Let It Be* came about,' he told me, 'as most people know, the Beatles were feeling the strain for various reasons. Turned out we all agreed that we'd come full circle, and were very aware of that. Hence the blue and red album cover, restaging the first album.'

In 1969 the band had re-enacted Angus McBean's 1963 photo for the *Please Please Me* LP, taken in a stairwell at EMI. They planned to use it for their next album, provisionally called *Get Back*. In the event, the shot was held over until 1973's release of the 'Red' and 'Blue' compilation records. Paul explained:

> There were the arguments, the business differences and all that. We were sort of coming to an end. Round about that time we made *Let It Be,* but because of the fraught personal relationships, the final straw that broke the camel's back was Allen Klein coming in.
>
> [He was appointed the Beatles' manager in February 1969; Paul's preference had been for Linda's father Lee Eastman, whose firm would indeed represent Paul's solo interests thereafter.]
>
> He decided that *Let It Be* wasn't good enough and that it needed strings. So he brought in Phil Spector, poor old Phil – it's not really his fault – to tart it up.
>
> But I'd had an early copy before any of that happened. We all had an acetate [pre-release test pressing]. Listening to it one night I thought, Jeez this is *brave*, but it's a great album. It really is just the Beatles stripped back, nothing but four guys in a room. Or five, with Billy Preston [their guest keyboard player].

It's almost scary, cos we'd always double-tracked, harmonised and so on, but this was a live album kind of thing.

I remember getting a thrill cos I was in this empty, very white room listening to this album – very minimalist – and thinking, great, very impressed. This is gonna be a great album. And then it was reorganised, re-produced for disc, reorganised for the shops, kind of thing. And I wasn't that keen on it. End of scene one, chapter one.

So was this the Glyn Johns version you were listening to? (Johns, a studio engineer who was then emerging as a producer, was asked to turn the initial session tapes into a coherent album.)

Yeah. It was the early takes.

With a different track list. I think 'Save the Last Dance for Me' was on it, for example. And the LP was to be called Get Back?

I think it was. It's the bootleg, isn't it? I mean, I'm not very clear, we just got our records, and this was our record. So I don't know what somebody was thinking of calling it. All these things get set in stone, like *Abbey Road* was going to be called *Mount Everest*, till almost the second we walked out on the crossing, because of [Beatle engineer] Geoff Emerick's cigarettes. Everything was always in a great state of flux, as it is when you're making an album.

So I don't know what we were going to call it, but you're probably right, it was gonna be *Get Back*. And it probably was Glyn's mixes, cos he'd done all of that. But the point for me was it was just the band and it was bare. That was it. End of scene one.

What had bothered McCartney most? Was it Phil Spector's extraneous production or the way that he hadn't been consulted? 'It was the two,' he says. But the answer fundamentally comes back to Allen Klein:

> The Beatles were getting ripped off, not just me, all of us. Certainly that was my opinion. So I *kept* asking, 'Don't give Allen Klein twenty per cent, give him fifteen, we're a big act!' And everyone's going, 'No, y'know, he says he wants twenty.'
>
> I say, 'Of course he does. He wants thirty really, but we give him fifteen. It's like buying a fucking car. You don't give the guy what he asks for.' So I was always trying to get us a better deal, not get ripped off. But it became impossible in the end, because it was three to one. I was like the idiot in the corner, just trying, I thought, to save the situation. And from Klein's point of view it looked like I was trying to screw the situation.
>
> He used to call me The Reluctant Virgin. I said, 'Fuck off, I don't want to marry you, that's all.' He's going, 'Oh, you know, he may, he maybe will, will he, won't he, that's a definite maybe,' he used to say about me. I was always trying to hedge my bets and not get in with this guy. I knew there was something wrong. However, the answer to your question . . .
>
> It ended up twenty per cent of every new deal he gets, was what I had to settle for. Nobody wanted the good deal, everybody wanted the screwed deal. It was really difficult. So the only thing I ended up being able to do was to boycott Apple. I just thought, I won't go in. I was going in every day, saying, 'Look, I think we got a problem here . . .' Fuck off. 'No, look, this guy's a used-car salesman.' The judge in the end said something like this. It was the prattling of a second-hand car salesman.
>
> That's how I felt. So I boycotted Apple. That meant I didn't go in and they had to come to me for decisions. That was very fraught.

The stand-off had the happy side effect of teaming Paul with a musician who became a lifelong friend, one whose timely intervention helped him let off steam:

> Steve Miller. I love him, he's a great guitar player and singer. We met when a session got blown out cos of an Allen Klein argument. The guys all came over [to Olympic Studios, 9 May 1969] and I wouldn't sign something. They wanted me to sign my life away. And I just decided, 'No, probably not a good idea, maybe Monday I'll do that.' They got pissed off with me cos I wouldn't do it Friday night. So they left, and the session was free. Steve popped his head around the door and said, 'Is this studio free?' I said, 'Well, I suppose it is. Shall we do something, man?' I said, 'Great.' I was in a mood for drumming, with a lot of fills, a lot of *bashing*. We did a track called 'My Dark Hour'. I drummed on it, played bass, a bit of guitar and singing. Steve did all the rest.

Miller's eventual record would credit McCartney as 'Paul Ramon', the whimsical stage name he'd briefly adopted back in 1960.

> I didn't want us to lose what we'd got, the Beatles' fortune. I didn't want *them* to lose it or me to lose it. When Allen Klein brought in Phil Spector, I said, 'I don't think we should do this. I vote against it.' And they said, 'Well, we vote for it.'
>
> So in answer to your question: I wasn't involved because of my boycott and I also wasn't consulted. You know: 'Is this OK? Do you like this? Is this arrangement OK?' In the past if you were gonna put strings on it, someone would run the arrangement past me. 'What d'you think of this?' And I'd say 'Great' or 'Not great' or 'Fix it'. As you do when you make a record.

Phil Spector's embellishments are maybe the least of *Let It Be*'s shortcomings as an album. The virtue of *Let It Be*, the movie, is that we see for ourselves what is going wrong:

> We got in touch with Michael Lindsay-Hogg, who had done a video. He certainly did 'Hey Jude' and 'Revolution'. I'm never very good chronologically, which came first. [He had also done 'Paperback Writer' and 'Rain'.] Michael I knew socially, he was one of the mates, an interesting guy. I said we want to make a film and he says, 'What's it gonna be about?' At one point we were going to take a boat, go aboard an ocean liner or something, make up a story about that, play in the ballroom. A bit like *The Last Waltz*. Just play, and make it up. We always liked the words *cinéma vérité*, that's why we worked with the Maysles brothers. [Albert and David Maysles, the documentary film-makers, had covered the Beatles' first tour of America.] It was this cool little phrase you heard around that time. Bohemian.

Wasn't the Houses of Parliament another suggestion?

> Ha! I think we suggested just about everything. This is what you do. You're talking about how things happen. You throw ideas into a hat. We could have easily thought of it, but we probably also suggested the Moon. No, seriously. You can, cos it's only a suggestion.
>
> Some you think are ridiculous ideas, but then someone goes, 'Well I know the guy from the Houses of Parliament and d'you know what? They have actually got a gig there.' You throw these ideas . . . Part of being artistic is you go too far all the time. You risk your believability by having daft ideas: 'What if we just burned this building down?' 'Well, actually, the insurance . . .' That probably *is* going too far.
>
> We probably did think of the Houses of Parliament. We certainly thought of an ocean liner and half a dozen mad ideas, but in the end we didn't go anywhere. We ended up on the

roof at Apple. Which again started as a silly idea: 'Let's go on the roof!'

At the time, you wouldn't have known for sure this was your last time playing together in public?

No. The most final we got was going back to EMI in Manchester Square and taking that photo [the restaged *Please Please Me* sleeve]. And we all felt spooky: 'This is pretty final. This is full circle. We've started and ended.' The other stuff was like, 'See you tomorrow.' That was a concert for the film.

Before the Apple rooftop session, on 30 January 1969, there had been a few weeks of filming in Twickenham Studios:

We got rid of those silly ideas and he [Lindsay-Hogg] said, 'Why don't you just go to Twickenham and a big studio?' The idea was to film the rehearsals and then have this ultimate, beautifully filmed concert at the end, and you'd seen it all develop. 'At the end the guys are gonna sing for you.'

Filming put their musical relationship under even greater strain. At one point, George Harrison walked out. As Paul recalls, it was not their first bust-up in a studio:

In the middle of that the group started to break up. So that became the film of the break-up. And we had some disastrous meetings. I got on George's wick, particularly. There'd been a few little things. The kind of thing that happened would be like in 'Hey Jude' [made the previous summer]. I had the idea to make it very simple and build towards the end. So I wanted, 'Hey Jude, don't make it bad, *duh-duh-duh*,' just very simple.

George, when we were rehearsing it, was going 'Hey Jude,' [*big guitar riff*] *dang-diddle-da-da*, 'don't make it bad,' *dang-diddle-da-da* . . . 'George, do us a favour, man. Don't play it. We'll have a solo later or something, but don't answer every phrase, it's gonna get boring very soon.' [*Sullen*] 'OK. Fuckin' won't do it then.' It was getting like that.

Locked horns. Young males was what it was. Now, knowing animals, stallions and rams, I know they're all at it. If they come of age, locked horns, it's what they do. Football, lager louts. That's my explanation, it's animal. Males, they do it.

So there we were, mature males locking horns. And George, one day [10 January 1969] he just wasn't there after lunch. It was like: 'Mee-ting! Shit, what have we done?' 'Well, he's real offended man, you've been over the top, bossing him around, and he's just as important as you are.' This is true, I needed telling off, I suppose.

We had a meeting round at John's house. And John, being very pragmatic: 'Well, we'll get Eric Clapton in!' 'Er, I don't know about that, man. We're the Beatles, it's different, you know?' I thought, No, I've overstepped the mark. I've got to apologise to George. So I did.

That was an intense period. It was the start of the break-up. After that it became a bit dodgy, cos we all wanted a say. Whereas in the past John and I had been able to write most of the stuff, get George to write one song, and write one for Ringo. That was the formula, because we figured Lennon and McCartney were the best writers and no one had really questioned that. But of course, after a while I think it wore on the other guys: 'Who *says* you're the best writers?' You can't just say, 'Well, we are, guys. We just happen to be.' You can't say that.

Towards the end of the Beatles, one of the reasons we broke up was, we'd organised it to be 'four Paul songs, four John songs, four George songs, four Ringo songs.' Which we can see wasn't going to be right. It wasn't the right balance. But it was getting too democratic for its own good, you know?

Me and John have some tense moments on film. Which, looking back I think is good. Normally you wouldn't allow it. Nobody wants to wash their dirty linen in public. But we were in the middle of a film, and while the guys are filming, John is, 'Well I don't agree.' Suddenly the music should have gone [*dramatic, cliffhanger sound*]. Then it got like the Troggs Tapes. [The Troggs were a band whose rancorous rehearsals were taped and circulated to universal mirth.] It got very . . . But we finished it, and I think it's a good film.

We got an Oscar for the music. It's my only Oscar, I amaze my friends with it. We didn't even know it qualified for an Oscar, but the Americans looked at all the films, and said, 'Well, the Beatles have a film, they're pretty good this year.' So we won. Heyyy! Got an Oscar, for nothing.

But it was a good subject for a film. We certainly didn't *intend* it to go that way, but it turned out to be good subject matter. 'World Famous Group Breaks Up On Film.' Not bad, you know?

Let It Be, the album and the movie, laid bare the fissures in the Beatles' foundations. It may not have been Klein's intention to break up the band, but he had hammered like a demon at the ampersand that once linked Lennon & McCartney.

The process had some way yet to run. The group reassembled to make *Abbey Road* – a truly worthy swansong, released before *Let It Be* but post-dating it in studio terms. The final catalyst for their break-up proved to be another record entirely: Paul's first solo album. The story of *McCartney*, as we shall see, is inseparable from the band catastrophe that was unfolding around it.

CHAPTER 7

Rage Against the Machine

It was the worst time of my life and the worst time of all our lives

In the last year of the Beatles, Paul experienced the contrasting sensations of a loving new family and the dissolution of an embittered band. His 1970 solo record was an attempt to escape the protracted battle, but it also brought about the ultimate crisis. At the time he was making *McCartney*, Paul thought the Beatles were still together. By the time it was released, however, the public heard it as a post-Beatle record: 'This is what Paul McCartney does after the Beatles.' That perception lingers, and makes the record seem insubstantial. But it was not framed as a grand, valedictory statement, nor as a bold declaration of his artistic independence. Paul told me, 'No. It was on the cusp.'

Legally, the predicament was that McCartney could not get free of a Klein-controlled Beatles without dissolving the partnership:

> There were a lot of funny things at the time. Allen Klein was the one I wanted to sue, to get out of it all. But everyone said, 'He's not party to any of the agreements, he's just an outside guy. You can't get out by suing him, you'll have to sue the Beatles.' So I got into this terrifying thing of having to sue them, scared more than anything that, as you say, people would see this album, hear my announcement, and then hear I was suing the Beatles, without knowing any of the context.

I couldn't have another band, because I wasn't sure the Beatles had broken up. We hadn't broken up when I started, it was just me doing solo stuff. Then we *had* broken up, but I wasn't sure we'd broken up.

It hung on from John's decision to leave the band, which came when I said I think we should get back and do some little gigs. He said, 'I think you're daft. I wasn't going to tell you until after we signed the Capitol deal [Capitol was the Beatles' US label]. But I'm leaving the band.' That was, like, The Moment When The Beatles Broke Up.

He describes the eventual *McCartney* album as 'a freedom thing. I wanted to get back to absolute basics, in the same way as I wanted the Beatles to go back on the road – just a little band again, try and remember who we were. In the same way, I'd liked the idea of the *Let It Be* sessions, where we'd do "Maggie Mae", just having fun as a band. This was me trying to continue that vibe.'

I didn't think it was going to be an album. It was just me recording for the sake of it. Then I started trying to put a few songs in it, alongside the instrumentals. I got things like 'Every Night', and 'Maybe I'm Amazed', so it started to have validity as a collection.

For me now, it's great memories of a happy period: getting with Linda, earliest days. She helped me, because I'd have a guitar and amp in the house and she'd say, 'I never knew you played guitar!' Yeah, I'd play a few blues licks, you know? I'd say I did this and that, did the 'Taxman' solos . . . She was very encouraging, and that led me to 'Momma Miss America', 'Kreen-Akrore', which were right off the wall. Then a few more normal things crept in, and it became an album.

Yet, despite the difficult business circumstances behind the album, many songs are positive, like 'Every Night', expressing how life has improved. And 'Man We Was Lonely'.

That was the truth. It had been a heavy, difficult period, but meeting Linda and starting a family was the escape. I'd see there was life out there. And little things, like I would get our own Christmas tree, instead of the office ordering it. We rebelled against that: 'You know what? There's a guy on the corner, he's got dozens of them, let's just go and we'll carry it home.' The whole spirit was that escape.

I said, 'How the hell am I ever going to get out of these heavy meetings?' And it was, 'Well, don't go.' *Ching!* Brilliant plan! Boycott them. That was like The Idea Of The Century. We did that, so they had to ring us up: [*moaning voice*] 'Oh, we're going to have a meeting, what's your decision?' 'No.' Or whatever. 'Yeah, go with that.' We just escaped, got out of Dodge, went and enjoyed life.

Because, Christ, I'd worked like a devil with the Beatles for all those years, and it didn't appear like there was going to be any *happiness* at the end of it. So, suddenly I found it, and grabbed it.

The album was my escape. We made it in the front parlour. Get home, new baby, it was that joy, it transforms your life. I hadn't had a baby before – we had Heather from Linda's first marriage – so home was great joy and solace for me.

Mary, who was Paul and Linda's first child together, was born on 28 August 1969. Heather was eight years old at that point. Their next baby, the future fashion designer Stella McCartney, arrived in September 1971.

Making this record was 'Yeah, this is what I love to do.' The rest, outside, was shit. I'd go out the front door and face all the shit in the world, but coming inside was like a cocoon.

Home was being natural, being myself. I either made it at home – I got a machine from EMI, a four-track – or went down to a little studio, Morgan in Willesden, just working with one engineer. Me and Lin and the baby in the control room. It was joyous. That was exciting, you know? Newlyweds. If you're lucky, it's a great few years. Young, married life is a very special time.

I'd go in for the day, like Monsieur Magritte. Go in and make something up, knock off in the evenings. I didn't have a recording desk, I was just plugging a mike into the back of a Studer machine. Put it up in front of the drum kit. Not enough bass drum? Just move the mike nearer. Very simple, about as basic as you can get. It was a joy to make.

'Glasses' . . . That was actual glasses, wine glasses. 'Kreen-Akrore' was about an Amazon tribe I'd seen, who were fighting for survival. I recorded the sound of a bow and arrow going past the mike . . . 'Hot as Sun' was around since the Beatles days.

'Teddy Boy' was good. I'd tried to make that with the Beatles but we didn't have enough patience with each other. It got on the *Anthology* – there was just enough to make a proper version. No one was having much patience with me, it never got made. So I pulled it over into this. And 'Maybe I'm Amazed' was about the biggest song on it.

Even now that album has an interesting sound. Very analogue, very direct.

When the time came to release it I had to deal with Mammon, which was Apple. Ring them up and say, 'Er, can I have a release date?' Neil [Aspinall] gave me a date. And suddenly Mammon decided to change my release date for [*sarcastically*] the massive *Let It Be* album. And I'm, 'You bastards! I've got a date worked out! How can you do this?' I certainly shouted loud enough.

It was Rage Against the Machine, me against them, the enemy, the fucking faceless suit out there. That's why it was a good album.

But it was in the middle of all the Beatle wrangles. So we had to keep it out of Apple, in case somebody burned the tapes. Booked studios ourselves, didn't show Apple the cover.

You really had to keep the album under wraps from Apple?

Everything you did at that time was a problem with Apple. 'Oh, I'm not sure you can do *that*.' Come on, man, with the Beatles we just said, 'We're doing that, this is how *Sgt. Pepper*'s going and you're gonna put these people on the cover, cos it's cool.'

It was always problematic. So I'd got the strategy then. If I go into Apple, it'll be the heaviest vibe. People will come out of the woodwork: 'You can't do that, we'll get the lawyers on this, wait a minute, let me get a legal opinion on what you're doing.' I thought I don't need all that. I'll just do it.

At the time, the actual music on *McCartney* was overshadowed in news coverage by the album's press release. In the typewritten sheets distributed to news media, Paul practically declared the Beatles to be over. How does he feel about this, in hindsight?

I issued the album and did this press release, which virtually had the announcement. I finally blew the whistle. And John was annoyed. He told me later that he wanted to be the one who announced it. But I felt that three or four months was enough to wait around. Either we were going to fuck about for another year, or we had to actually say to people, 'You know what? About three or four months ago we actually broke up. I haven't worked with them or spoken to them since then.'

A collective paralysis had overtaken the group. Each of its members was now preoccupied by solo ambitions and – certainly in Paul and John's cases – by the lives they sought to build with their new partners. Paul had been avoiding Apple for months, but the company would still be releasing his album, and he was obliged to use their promotional process.

We discussed this at more length for the 2010 reissue of *McCartney*. The 1970 press release was in questionnaire form. Had this been done with his Apple lieutenants of the day, perhaps Derek Taylor or Peter Brown?

I'll tell you what happened, from my recollection. Peter Brown said you're putting a record out, so you'll need to do publicity. There was no way I could sit around and do a press conference. But I recognised the need for some publicity. So I said, 'What?' He said, 'Well, press conference, interviews, like you normally do.' I said, 'I can't do that. Why don't you do some questions for me and then stick that out, make that into a press release or something.'

So he did the questions that are on that sheet, and sent it round to me with a space. I just put in, you know: 'Are the Beatles going to re-form?' Now, the thing with the Beatles was, we weren't telling anyone. Because this certain American businessman had said, 'Don't tell anyone, because I'm gonna renegotiate the contracts with Capitol, et cetera, and they don't need to know you've broken up. That would make it difficult for me to renegotiate a new deal.'

So we were all keeping schtum. But I was pissed with that idea, because I thought the Beatles have always been about honesty, and here we are skulking round like a bunch of wimps, not telling anyone. But we'd broken up. And believe me, I went back and George went back and we all went back and said, 'Hey, shall we *not* break up?' But it was like, 'No, we're breaking up.'

So when the question came up in the questionnaire, I said, 'No, we're not re-forming.' Or whatever. I dropped the truth into that interview.

The idea came up. Just slip it in the press releases. You don't need to do a publicity thing; all the people in the press would get free copies, as they always did and still do. So it was a press release. But it looked like it was part of the album. I don't think people got it in the shops, to my recollection. It was just the press copies, and I thought, well, that'll do it. If the *Evening Standard* wants to know what's going on, there's my press release.

So that was that. But the perception of it looked cold and calculating. 'He's just stuck this in. What is the guy on? *And* he's suing the Beatles! What a bastard.' I caught it in the neck for that. I had to ride that wave of antagonism, knowing what I had done was right. And that in a way, I was just answering the questions that this guy had set me, like an exam.

Sooner or later, it always came back to that 'certain American businessman', Allen Klein. As Paul's legal relationship was with the Beatles, not their contentious new manager, it was the Beatles that Paul was obliged to take to court:

It was a nightmare. I don't really like talking or even thinking about it. In a nutshell this guy came in to rob the Beatles. A certain American manager was burgling the Beatles. And I spotted the burglar. Nobody else did. They rather liked this guy, and they welcomed him in.

I had the choice of busting the burglar, or allowing him to take everything from the house. I need to bust this guy or there'll be nothing left. I said to people, OK, I'll sue this guy. They said, 'You can't. If you do anything you have to sue the Beatles.' I couldn't do that. It was a good few months before I could even get my head around it. Meanwhile he was in the drawers and nicking everything.

Eventually I got around to doing that. But it created real bad feeling between the Beatles. It created bad feeling in the public arena, because all they saw was me suing the Beatles. You couldn't explain to people why. I think people understand it now. But at the time it was a nightmare.

I tried my best in the press to say, Oh, blah blah blah, I couldn't sue Allen Klein, blah blah. It was a shitty time for me. The only option was to either let him take it all, and all of us just swim along with him . . . but the truth of the matter is that he was a total cunt. He said I was fine: 'Don't worry, McCartney loves me.' And I knew I was hating the bastard. He was a crook and I could see it.

But to get away from him I had to sue the guys. And as *you* know, Liverpool, the mates, no matter how much we were arguing, it's one thing you don't ever want to do.

I knew the perception of me would be deadened from there on. And I suppose in many ways I've been fighting that for twenty years. I knew that would happen. But it was a clear choice: do that and possibly save it all, or lose it and pay the lawyers' bills, which was not a terrific option. Or just let Klein take it all. Cos the others were with him, gung-ho.

I took the option of suing him and had to live with that perception: 'This [the solo album] is what Paul's done as his first move after leaving the Beatles.' Which was actually the nicest bit, I did an album after the Beatles. So what? The worst thing was, I sued my best mates. But looking back they now say, 'Thank you, you got us out of it.' We wouldn't have Apple, there'd be no *Anthology*, no *Number* 1 record. It'd all be in someone else's pocket now. It was the right thing to do, but I knew I was walking into that Valley of the Shadow of Death. It was scary, but it was one of those moments in your life when you've gotta do it.

It was a choice of getting burgled, or nicking the guy. To do that, the choice was obvious. I had to get the scuffers [police] in. It led to so much bad feeling that didn't heal for a couple of years. Thank God it did heal, that was the great thing. We re-established our relationships. Even though I had to go through all of that shit, it was right to go through it.

It was the worst time of my life, really, and the worst time of all our lives. The whole thing had gone sour. This battle was there, and I was just trying to save *our* fortune for *us*.

⁓

While *McCartney*'s lo-fi simplicity is increasingly praised today, it was not so well-received in 1970. The record was born into a world that still expected Beatles to deliver tablets of stone from the mountain-top. Only the grand finale, 'Maybe I'm Amazed', sounded like a Beatle classic, and the rest were considered as casual throwaways. At that point in time the last thing most people had heard from Paul was side two of *Abbey Road* – a very different proposition.

'Very produced, yeah. Quite sophisticated in comparison.

We put it out, enjoyed it. It got mixed reviews, some of which were dynamite. I think John thought it was crap; I spoke to someone yesterday and they said John said it was rubbish.

Now I like its bare bones. I mean, you couldn't get more honest than plugging right in the back of the machine. I like it – and I think John was wrong.'

For all its backstage tensions, Paul had at least made *McCartney* as a Beatle. What he had to learn now – for the first time in his life – was how to be a musician who *used to be* in the Beatles.

And given the band's unsought position in history, this was more than a minor show business conundrum.

CHAPTER 8

The Astronaut and the Moon

Is there life after the Beatles?

McCartney's London house had been a salon for Swinging London; it then became a sanctuary from the fallout. But now, as the Seventies dawned, he felt increasingly drawn to his Scottish farm.

Paul was not unique in embracing rural life: Dylan and Van Morrison were famously holed up in pastoral idylls, while English bands such as Traffic made a fetish of 'getting it together in the country'. John Lennon was actually unusual in moving from London's leafy outskirts to the most urban environment possible, New York City.

In 1989, Paul described for me his early post-Beatle life: 'It's like if you've been an astronaut,' he said, 'and you've been to the Moon. What do you do with the rest of your life?' He shrugged. 'Get religion, most of them do. And go on lecture tours saying, I saw God on the Moon.

'It's surprising how things go. There's always young people coming up and they don't know the legends that have gone by.'

He'd just been interviewed for the teenage pop magazine *Smash Hits*, whose writer told him they received letters asking who George Harrison was.

'That's what time does. They're little kids, they don't know. You thought there would never come a time when people wouldn't know who George Harrison or the Beatles are. Yet there it was. People asking, Who is he?'

(In 2015, when Paul joined Kanye West for the track 'Only One', fans of the rapper were reported as tweeting 'Who is this guy?')

'I always found that optimistic, actually. Particularly if you're trying to do something after the Beatles. Is there life after the Beatles? It was good that there were young people coming up. You could play to them and not feel like you were trying to outdo your own legend.'

After *McCartney*, the solo debut that was never quite planned as such, Paul sailed with Linda to New York. Like John at that point, he must have seen the USA as a comparative refuge, far away from Apple and its problems, far away from English antipathy to his new foreign wife.

Four years earlier, the Beatles' last US tour turned sour after Lennon's quip that they were 'bigger than Jesus'. Still, America had been their inspiration, musically and culturally. Conquest of the States was their greatest symbolic achievement. Both Paul and John's wives had once called New York their home. And recent Beatles were somehow more revered here than in their homeland.

England in 1970 was itching for the newest pop sensation. The Beatles were not forgotten, but as yet, rock had not begun to fetishise its founding fathers with the tribute bands, award ceremonies and stylistic recycling that later became standard. It was too soon to feel nostalgic, and fashions moved on with unforgiving swiftness.

Lennon's move to New York would prove permanent, whereas McCartney's was temporary. Some might say this difference stemmed from their contrasting personalities – John the wild rover, Paul the homebody. But it was probably only circumstantial.

As events played out, the bass player never surrendered his London home, nor his Scottish estate, and would revisit Liverpool constantly. If Lennon stayed Stateside, it was through a mixture of choice, inertia and legal necessity.

Paul and Linda, meanwhile, had music to make:

> We were thinking of forming a group. I didn't want to end my career and I figured, Well, you'd better sing live then, because if you go into a closet you'll vanish up your own trouser leg. We went to New York first of all. It was great getting there. We took a French cruise liner [SS *France*], a posh old-fashioned one. You had a French maid with a little hat and apron. Like *ooh-la-la*! It was an adventure. [This trip, from October to December 1970, was followed by other US visits in early 1971.]
>
> We took that from Southampton and started to organise some songs. We found a grotty little basement and auditioned a bunch of people. We got someone to throw a lot of drummers at us, out of which we picked Denny Seiwell, a really good session guy, a fun person that you could get on with.

Adding a second session wizard, the guitarist Dave Spinozza, Paul made his first solo single, 'Another Day'. A safer choice might have been the widely admired 'Maybe I'm Amazed', but he went for this self-effacing song that was once intended for the Beatles. It was exquisitely played, with impressive vocal backing by Linda, and was indeed a hit. But its sweetly melancholic mood, and classic McCartney regard for the anonymous loner, drew derision from John Lennon and other critics. In John's most cutting anti-Paul song, 'How Do You Sleep?', there was a sideswipe referring to his departed partner as 'just another day'. The line was suggested to him, in fact, by one Allen Klein.

Spinozza had other commitments, and after a few more tracks his place was taken by another New York fixture, Hugh McCracken. Both guitarists would also figure in John Lennon's solo work.

Paul and Linda, meanwhile, spent their leisure hours in dressed-down anonymity:

> We'd go up to the Apollo [the Harlem venue renowned for its R&B history] and things like that. Whereas with the Beatles they'd always said, 'No, we don't want you going to the Apollo, it's not safe up there, guys.' Oh man, we've heard about the Apollo all our lives, we gotta go! 'No, it's blacks, you know, dangerous up there.'
>
> I had a beard back then, looked fairly anonymous anyway. I used to wear a combat jacket and jeans, and in New York you looked just like any junkie on the street. So you don't get noticed. But she's very ballsy, Linda. So we went up there.
>
> We were late, it was talent contest night, and they'd just closed the door. And Linda was, 'Oh no, man, he's come all the way from England, you gotta let him in, he'll love the Apollo.' 'I'm sorry ma'am, we're closing.' 'No you gotta.' She gave him so much of this he just said, 'Shit, all right, get in.' I think we might have been the only two white people in there. But it was cool.
>
> It was nothing like an English talent contest, because nearly all of them were *very good*. It was soul, and it was New York, so it would be good. There was just one guy, from Kentucky, who got booed off. He was singing 'That's Alright Mama' and these guys in front of us, smoking grass, go 'Try singin' it walkin' off!'
>
> There was a little guy up in the box with a trombone, and if he didn't like an act, it was like *The Gong Show*. *Brrrpp, brrppp*! They just had to go. The great thing was if they liked them, the record producers would run on: 'I'm Arista Records, offerin' a contract! Aaright!'

We did a lot of that, just bombing around. Once we were in Harlem, 125th Street. Cos I'm fascinated by all that, coming from Liverpool. Linda said, 'I've got to pick up Heather from school, but I'll see you here in about an hour.' So I was wandering around. I saw this playground full of kids, and it was great. These black kids, doing skipping games – I can't do it, but it was like R&B rhyming slang – early rap, I suppose. There's a famous record . . .

Three-six-nine, the goose drank wine . . .

'The monkey chewed tobacco . . .' ['The Clapping Song', a 1965 hit by Shirley Ellis]. And this black guy walked up: 'You a teacher?'

'No, I'm just watching the kids, you know?'

'You ain't a teacher? You better get off this block, man.'

'What are you talking about? I'm a tourist.' He obviously didn't recognise me, I was looking pretty funky.

'You're kidding aren't you? It's a free country.'

'You better get off the block, man, or I'm gonna *put* you off.'

He started walking off, so I'm walking along with him, like Ratso in *Midnight Cowboy*. 'Look, man, I'm from England. We love this. I'm a musician, I'm into R&B and this is fascinating to me and it's very bad of you to try and chuck me off the block' and all that.

He says [*low menace*]: 'You'd better be gone, motherfucker.'

Well, believe me, I got off that block.

But I wandered around and went into a record shop. I was really brought down. All your life has built up to this, and this guy thinks you're a perv. I was telling the black guy in the record shop. He says, 'Don't worry, man, we ain't all like that, there's just one or two guys, they uptight.'

But it was exciting, really. That was the flavour that we did *Ram* under.

Ram, Paul's second post-Beatles LP, is a fabulously ramshackle affair, maybe the craziest and most tuneful of his career. Its posthumous reputation has grown steadily, though the initial reception was muted. John and Yoko listened carefully, and scrutinised the artwork, and decided it was a litany of insults. But in truth the record is wonderfully messy and unpremeditated. It bristles with hooks; songs collapse into one another like a row of drunken sailors, half-realised ideas are tossed around with insolent ease.

'I worked in Phil Ramone's studio and in CBS for a while,' he recalls, 'and then went out to LA to do 'Back Seat of My Car', with [producer] Jim Guercio, to finish it off. Did some work there, got a bit of sunshine. It was hard work because it was mainly just me and Linda doing it. But it was OK.'

Such was the soap opera that attended the Beatles' separation, critics scanned their solo music for signs of a semaphored Lennon–McCartney conversation. And in *Ram*'s case, Lennon led the way.

'Too Many People,' Paul admits of the opening song, 'was a bit of a dig at John, actually, because he was digging at me. We were digging at each other in the press. Not harsh, but pissed off with each other, basically.'

How does it start? Are you singing 'Piss off'?

> Yeah . . . 'Piss off, cake.' Like, a piece of cake becomes piss off cake, and it's nothing, it's so harmless, just little digs. But the first line is about too many people preaching practices, you know? I felt John and Yoko were telling everyone what to do. And I felt we didn't *need* to be told what to do. The whole tenor of the Beatles thing had been, like, each to his own. Freedom. Suddenly it was 'You should do this.' It was the wagging finger. I was pissed off with it.

So that one got to be a thing about them. But then the ball starts rolling. And there was a picture that we had for Hallowe'en, of the two of us [Paul and Linda] in silly masks. I'm Wimpy out of Popeye, just masks we picked up in a kids' shop in New York. And Linda was another character, which looked a bit oriental. We heard later they thought that was a dig at them, but it actually wasn't. Some of the digs that weren't digs got taken for them.

He explains that the song 'Dear Boy', for example, was not about John – the character who 'never knew what you had found' was Linda's ex-husband.

So then John did a piss-take, he held a pig instead of the ram. [A postcard, issued with Lennon's album *Imagine*, parodies Paul on the cover of *Ram*.] This wasn't posed. Me and Linda decided to photograph our sheep, so every bloody sheep in the flock that year, there's a photograph of me holding each one. Over a hundred pictures. I was supposed to be cropped out!

We were driving up to Liverpool and deciding that *Ram* would be a good title for the album. Then the picture came: you can ram a door down, and a ram is a male thing, like a stag. It just seemed like a good word.

'Monkberry Moon Delight' I liked, so much so that it's in my poetry book. 'Long Haired Lady' is very period piece, [*fey Californian accent*] 'My long-haired lady'. Very Seventies. 'Ram On' is a cute thing on a ukulele, cos I used to carry one around with me in the back of taxis in New York, just to always have music with me. They thought I was a freak, these taxi-drivers.

'Uncle Albert/Admiral Halsey' was an epic, number one in America, surprisingly enough. I like the little bit that breaks in: 'Admiral Halsey notified me, da-da-da, had a cup of tea and a butter pie.' It's a bit surreal, just coming out of left field. But I was in a very free mood, and looking back I like all of that. It must have freaked a few people, cos it was quite daft.

It was like you had enough songs for two albums, so you used fragments or medleys, like a patchwork. One part of 'Ram On' becomes 'Big Barn Bed' on a later album.

Yeah, 'Long Haired Lady' goes off a bit, 'Big Barn Bed' comes off 'Ram On', that's right . . . 'Back Seat of My Car' is very romantic: 'We can make it to Mexico City.' That's a really teenage song, with the stereotypical parent who doesn't agree, and the two lovers are going to take on the world: 'We believe that we *can't* be wrong.' So it's corny but I like the underdog making it.

There's a lot of pent-up energy on Ram. *You were out of the Beatles now. Were you feeling in competition?*

Yeah, we were all in competition, trying to avoid each other's release dates, like we'd avoided the Stones' release dates in the Beatles. Obviously when John or George released an album, I'd check it out and see where he was up to. The truth, as a lot of people have said, is that we were missing each other. A big comment about all of us was that we missed the collaborative thing, of John saying 'Don't do that' or 'Do that'. Sparking each other off.

For a while I was very conscious of that. It was a pretty big shock. You know, not to be hanging out with these guys? I'd hung out with them since I was seventeen or eighteen.

It's odd looking back, but of the four ex-Beatles, George and Ringo got off to the strongest starts, commercially.

Yeah, George's *All Things Must Pass* . . . As he said, it was like diarrhoea: he must have held it in for so long. He had Phil [Spector] and a lot of really good people. And George was *so* pissed off with us. I mean, *all* that anger came out. Which is a good thing for an album. The 'I'll show you' factor, which I had later in *Band on the Run*. 'Oh, we need *you*, do we? Oh yeah?' So George and Ringo did get off to very good starts. John and I took it a bit hard, but throughout the years we all did pretty well as individual acts.

What I love now is you get younger generations who are going through what I was going through. Twenty-something, they're looking for where they're gonna go, as we were looking at hippifying things a bit. Getting away from authority and learning how to do it yourself. I think that's what kids relate to now. There's something innocent about it. It's young. It's younger than the Beatles' music.

CHAPTER 9

Starting From Scratch

I knew the minute I tried it wasn't going to be easy

Wings were a band who seldom felt the feathery end of the critic's quill. And their line-up was unstable, fluctuating around a core trio of Paul, Linda and Denny Laine. Even so, their commercial achievements were enormous, and their posthumous reputation has steadily grown. What are we to make of McCartney's second full-time group?

They operated for eight years, from 1971–9, which was only a little less than the Beatles. McCartney led them with bravado, barely disguising that he was lurching through the least strategic career in rock history. A wilfully chaotic project that featured his wholly inexperienced wife, Wings began with unannounced shows to small halls of bewildered students.

They progressed to the sunlit uplands of stadium rock. They made a biting protest song called 'Give Ireland Back to the Irish' and followed it with the stubbornly childlike 'Mary Had a Little Lamb'. They recorded a classic Bond theme in 'Live and Let Die', and eventually sputtered to a close with a bizarre LP named *Back to the Egg*.

Paul has defended their memory ever since. Yet sometimes he reveals those years to have been a rare period of professional pessimism.

He always yearned for the solidarity of a band, but Wings were too combustible. Longing for the comfort blanket of another 'gang', with some of the democratic quality the Beatles initially enjoyed, he envisaged Wings as part of his quest for free-spirited spontaneity. But ultimately, even the absence of a plan can unravel. As ever in McCartney's story, what survives is some music of surpassing beauty.

After *Ram* he decamped to Scotland, bringing with him two American stalwarts of that album, the drummer Denny Seiwell and guitarist Hugh McCracken. Only one of them, however, would join the new group that was taking shape: 'Hugh came to Scotland to rehearse,' says Paul, 'with a view to being in the band. But he was such a New York guy that he didn't really like to be away from America. And I can see that. New York is a satisfying town, you can walk one block and get anything, whereas you can't do that in the Mull of Kintyre. So Hugh got withdrawal symptoms, and he said to me, "I don't think I can do this." But we made good music together.'

In McCracken's place came a second Denny. 'Denny [Laine] came in from the Moody Blues. I'd seen him when we were out on tour with the Beatles.'

> My most enduring memory is of one night up in somewhere like Edinburgh on tour. We'd had a few drinks and decided that the Moody Blues would play the Beatles at snooker on this very beautiful, full-sized table. Instead of being sensible and playing one at a time, against each other in a kind of league, they all got at one end of the table and we all got at the other, and I'm afraid the table got trashed. Oh shit. But we did have a laugh.
>
> So I knew Denny from then. I knew we could get on personally and I liked his voice very much, particularly *Go Now*, which I championed. I remember taking that around the BBC in its early days and saying 'Have you heard *Go Now* by the Moody Blues? It's my favourite record of the moment.' And those producers would take notice. So I got him a few plays. I knew he had a great voice, good guy, good guitar player, so he became

> the first guitar player. I was used to having another lead voice in the group with me, so Denny became that.

And there on the keyboards, a fully-fledged band member, was Linda. To many people, this was a slightly peculiar line-up. 'It was ballsy to do,' Paul counters, 'but I couldn't think of anything else.'

> It didn't feel ballsy at the time, it just felt like, Well, what else do I do? The options were to get together a big famous group with Jim Keltner [the revered American drummer]. The other guys did that all the time, which is why I probably didn't want to do it. I felt, [*wearily*], 'Oh fuck it, all the ex-Beatles are going to use Jim Keltner.'
>
> It just felt too safe. Got to risk it a bit more. I thought, Nah, we've got to get good, not unknowns – cos Denny Laine wasn't – but we've *not* got to get a kind of Blind Faith supergroup, type of thing.

Christened Wings, the new group made a faltering start with their first LP *Wild Life*, released in December 1971. The reaction among my friends, and in the hugely influential music papers that we were just starting to buy, was one of sincere disappointment. In his haste to be up and running, perhaps, Paul had neglected songcraft and studio finesse, and the result was a sketchy collection of half-realised ideas. In contrast to the riotous variety of *Ram,* everything lasts a little longer than it ought.

Still, McCartney's inherent melodic knack holds it together and I always found the record fun, in its own wonky way. By his own admission it contains one of his worst songs, 'Bip Bop', but there are also two of his most underrated.

In 2001 I took along the vinyl copy that I'd bought thirty years earlier in Rushworth's store, a few doors down from Brian Epstein's old family business, NEMS. Paul examined the ancient artefact with great curiosity. 'From when you were in Liverpool?

What's the label like? Yes, right down to the label . . . Sleevenote by Clint Harrigan. Damn fine writer if you ask me!' Harrigan was, of course, Paul himself: 'I just couldn't own up to it.'

Turning to the track list he recalled the music itself. The opener, 'Mumbo', is a pure slab of noise that sounds, if anything, wilder as decades pass:

> 'Mumbo' is just a big scream of no words. A wacky idea, cos it was just 'Whuurrrgghh A-hurrgghhh!' and we mixed it back so it was like 'Louie Louie'. Everyone's going, What are the words of that? Just hope they don't ask for the sheet music. Which no one ever did, luckily.
>
> 'Love is Strange' was a song Linda and I had loved from the Fifties. 'Wild Life' was about a visit of mine to a safari park in Kenya, where I saw a sign that said: 'Elephants have the right of way'. 'Some People Never Know' was just me and Linda's love song, us against the world. 'I am Your Singer' is similar. 'Tomorrow' – 'bring a bag of bread and cheese' – which is what we used to do around southern France, go in a little shop, buy a baguette, a bit of cheese, a couple of tomatoes, bottle of wine, go in a field.

Probably the album's real triumph is its plangent six-minute finale, 'Dear Friend': 'A bit of longing about John,' is Paul's description. 'You know, "Let's have a glass of wine and forget it." A sort of make-up song for John.' Alas, this nakedly personal song – as touching a plea for reconciliation as any Beatle fan could wish for – attracted far less attention than the supposed slights and barbs of *Ram*.

By the 1970s there were suddenly a lot more superstars around. The Beatles had occupied the peak of pop's pyramid. But now they were gone, and rivals like the Rolling Stones and Bob

Dylan were still productive. There were new comets in the firmament: Led Zeppelin, David Bowie, T. Rex, even the Osmonds in their own way, or the Jackson 5, or Abba. For Paul McCartney it must have been a time of readjustment. Did he find that difficult?

> I knew it was going to be difficult. There was this thing of 'Follow The Beatles'. I knew the minute I tried it wasn't going to be easy. You found yourself just one of the acts in the hit parade, rather than the undisputed leaders. But it was something I knew was going to happen. It wasn't like it surprised me. I didn't go, 'Oh God! We're not as big!' I knew by starting the group from scratch that we had to work our way up.
>
> Anyone like Zeppelin or Bowie, who'd been building during the Sixties and had now arrived, naturally took precedence. You had to understand that, if you wanted to live in that climate. You had to know there are people bigger than you. And it was good because it gave us a benchmark. We thought, we'll be as big as them one day.
>
> It was weird starting all over again. But it wasn't the world's worst thing. It was sobering. It's good to be knocked off your perch, to get your feet on the ground. There was a lot of that with Wings. Not only was I doing things for myself with the band, I was personally doing a lot of things for myself, living up in Scotland, mowing the field with my tractor.

McCartney can often display a strange combination of caution and reckless daring. There's something of both in Wings' inaugural tour from 11–25 February 1972, when they tried to avoid the world's merciless scrutiny by simply turning up in random British colleges. He charged admission – for one thing his money was still locked up in Beatle hell, for another he loved the romance of a baby band. Pragmatically, he toughened up the sound by acquiring Irish guitarist Henry McCullough, a bluesy player well-respected for his time in Joe Cocker's Grease Band:

We got a band and hatched the plan of the university tour. Didn't want to have a big supergroup, just wanted to try and learn the whole thing again, hopefully learn some new things rather than repeat the Beatles. Which has been about as successful as anyone in the world was ever gonna get with anything. The theory was that by going out and looking at the whole deal again, you might get a few new clues.

So we literally took off in a van up the M1, got to Ashby-de-la-Zouch [in Leicestershire], liked the name. Great! Turn off here. But there wasn't a gig, just a little village. It was a signpost. We kept going until we got to Nottingham University, and then it suddenly hit. 'Ah, let's do universities.' Otherwise there weren't any gigs. That's a captive audience. There's people.

I remember thinking one good thing that might come out of this, in future years we'll meet people who'll say, 'I was a student when you came.' They might go on to be something, and we'll be infiltrating with them now. 'Give Ireland Back to the Irish' was the message on that tour, so they'll know we were being a bit political. If they become a big whizz at the BBC or something, they'll be able to say, 'I was there, way back when.'

For us it was just to get road experience. We showed up at these places and it was crazy. If we've got five hours some time I'll tell you about it. It's a whole saga. I remember telling it to John Schlesinger [the film director] and he said, 'Oh, I wish I'd been there, I would have loved to have filmed that.'

You took the casual approach to extremes, didn't you? Not even booking hotels? (Nor, of course, did McCartney have a manager.)

No gigs or hotels or anything. Looking back, I don't *believe* we did that. In the van we had the band, the dogs, the kids, it was madness. But we had fun times, and we did learn new stuff. It really was like I'd never been in the Beatles, couldn't rely on any of that fame as a crutch.

We went up to these universities, and of course fate had it that a lot of them were having exams. We didn't ring them up, and we forgot to ask if they'd be ready for us. But we found a couple. Nottingham, Lancaster, Newcastle City Hall, Durham. When we did find 'em it was cool. The students had a good time.

We only had eleven songs, which wasn't enough for an hour. So we'd do long versions and repeat them. And we just lied. Having to repeat 'Lucille': 'It's a request from so-and-so in the Upper Sixth, science student.' We just made it up. We came away with these bags of coins, which reminded me of Peter Sellers in *Tom Thumb*: 'One for you, two for me . . .' We counted them out in the van afterwards.

I remember you saying you'd been physically distanced from money for a long time.

Yeah, it was all cheques and accounts and stuff, bank statements. And suddenly there it was, we had to somehow change all these half-crowns. Or 50p's? Nah, must have been 50p but it felt like half-a-crown. [Britain had switched to the new decimal currency one year earlier.] Good experience, and it got us together as a band, going through all those hardships, like a young band does. It brought us together.

After their adventures in academia, Wings began work on a more considered album. *Red Rose Speedway* recovered some of the poise and consistency that was expected of Paul. But his singles of the period were impossible to categorise: the playfully innocuous 'Mary Had a Little Lamb' seemed a riposte to the BBC ban he'd received for 'Give Ireland Back to the Irish'. The double A-side of 'C-Moon' with 'Hi Hi Hi' married a reggae singalong of young romance with a throaty rocker whose sexual innuendo earned another BBC ban.

In this erratic time, *Red Rose Speedway* sounded straightforward, especially its crowning achievement 'My Love' – a classic McCartney ballad of immediate appeal, further elevated by Henry McCullough's heart-rending guitar solo. Despite the inclusion of a few leftover *Ram* numbers, the sense was of Paul's commercial re-emergence. In the same sessions he agreed to write the next James Bond theme, 'Live and Let Die', which proved a dependable spectacle of his live shows for decades to come.

The band began to play more rational tours, too. Wings Over Europe in 1972 was followed the next year by a trip around Britain's bigger halls, sealing Paul's return to mainstream acceptance. In May of 1973 I saw my first-ever McCartney show, at the same Liverpool Empire where the Beatles had played their last home town show eight years earlier. The emotional freight of this return – in the city, the audience and doubtless in McCartney's heart as well – was extraordinary.

So far, so good then? Wings had certainly taken the scenic route in getting themselves established. It should have been plain sailing from here on.

It wasn't.

CHAPTER 10

Soaring

I've got to turn this around, or I'll just dig a hole for myself

Wings' next LP, *Band on the Run*, was the first of Paul's post-Beatle records to sound as fully developed as *Sgt. Pepper* or *Abbey Road*. It was eccentric, but its whimsy was kept in check by sophisticated songcraft. This was in fact the sort of music he was *expected* to make, and his reward was a welcome spell of both commercial and critical favour.

In its making, though, *Band on the Run* was a tale of serial disasters. It was literally the album that almost killed him.

Rehearsing new material up in Scotland, Paul's thoughts had turned to a recording venue:

> I thought any studio that EMI's built, the conditions will be OK. And George had worked in Karachi or Calcutta, so I knew they had studios in all these far-reaching places. I asked EMI for a list and it was great: Rio de Janeiro, Lagos, France, they've got studios everywhere. The other temptation was China, that was on the list.
>
> I thought Rio or Lagos, because of the rhythmic element. I don't think I was necessarily thinking of using locals as much as absorbing the atmosphere. Being in a climate, you know: if you are in Brazil there's no escaping it, same with Africa. I thought, Africa, yeah, it'll be a great vibe.
>
> Of course they were *building* Lagos when we got there. It

was before oil. Now apparently it's a big city but it was mud huts, a couple of BOAC [British Overseas Airways Corporation, now BA] buildings. It was monsoon season, pissing down with rain, so it wasn't even sunny most of the time. That song 'Mamunia', 'rain comes . . .' was the vibe.

They were building the studio when we got there and they didn't know how we recorded. 'We hear you want booths. Booths? What is this?' We'd say, 'You know, like a sound booth?' Well they built them, they were like big boxes but they hadn't put glass in them, they didn't understand what we wanted them for.

It was just a different mentality. 'You've got to have glass in them, it's to stop the sound.'

'Oh! Sound booths! Very good.' And they'd build it.

But the problems had begun even before the flight to Nigeria. Henry McCullough left the band a few weeks before departure, and Denny Seiwell followed suit with only twenty-four hours' notice. It would seem that disagreements over pay and musical policy both played a part.

'Only three of us made it down there,' Paul recalls:

Me and Linda and Denny [Laine]. A couple of the guys said, 'We just don't wanna go.' Well, thanks. I hated that. I like an easy life, like most people.

After feeling deflated for a number of hours, I then thought, right, OK, we'll show you. And that was it, very much a motivating drive. We will now make the best album. And when these guys hear it, they will go, 'Shit, we should have gone.'

It wasn't vindictive but it was motivating – I've got to turn this around, or I'll just dig a hole for myself. We are *going*. Our only alternative was to cancel the whole trip, not make an album, go into a depression. So I said, 'Fuck it, I'm not gonna let that put me off my stride.'

The first fruit of this unpromising start was a rollicking track, with Paul on drums, called 'Helen Wheels', which was a hit single in October 1973. Named after the McCartney family's Land Rover, the song celebrates their regular migrations northward:

> I like that because it's a British road song and there's not many of those around. It's always Route 66. How many songs have got Carlisle in them? And Birmingham, not Birmingham, Alabama. The M6 . . . Linda loved Scotland. I still love setting off in London, going up the motorway, and you see the land change. It's like going all the way through America. We always cheer as we go over the border then around Loch Lomond. It's got a lot of memories for me, that Land Rover with everything in the back, dogs, kids, us all up at the front, and me, driving on this epic journey.

Nigeria turned out to have a few more surprises in store:

> One of my habits is not to work things out, to let things happen. That has its advantages and its disadvantages. We went expecting blue skies, green jungles, and it was like, *No.* This was inner-city Lagos, with dead people lying by the road, and the brown clay spitting up at you, driven by the monsoon.
>
> Everyone was freaked out. Good old Geoff [Emerick], the engineer on that album, he freaked cos he hates spiders. The road crew put a spider in his bed. So we were all [*thumps heart frantically*] . . . It was buggy, too. Everywhere was like an airport lounge, bare, never any furniture, and fluorescent strip lighting with millions of bugs. It's not my idea of comfort.
>
> We got mugged one night. Six guys leapt out of a car. We'd been told not to walk anywhere: 'This is Africa, man. Take a car everywhere.' But you know, that's what they say in Harlem, and you've got to experience the place.

Me and Linda were walking half an hour from the mate's place to our bungalow. It was a beautiful night, cameras, tape recorders all over us, just prime mugging targets. And this car pulled up, Linda got a bit apprehensive.

The window came down. 'Are you travellers?'

I said, 'Er, yeah, we're just walking, you know?' So the car went on for a few yards and then it stopped again. They'd obviously had a discussion, and one of them got out.

I said, 'Listen mate, it's very nice of you to offer us a lift, but it's OK, we're walking.' The fuckers were gonna mug us! And me, soft-head, you know, is going, 'That's a really nice offer, man. Fine. Off you get back in.'

And I pushed him back in the car! Another discussion, another few yards. Next time, all the doors went, six people jumped out, the little one had a knife, he was shakin', he was shittin' himself and so was I. There was no mistaking it, this wasn't a lift.

Linda, who's a dead ballsy chick, she's screaming, 'Don't touch him! He's a musician! He's just like you! He's a soul brother, leave him alone!' She's screaming at the top of her voice. 'What do you want, man? Money? Here. You can have it. The tape? Sure! Take it. Camera. Yeah, go on, you can have it all.'

They left. I said, 'Right, we walk *fast*, very fast and don't stop for anything.' Got back to the villa. The minute we got back, [*gasping*] cup of tea, the lights went, all the lights went out. Fucking 'ell.

It turned out to be a power cut, but I said, 'They've followed us. They're gonna do us.' You know how you think. It's not rational. And you know what we did? I said, 'Let's go to bed.' That was the best we could think of. We just pulled the bedclothes over us and stayed there till morning. Praying that morning would come. And it did.

I was a nervous wreck. We got to the studio the next day and the guy who owned it says, 'You're lucky you're white. They would have killed you if you'd been black, because they'd have figured you would have recognised them.'

When you were robbed, didn't they take your actual tapes as well?

Yeah, they took the demos of *Band on the Run*. I thought the joke would be that the guys who robbed us probably recorded over them, or chucked them in a ditch as being of no value. It's kind of ironic. You have to laugh. But I certainly wonder what happened to those little cassettes.

Shortly after that I fainted. I'd had it up to here with this thing. Linda thought I'd died and they took me off to a doctor. It was some kind of bronchial spasms, I could hardly breathe. You're going to the hospital in the back of a taxi, through this hub of the city of Lagos and it's a night [*frantic foreign voices, sirens and car horns*]. Oh fucking hell, I'm dying.

A source of further anxiety was Nigeria's music legend Fela Kuti. 'He accused me in the local newspaper of "stealing the black man's music".'

I said, 'What are you talking about? I've written it all myself.'

'Yes, but you have come to steal the vibe, and the African, we get no money.'

'Well, come round to the studio, I'll play you some stuff.'

I don't know if I've told you the story. But they did show up, mob-handed. I played him a couple of tracks and said, 'Where's the influence there, man?' Cos *Band on the Run* isn't African. 'You show me, where have I stolen your music?'

He was all right. 'You are good man. Is OK.' We became friends because he realised he'd got the wrong end of the stick.

That was a crazy trip. We got back and I opened a little note that I'd just missed. It said, 'Len Wood, Chairman of EMI. Dear Paul, I understand you're taking your family to our Lagos studios. Would advise against your going there as there's just been an outbreak of cholera.' So that's where we were going.

When we got back people would say, 'Ah, out of adversity has been born a good album.' I hate that theory. It may be true, as well. I hate the idea that you've got to sweat and suffer to produce something good. It turned out successful, anyway.

The record was completed at AIR Studios in London. And then it was packaged in the most memorable LP cover since *Abbey Road* – a strangely random group of famous people caught in a prison spotlight. The session was actually shot in the mansion grounds of Osterley Park, west London, where Paul remembers, 'everyone choosing their costumes, Kenny Lynch, Michael Parkinson as a young cat. All of us looking like delicious young men, with bodies to die for, standing around talking to John Conteh.'

Listening to it, as I did last night at Abbey Road, what struck me was its quirkiness. Most people don't arrange songs that way any more. People often have a straightforward approach to a song, but *Band on the Run*, it's editing, it's cutting. It's like a radio play that moves around. 'Band on the Run' itself sets the tone for that. It moves in and out of beats, genres, and just seems to work. It made me think, we didn't give a damn then.

Among the last things you'd done before was the Bond theme 'Live and Let Die', *which similarly has sections and a narrative. Did that put you in a mindset for* Band on the Run? *In fact you sat down and read Fleming's book, I think.*

Yes, I did, on the Saturday and wrote it on the Sunday. I hadn't thought of that but I think that might be true. Having to write something for a film reminded me what degree of licence you had to play around with structure. I did 'Live and Let Die', as you say, which has various parts stitched together, and that probably encouraged me to think about *Band on the Run* in the same way, as a kind of epic adventure album.

I was always pleased with the success it had, because we were building Wings and doing that, post-Beatles, was almost impossible. It's nice to look back and see that somebody thought we actually succeeded. They heard it and thought, I love that song. I remember I was going on the ferry, or I was dating some girl. It was the soundtrack to a lot of people growing up.

Aiming to take Wings back on the road, Paul now added a new drummer, Geoff Britton. On guitar there came the young Scots prodigy Jimmy McCulloch, formerly of the briefly successful pop band Thunderclap Newman. During a summer sojourn in Tennessee they recorded a storming single – with its own lyrical quotient of sheer strangeness – called 'Junior's Farm'.

The new band's earliest rehearsals were captured in a short film *One Hand Clapping*, made in 1974, but never commercially available until a deluxe reissue of *Band on the Run* in 2010. 'It's nice to see that resurfacing,' he told me at the time. 'It was David Litchfield. He produced a little magazine that was funky.'

Ritz *magazine, with David Bailey.*

'Yeah. He was a friend, and we decided that he would shoot a simple piece on video. We would go into Abbey Road and play basically what we'd rehearsed. We called the film *One Hand Clapping*, for absolutely no reason, and not a lot happened with it. But that is the beauty of these reissues, that suddenly these things find their home.'

Paul was not cured of his taste for unfamiliar recording venues, and the next LP was made in New Orleans. Still, *Venus and Mars* was nearly as winning as its predecessor. There was a great saxophone waft of Mardi Gras in the hit single 'Listen to What the Man Said', and more local colour in a tremendous out-take,

'My Carnival'. There was a name-check for Led Zeppelin's Jimmy Page in 'Rock Show', as if to acknowledge the new rock hierarchy that Wings were up against, plus some strong ballads and a sly, funky standout in 'Letting Go'. Of course there also had to be something baffling – here it was a version of the theme to Britain's cosy teatime soap show *Crossroads*.

Mid-sessions, the drummer Geoff Britton had been replaced by an American, Joe English. For all its temperamental volatility, this new line-up was probably Wings' finest. It emboldened Paul to undertake their biggest tour so far – the global trek of 1975–6 that included almost thirty shows in the United States – his first appearances there since the Beatles abandoned live work in 1966. The set list took in Wings hits and, for the first time, a handful of Beatles songs, though their split was still keeping some lawyers employed. There was also material from a new album, made at Abbey Road between stages of the tour, called *Wings at the Speed of Sound*. And there would soon be a triple live LP, *Wings Over America*.

In the ten years since those last American shows, the pent-up passions of Beatlemania had never found proper closure. Paul's tour was all the more triumphant for managing to honour that past without being trapped inside it. He recalls with special pleasure a gig at Seattle's Kingdome on 10 June 1976, where the attendance of 67,000 surpassed the Beatles at Shea Stadium:

> We broke our own record. That was a big pay-off for Wings after all that terror, post-Beatles.
>
> We have this big tour, and at first everyone wants to know [*US announcer voice*], 'Is this gonna be a Beatles reunion? It's rumoured that McCartney, George Harrison and Ringo Starr are apparently going to join him on stage, and . . .' Was John alive then? I'm terrible at chronology.

He was alive until after Wings.

Of course. I'm hopeless on dates, as you can see. It was rumoured the Beatles were going to re-form. So it bugged us – even in Wings' most successful year they were taking our success off us: 'Well, maybe the Beatles will re-form. *That* would be good, wouldn't it?' The great thing was that a few weeks into the tour, it was, 'Who cares? It doesn't matter! This is a great band.'

It *was* a good line-up, with Jimmy and Joe and the brass section. It sounds good and looks good, and we did this thing that we set out to do. And we needn't have worried. You always think nothing will ever take over from the Beatles, but it's funny what time does. It's a bastard, because I meet people now who say, 'I was a real Wings fan.' You never thought anyone could ever say that.

CHAPTER 11

Wings Folded

We lived in fear, all those years

The first phase of Wings' career was eccentric. The middle years were comparatively conventional – and massively successful. But the closing scenes would prove as strangely chaotic as the band's beginnings.

Their 1976 album, *Wings at the Speed of Sound*, was a worthy move towards band democracy, with showcase tracks for every single member. Yet the cover of its follow-up, *London Town*, revealed a line-up cut back to the core trio that had made *Band on the Run*. Paul, Linda and Denny Laine were pictured by the wintry River Thames. On the reverse they wore tropical togs, befitting the recording location, a yacht in the Virgin Islands. Somewhere along the way, Jimmy McCulloch and Joe English had become men overboard.

English, it was reported, had left mid-sessions because he missed his native America. The volatile McCulloch had resigned to join a re-formed version of the Small Faces. Recording was further interrupted when Linda gave birth to the McCartneys' son James, their third child together, after Mary and Stella. Somewhere in the confusion, Paul and Denny wrote a lilting Scottish waltz called 'Mull of Kintyre', which became one of the biggest-selling singles of all time. This it achieved at the zenith of punk rock, and it likely surprised Paul as much as anybody. The track was planned only as a double A-side with the now-obscure rocker 'Girl's School'. For a man who is sometimes accused of knocking out hits to order, McCartney's career really is a monument to serendipity.

London Town was released into the wild in early 1978, and the pop world had utterly changed since the band's last studio album. The Christmas success of 'Mull of Kintyre' had naturally nailed Paul back to the middle of the road; like any huge phenomenon, it bred a vociferous antipathy in some listeners. The Scottish song played to Paul's most innocent instinct: a generic homage to the district he'd made home from home. It was sublimely detached from anything that was hip. Meanwhile the new album had his usual quotient of melody, whimsy and grit. But in the new age of punk rock, not to mention disco and heavy metal, Wings were more of an oddity than ever.

The kudos of being an ex-Beatle was now at its lowest ebb. John Lennon was responding to public indifference with indifference of his own, sequestered with a tape machine in his New York apartment. Paul, however, was determined to stay in the game. *London Town*'s title track has a surreal charm, and its outstanding song 'With a Little Luck' captures quintessential Macca hopefulness. It's generally a low-key collection, but Michael Jackson, or at least his producer Quincy Jones, was certainly paying attention – he picked its prettiest cut, 'Girlfriend', for his next project, the monstrously successful *Off the Wall*.

In 1989 I asked Paul about Wings' line-up changes; he was then rehearsing his new band, itself not destined for permanence. At this point, Wings' apparent instability was a charge he seemed unwilling to accept:

> Fairly unstable, but not half as unstable as some people. To get a group is a difficult thing. Groups are always chopping and changing. The Shadows, that great stable pillar of British society, d'you know how many changes they've had? Well I do, cos I'm

a fan of theirs: Brian 'Licorice' Thingy [Locking] and Brian Bennett and Jet Harris . . . So I don't think it's *that* unstable.

What do you do? Stay stable with a bad group? I just wasn't happy with the people. So you try and do better. I probably only had about three line-ups of Wings, it's not that many.

It did get me, 'Oh, he's hard to work with.' But you can look at it another way. They weren't that good, maybe. Either I'm a bit of a sod, or, whoever it was, wasn't that good. I'm not sure which it is, but I can remember what happened, why we broke up in each instance. Once, I was trying to get the guitar player [Henry McCullough] to play something and he said, 'It can't be played.' Oops. Oh dear. It can, you know. It got to be one of those, so it was like the Troggs Time really. [Another reference to the infamous Troggs Tapes.]

Obviously I'd have liked to have just had the Beatles, one line-up of Wings, and this new band. That would be terrific.

A little later in 1989 we returned to the subject and he acknowledged that musicians might find it challenging to play for Paul McCartney. Was that to be a regular story through the Wings years?

The difficulty was that after the Beatles, what do you do? I think that any band felt a bit not up to it. If you had any sort of argument it was amplified because they were insecure anyway. So, a regular thing? There were quite a few line-up changes. There were some crazy line-ups. I mean, *this* band feels very stable [the 1989/90 tour band group], just in their personalities. There's no piss artists. We all like a drink but there are no really serious piss artists. There's no really heavy anything, really. Which you know, bands used to be more. They're not like that so much now. Which I'm more comfortable with.

But someone like Jimmy McCulloch was an erratic personality, if you want to put it nicely. A great little player, lovely bloke, but been brought up in Glasgow, so he was a boozer *par excellence*, and a stayer-upper-later. Jimmy wanted it all and he wanted it now, one of those guys. Which was awkward, because you'd want your kip and he'd be in the next hotel room to you, blasting music after coming in off the piss at four in the morning. I'd have to go into him: Hey, Jim, do us a favour man. 'Oh, sorry man, were ye asleep? Oh OK, aye.' He was out of it and he'd be out of it on sessions, so I'd have to play the stuff.

From the perspective of now, it's lucky that we *ever* held a group together. Cos it was a raunchy mob, actually. Henry McCullough was a raunchy character, Denny was quite get-at-it.

Twelve years later, in 2001, I found his attitude to Wings' impermanence was perhaps more philosophical:

I knew it happened and people always asked me, but I blanked it. Probably in my mind a band is a democratic unit. Everyone has an equal vote, and in the Beatles for ten years that had been the case. If Ringo didn't like one of our songs, which wasn't often, Ringo could veto a Lennon and McCartney song. He had the right to do that.

That was good, everyone felt good about themselves. But in Wings that wasn't the case. I was an ex-Beatle. So I saw myself as the leader of the group, which I'd never been in the Beatles, where the leadership had sort of moved around. There wasn't a leadership in the Beatles. People had said that John was, and later people said that I was, but neither of us ever acknowledged it. People would say, 'Who's the leader of the group?' We'd say, 'There isn't one.' So it became a democracy.

But Wings wasn't. Looking back, that could be why. I think a democracy works better. It wasn't as if it was a dictatorship, but we weren't all equal. Musically, we were various degrees of musical experience. And it might have been that that's what did it.

Still, Wings had one more act to play. By May 1978 Paul was recording with two new members, drummer Steve Holley and guitarist Laurence Juber. They repaired to Kintyre, where Paul was adding adjacent land and buildings with extra musical facilities. Here they began what turned out to be the band's last album, *Back to the Egg*. Further recording took place at Lympne Castle in Kent, and in a small studio in MPL's London office.

But from its frankly awkward title onwards, *Back to the Egg* remains a head-scratcher. Indeed it was among the first LPs I was given to review by the *NME*, and I found myself nonplussed. I loved the melodic grace of numbers like 'Arrow Through Me' and 'Winter Rose/Love Awake' and admired the perverse commitment he could show to a lyric such as 'Old Siam, Sir', and the wilful use of fragmented recitals. But would the *NME* readers be as tolerant?

By this stage, mid-1979, punk had evolved into new wave, still tough but commercially sleek and disciplined. When *Back to the Egg* was not given to mysterious self-indulgences, it was lurching into formulaic big rock, especially in a multi-superstar line-up – the 'Rockestra' – that Paul convened for a few tracks.

The general reception was sceptical, and a decade later Paul was suggesting to me it was one of his worst records. By 2001, however, he had promoted it to the category of 'most overlooked.'

Probably nothing on *Back to the Egg* was odder than 'The Broadcast' – over a pretty piano and some languid strings, a well-bred Englishman reads extracts from a few books:

> The two people who owned the castle we were recording at [Harold and Deirdre Margary, at Lympne] . . . We set up a little mobile unit and they used to invite us in for a drink every

evening. Me and Linda would sit in their sitting room and they were [*gently upper-class accent*] 'very lovely people, very far back.' We got a great relationship with them. Even though we were different generations and classes, we just had a lot in common. And I hit on this idea, I asked them would you select some favourite prose or poetry, just read it for me and I'll use it in a collage. So that became 'The Broadcast'.

The 'Rockestra Theme' has good memories for me, of John Bonham in particular on drums, cos he's the powerhouse behind the rhythm section. And all the great guys who showed up, [Pete] Townshend, Hank Marvin, a lot of really cool people. The idea was funny, but we were thinking recently of trying to revitalise it; every city has millions of people who play guitar, loads of drummers, and they only ever get together in really small units. Every city's got millions of people who can play violin, viola and cello, and percussion, but *they* get together in large units. It was like an us-and-them thing. Why don't *we* get together in large units?

That was the idea I was trying to float. I was hoping it would take off so much that people in Cleveland and people in Carlisle, kids would all get together and form rockestras, and do things like 'Lucille'. Imagine twenty bass players – *dum-dum-dum* – ten drummers – *bash bash bash* – it would be a great scene, man, so someone's still gotta do that. I may not get round to it but someone will, and I want inviting to it, please.

I first met Paul McCartney on the night that Wings played their last Liverpool show. I was twenty-three and working for Britain's biggest music paper, the *NME*. While this assignment seemed to me a dream come true – the opportunity to meet an actual Beatle – I don't think my editors saw it as particularly important in the post-punk musical climate of the time. They happily sent their least experienced writer.

On the other hand, nobody knew the band would not tour again. We weren't aware that he'd spent the months since *Back to the Egg* recording alone. It was now late 1979 and although the jaunty new single, 'Wonderful Christmastime', was credited solely to Paul, the band were still employed to promote it. In other words, we were at another point of some uncertainty in Wings' career.

This being the homecoming concert – held as a benefit for the then-struggling Royal Court Theatre – none of that unease was evident from the stage, and I recall a happy night. It could hardly match the euphoria of that Liverpool Empire show six years before, but what could? The newest material available was from *Back to the Egg*, which had captured very few hearts, and the latest line-up was not road-trained. He played only a few Beatle songs. But, you know, it was still Paul McCartney. Back in Liverpool. That sounded like a party in anyone's book.

After the gig there was a small press conference in the Royal Court's art deco bar. Fans were thronged around the entrance; some had paid the Scouse touts extortionate sums for tickets. Characters from Paul's past, like the Beatles' early manager Allan Williams, were turning up in readiness for a knees-up. But the press chat was nothing much. With hindsight I wonder if Paul was already detaching himself from the whole Wings project.

He bore with patience the usual questions about a Beatles reunion; the band were at least on speaking terms by now, but not much more. This, in any case, was just a year before the fatal night in New York City that would make the whole idea redundant. I blundered in with some banal enquiry or other, which Paul answered politely. When I left the theatre, nearby Lime Street was barricaded by taxis; nothing to do with McCartney's visit, just the result of another Liverpool cab strike. For me it meant a long walk home in the bitter November cold, yet I felt elated – Christ, I've just spoken to a Beatle.

Wings lacked a definite ending. During that final UK tour they played one of Paul's new solo recordings, 'Coming Up' – the band's live version, from Glasgow, was so acclaimed it was made the B-side of the eventual single. But there were no more Wings releases. They had some rehearsals in 1980. But after a last benefit show for Cambodian refugees in December of 1979, there were no more Wings shows either.

The immediate reason is not hard to spot: Paul's infamous 'Japanese episode' at Tokyo's Narita Airport on 16 January 1980, when he was arrested for possession of cannabis. The band's intended tour of that country was abruptly cancelled.

Speaking to me in 2010, he seemed unsure of what was going through his mind on that occasion, thirty years before:

> I think the Japanese 'episode' as we can call it, was the end of Wings. It's strange, that period for me. I didn't want to go to Japan with this band. I felt under-rehearsed. And I don't like that feeling at all. I will normally rehearse so I feel, We've got a great show. Then I'm happy to go. We were going to rehearse in Tokyo, and I thought, Oh, a bit last minute . . . So I was panicking about it all.
>
> And suddenly, I get busted. And I don't know, it feels strange. It's almost like I got myself busted, to get out of it. I really don't know, to this day. I also think, did someone put that stuff in there? To bust me? I don't know. It's very psychodrama. Anyway, the upshot was, we got there, I got busted, and I really thought, this band isn't gonna work, I'm not happy with it.
>
> Why weren't we rehearsed? There was something going wrong, something was trying to tell me something. So that was the end of Wings. Since Wings had started, I must say I was looking forward to the day it ended – just to be able to say: 'Wings

> Folded'. I do remember wanting to say that. I'm not sure if anyone ever used it.

At the time, he wrote a short book for his own diversion, *Japanese Jailbird*, that detailed his nine-day spell in prison: 'I never did anything with it. I made copies for my kids. I like it as writing, it's a slim volume, twenty thousand words, but for me that was a lot of writing. Cathartic.'

His next move was to put out a new album, *McCartney II*, issued in May of 1980. Its core was the home recordings he had made the previous year, just before Wings' final tour. It struck me that there was an echo of his first post-Beatles album, *McCartney*, from 1970; both were made by Paul alone, while he was officially still in a band that wasn't destined to record again. Was he effectively – and perhaps subconsciously – giving up on Wings, just as he had the Beatles, and falling back on his own devices?

'Yeah. And wanting to continue making music. With Wings . . . It's not easy to just ring up a bunch of people and say, "We won't be a band." It takes a bit of time. So during that time you either don't do any music or you think of some project like this. I think that's what I did with *McCartney*, just to keep making music. And I think it was the same with this.'

And how do you feel, now, about what Wings achieved?

> It's nice, there was something there. I *now* know that, but I didn't know it then. We lived in fear, all those years, we just thought what we were doing was bad. We listened to our critics. We never thought we did anything good, which is a pity, because there was good stuff there. Now there are some people liking it as much as the Beatles. There are people whose age made them actually prefer it. But we'd get slagged off everywhere and it was intimidating. It is nice now to come out of the tunnel and feel we did something good.

The big thing about Wings was that we bought into the myth that it could never be as good as the Beatles. I knew it was the world's most difficult thing to bite off. Everything we did was in the shadow of the Beatles, which had recently been this phenomenal band. We did everything with quite a lot of paranoia. Even if we did something innovative, or broke a record that the Beatles had had, it was still, like *Woah* . . .

Something like 'Coming Up' was very me, not very Beatles. And that's what I was trying to do with Wings. People would say, 'Why don't you do Beatles songs?' We'd go [*gruffly*] 'We don't do Beatles stuff, we're Wings.' We were trying to get our own identity. I was trying to strike out with something new. I thought there's not much point doing the ten years after the Beatles, and just repeating it all. Some of these would have worked with the Beatles, some of them wouldn't.

If 1980 had started badly, in a Japanese jail, the year would end tragically, with John's murder on 8 December. In the space of twelve months, McCartney had lost the band he had planned his second career around, and the artistic soulmate who had made his first career conceivable. (We shall, of course, return to this catastrophe soon.)

If McCartney was truly irrepressible, now was the time to prove it. He had been a recording artist for eighteen years, but his career had not even reached its halfway mark.

CHAPTER 12

Of Frogs and Firemen

Macca gets back to work

Rupert the Bear was a small furry animal from newspaper comic strips, familiar to every child in Britain since the 1920s. Along with his well-dressed friends, who included a badger and an elephant, he roamed a dreamlike English countryside, enjoying far-fetched adventures that always brought him home in time for tea.

Paul rediscovered the yellow-scarfed little fellow when reading stories for his own children; he thought of writing soundtrack music for an animated film. He actually attempted some tracks with the final line-up of Wings, though these remain unreleased. But the whole project was sidelined in the confusion of 1979/80.

Eventually, as Wings were fading from Paul's plans, he pushed ahead with that film idea. Now a thirteen-minute short, titled *Rupert and the Frog Song*, it finally saw release in 1984, complete with a croaking choir of cartoon amphibians who spawned – if that is the word – a hit single called 'We All Stand Together'.

Credited to Paul McCartney & the Frog Chorus, this oddly grandiose number reunited him with his old producer George Martin, secured another Top 3 hit and became a perennial Christmas favourite. It has the enduring quality of all those animal songs that BBC radio used to serve up to children on Saturday mornings, from 'Nellie the Elephant' and 'Little White Bull' to 'The Ugly Duckling' and 'Tie Me Kangaroo Down

Sport'. Personally I've always found the frog song charming. But something about its anthropomorphic innocence struck a bum note with Paul's detractors.

The same detractors were no less forgiving of 'Ebony and Ivory', the Stevie Wonder duet that closed Paul's 1982 album *Tug of War.* He'd even had to weather criticism of his response to John Lennon's murder. He could have been forgiven for wondering if the 1980s were going to be one of those decades when you should really just stay in bed.

Wings were over. Its nucleus of Paul, Linda and Denny Laine could still be heard on various *Tug of War* tracks, but from now on the albums bore Paul's name alone. And there would be no more live shows for a long time to come.

On the other hand, lacking a regular band, he was free to pursue whatever collaborations he fancied. He and Stevie Wonder concocted a funky track called 'What's That You're Doing'. Elsewhere in the *Tug of War* credits we find well-known names like the rockabilly pioneer Carl Perkins, 10cc's Eric Stewart and the peerless American bass player Stanley Clarke. George Martin produced the whole affair and it was engineered by another Beatle stalwart, Geoff Emerick. As ever, Linda was there to sing backup.

So Paul had some dependably familiar faces around. Much of the same personnel were on his next album, *Pipes of Peace* (1983), whose sessions overlapped with *Tug of War.* This time, even Ringo Starr showed up. But the starriest guest of all was Michael Jackson, co-writing two songs, 'Say Say Say' and 'The Man'; Paul repaid the favour with a duet on Jackson's own number 'The Girl is Mine', destined for the biggest-selling album of all time, *Thriller.*

So far, so good, even if *Pipes of Peace* seemed like a slight tailing off. The reputation of his next LP, *Give My Regards to*

eenage rebel: a young aul McCartney plays lunchtime session at e Cavern Club in iverpool on December 1961.

Paul with his father, Jim, in 1967. 'Learn to play the piano', McCartney Snr had once advised him. 'You'll get invited to a lot of parties'.

Paul and George with Richard Lester, director of the Beatles' early films: 'Rock and roll movies were traditionally bad. We held out for something good.'

A Liverpool airport press conference for the northern premiere of *A Hard Day's Night*, 10 July 1964. Typically, Paul looks the most at home. But today the same airport is named after John Lennon.

Following a triumphant motorcade from the airport, the Beatles greet the crowd and meet the Lord Mayor at Liverpool Town Hall, before the premiere of *A Hard Day's Night*.

The Beatles hit the beach at Miami, Florida, 13 February 1964, before filming the second appearance on the Ed Sullivan TV show.

The dawn of the music video: filming a TV promo clip for 'Help!' at Twickenham Studios on 22 April 1965.

'And then, of course, the deafening din, like a million seagulls.' A dash to the stage of New York's Shea Stadium on 15 August 1965.

British bobbies hold the line – just – outside Buckingham Palace as the Beatles collect their MBEs from the Queen on 26 October 1965.

Sgt. Pepper was launched at Brian Epstein's London house on 19 May 1967. The picture was taken by Linda, just four days after she met Paul for the first time

The band took their Sgt. Pepper costumes out of mothballs to film a clip for 'Hello, Goodbye' at London's Saville Theatre on 10 November 1967.

'he cartoon Paul om *Yellow Submarine*, eleased in 1968. 'We id it begrudgingly... ut it has a sort of ippiness that looks ice now.'

Playing his Fender Jazz bass at Abbey Road, during 1968 sessions for the White Album.

Nonplussed office workers were lured to Apple's rooftop by the impromptu gig, held on 30 January 1969, that would be the band's last performance in public.

Mixing at Abbey Road with Ringo and the Beatles' producer George Martin: 'It's always been good for me to have someone like George, who actually knows music.'

Broad Street, was diminished by the problematic movie it soundtracked. It was also a bit of a jumble – mostly re-recorded songs from Paul's back catalogue, plus some of George Martin's orchestrated score. Still, there was the majestic 'No More Lonely Nights', some tight rock-and-roll sessions with Ringo and the guitarist Dave Edmunds, and a lovely finale called 'Goodnight Princess', played in the old-time dance style that Paul's father had loved.

The decade wore on and pop music was reinventing itself, especially under the impact of hip hop. What was Paul McCartney's place in it all? There was no particular answer to that question in the 1986 record *Press to Play*. Like the rest of his less-acclaimed albums, *Press to Play* has tracks that are ripe for rediscovery, but a brief writing partnership with Eric Stewart did not blossom. The most memorable aspect of the album was its romantic cover shot of Paul and Linda, by a photographer from Hollywood's golden age, George Hurrell.

Press to Play, in its defence, was not a complacent piece of work – in fact, it's bursting with the urge to experiment. But there were no crowd-pleasing singles in the mix, and Paul failed to find the right chemistry with his new producer Hugh Padgham. Another project, with the producer Phil Ramone, was to be called *Return to Pepperland*, twenty years on from that first high summer of psychedelia. But it was not to be, though some of its new songs would find eventual release on later records.

More successful was a return to Paul's deeper roots: *Choba B CCCP*, which in translation, of course, means 'Back in the USSR'. This red-blooded blast through some rock-and-roll oldies was recorded in two days with a scratch band. For McCartney it was a useful way of blowing away the mental cobwebs.

And, in the meantime, he got in touch with Elvis Costello.

Towards the end of the 1980s McCartney found fresh impetus. Songwriting sessions with Costello produced useful material for both men. On Macca's side, it racked up his tally of new songs for the next album, 1989's *Flowers in the Dirt*. And from these sessions came the touring band that would put Paul back on the road. With these players, and Linda, he undertook world tours that opened up a new phase of his career.

The next decade saw novel demands on Paul's time, whether it was full-blown classical commissions like the *Liverpool Oratorio* or his commitment to the Beatles' gargantuan *Anthology*. And between those planet-straddling tours he made another studio album, 1993's *Off the Ground*. Again the impression was of a hungrier McCartney, re-energised by a roadworthy band, his lyrical backbone stiffened with more Costello collaborations.

Admittedly, he could no longer count on VIP access to the singles charts. Those markets and their media belonged to another generation now, and they marched to the beat of a different drum-machine. At the same time, for anyone with sufficient curiosity to listen, it was apparent that 'Macca' – the old Scouse nickname was suddenly being adopted everywhere – was not finished yet. He weighed in with further classical compositions, some dance-club wildness as The Fireman, and a radio series called *Oobu Joobu*. We'll revisit all these in due course.

By the time of the *Flaming Pie* album in 1997, Paul's children were grown up, close friends (like Ivan Vaughan, the Quarryman who had introduced him to John) were dying, and on his mantelpiece there was a knighthood from the Queen. In Britain's imagination McCartney was changing from rock star to a mixture of elder statesman and kindly uncle. And at this point he turned in some of his most deeply felt songs, free of easy optimism but full of spiritual encouragement.

From the album's title – 'flaming pie' is taken from an old John Lennon quip – to its mood of wary stoicism on 'Somedays', and wistful reminiscence, 'The Song We Were Singing', it represented a ceasefire in the war between Paul's past and present.

Post-*Anthology*, he could at last present himself in full, with due acknowledgement to all periods of his life.

In line with its laid-back ethos, *Flaming Pie* was made without a band but with the help of Jeff Lynne, who had just done production work for the *Anthology*'s 'new' Beatle tracks, plus old comrades Ringo, George Martin, Steve Miller and Geoff Emerick, as well as Linda and the McCartneys' son James, who was now emerging as a musician in his own right. Among the most affecting tracks, 'Little Willow' was written for the children of Ringo's ex-wife Maureen, who had recently died.

Within a year of *Flaming Pie*'s release there was another funeral, this time for Linda: after three years of illness, she succumbed to cancer in April 1998.

In that light it was natural to hear his next rock album – 1999's *Run Devil Run* – as a clearing of the emotional decks. Paul assembled a squad of grizzled, if distinguished, rock-and-roll pugs to help him through a storming set of Cavern-era cover versions with a few new songs thrown in. Of the latter category, 'Try Not to Cry' is a lovers' break-up story that doubles for the real bereavement he was enduring that year.

Thrown riders like to get back in the saddle. *Run Devil Run* declared that Paul was still in the game. Elvis Presley and Chuck Berry chestnuts were attacked with a passion to shame rockers a third of McCartney's age. He sounded as thrilled as he did on 'I Saw Her Standing There'. Whatever life might bring his way, there was something indestructible in McCartney's spirit, at least where music was concerned. The record rocked like a bastard.

One would imagine that being Paul McCartney was a full-time career. And yet he's often run some parallel operations, often as one half of The Fireman.

In partnership with the producer Youth, alias Martin Glover, formerly of the band Killing Joke, he has made a series of records that began in 1993 with *Strawberries Oceans Ships Forest.* The Fireman name was initially a subterfuge – though the duo's anonymity was short-lived – allowing Paul to step outside of his more conventional range. As The Fireman he could experiment with sounds that his mainstream audience might find rather strange, especially if they'd bought it expecting something more characteristic.

It was a variation on the same ruse he'd conceived with *Sgt. Pepper* – an alter ego that could be more daring even than the Beatles.

And *Strawberries* was indeed a long way from Paul's normal output, harking back to his avant-garde dabblings in the 1960s. The starting point, this time around, was an invitation to Youth to remix tracks from *Off the Ground*. The plan morphed into a full-blown album of ambient and techno tracks that revel in samples and loops, massive drumbeats and tribal celebration. Amid the explosive rhythms and trance-like drones you will even hear snippets of the upper-class dialogue from *Back to the Egg*: 'I think I sense the situation . . .'

It was a record whose natural habitat was the dance club rather than the home hi-fi, but it's a sledgehammer finished with intricate decoration, and not without McCartney's trademark qualities of swing and exuberance.

The Fireman project was resumed with *Rushes*, in 1998, rather more approachable than its predecessor in the variety of textures and instrumentation. 'Watercolour Guitars' has the drum-free acoustic prettiness that its name implies; 'Palo Verde', one of three cuts to pass the ten-minute mark, has spectral interspersions by Linda (it was recorded in her final weeks); 'Bison' is a lopsided monster, bass-heavy and huge, featuring Paul on drums. Another track, 'Fluid', builds from a gentle piano figure into something dark and ominous, enlivened by moments of erotic moaning.

Youth was again on hand, along with Welsh band Super Furry

Animals, for what's probably the least accessible record of McCartney's career, 2000's *Liverpool Sound Collage*. Conceived to accompany a pop-art exhibition staged by Peter Blake, the *Collage* mingles snippets of the Beatles' studio banter with snatches of Liverpool street talk, abstract washes of sonic distortion and slow, loping beats.

Paul's next collaboration in this off-the-wall tradition was *Twin Freaks* (2005), put together with Roy Kerr, a DJ and producer who traded as Freelance Hellraiser. Applying Kerr's mash-up skills to existing McCartney numbers, the tracks were played as a curtain-raiser for the 2004 European tour. The effect is often thrilling: 'Long Haired Lady', off *Ram*, gets chucked inside a blender with an obsessive guitar riff from 'Oo You', off the *McCartney* album; 'Live and Let Die' is entirely taken apart and reconstructed with fragments of speech, new percussion and a general mood of anarchy. The early Wings track 'Mumbo' – which was bonkers enough to begin with – pushes out to the borders of madness. Elsewhere are numerous tracks from 'Temporary Secretary' to 'Rinse the Raindrops', and 'Venus and Mars' to 'Coming Up', circling and colliding in febrile panic.

The Fireman's third album, their last to date, was *Electric Arguments*, and it seemed almost conventional. Although the songs are often ragged, they *are* songs, with plenty of melodic force, and McCartney's voice is finally back in charge. An addictively chunky rocker like 'Sing the Changes' could sit quite easily on one of his mainstream albums. 'Highway' and 'Nothing Too Much Just Out of Sight' are equally red-blooded. The roughness and spontaneity do not disguise the strength of this material, which could pass for the near-complete demos of a classic McCartney solo album. *Electric Arguments*, in fact, is possibly the finest record that a lot of his audience have never heard.

In the twenty-first century, Paul McCartney's public profile seemed higher than at any time since the Beatles. Given the media's ever-closer embrace of celebrity culture, he could not escape a surfeit of personal coverage when he started dating Heather Mills. The couple duly married in 2002 and, just over a year later, they had a baby daughter called Beatrice. But the marriage was fated to end in a widely reported divorce case in 2008.

By that point Paul had already met an American woman, Nancy Shevell, whom he went on to marry in 2011.

Reviewers and fans were naturally tempted to trace the influence of these events in each album of new material – and there were indeed songs with a direct relationship to McCartney's emotional circumstances. But it's seldom his policy to spell out an autobiographical story. Lyrically he's just as likely to take pleasure in the simple sound of words and the images they create.

Driving Rain (2001) was Paul's first full set of original songs since *Flaming Pie*, and proved another turning point in a career that showed no signs of slowing down. On the personal level there was a tender recollection of his first meeting with Linda, 'Magic', and songs like 'Lonely Road' and 'From a Lover to a Friend' that expressed the pain of loss, redeemed in time by new love. And the sense of spiritual resilience was underscored by the record's energy and freshness. With his new producer David Kahne, who'd later steer Lana Del Rey's breakthrough album, McCartney again felt the urge to gather a working band around him. Within six months he was back on the road for a full-scale tour, Driving USA.

In the years ahead I was kept pretty busy myself with the stream of editorial tasks that sprang from Paul's work-rate, with regular tour magazines, website updates, a lavish hardback book, *Each One Believing: On Stage, Off Stage, and Backstage*, PR materials, and liner notes for new and reissued albums.

McCartney's recording plans took a detour in 2003; after a

few more sessions with David Kahne – forming in the process a new band, whom we'll meet presently – he followed George Martin's recommendation of a new producer, Nigel Godrich. Best-known for his association with Radiohead, Godrich talked Paul into a multitasking studio method, reminiscent of the 'true' solo albums *McCartney* and *McCartney II*.

In the event, Paul adopted both approaches – working alone with Godrich and staying in touch with Kahne and the band. The former sessions became the basis of his 2005 record *Chaos and Creation in the Backyard*, while the latter led to *Memory Almost Full*, released in 2007.

Chaos and Creation was a dense and typically varied collection of songs that touched on nearly every Macca reference point, from pounding bass and delicate acoustic guitars to whimsy, uplift and resilience. Its cover shot was an early photo by Mike McCartney, of Paul on a deckchair in their Liverpool garden, strumming a song beneath the washing-line.

In a sense this picture might have been more fitting for *Memory Almost Full*: as its title hinted, here was the author of 'When I'm 64', written when he was a teenager, now approaching that very milestone. In songs like 'Ever Present Past', 'That Was Me', 'Feet in the Clouds' and 'Vintage Clothes', we hear a man coming to terms with his whole life, and the baggage it represented – happy, sad or simply bewildering. In the magisterial 'The End of the End', we find him pondering mortality itself.

This impulse to take stock of his life would re-emerge on 2012's set of venerable homages to early popular music, *Kisses on the Bottom*. It hadn't escaped McCartney's notice that contemporary rivals like Rod Stewart and Robbie Williams were presenting their own takes on the Great American Songbook. At the same time, he saw the songs of that bygone era as a cornerstone of his musical education, as well as an emotional link to the family warmth of his childhood.

Paul avoided numbers he felt were too well-known, and wove in new material like 'My Valentine', written for his fiancée Nancy (it was first played at their wedding). Late in the day, the album's title was fixed as *Kisses on the Bottom*; not a classically romantic name, perhaps, but a line from the song 'I'm Gonna Sit Right Down and Write Myself a Letter'. McCartney took a puckish delight in its abrupt subversion of the record's quaintly old-fashioned leanings.

But McCartney's career never travels in a single direction. For every 'Honey Pie' there was a 'Helter Skelter', and for every 'Blackbird' a 'Why Don't We Do It In The Road?' In a few years either side of *Kisses on the Bottom*, he was making further experiments in noise with The Fireman and challenging himself with long-form compositions such as *Ecce Cor Meum*; in 2014 he recorded a score for the video game *Destiny*; soon after that came singles with artists far beyond his ordinary orbit, Kanye West and Rihanna. And somewhere in between, he reaffirmed his 'core' career with the 2013 album *New*.

Despite a trio of numbers with lyrical roots in his Liverpool youth – 'Queenie Eye', 'On My Way to Work' and 'Early Days' – the tone of *New* was energised and contemporary. Paul was doubtless helped by his decision to use four young producers across the record: Giles Martin and Ethan Johns were both the sons of producers with a Beatle pedigree (George and Glyn respectively), while Mark Ronson and Paul Epworth were building reputations too. McCartney and his team made vibrant, adventurous pop, rich in playful detail.

Some listeners thought that Paul's voice was losing the elasticity and strength it once had; he was, after all, now in his seventies. But a couple of *New*'s songs, like 'Early Days' and the 'hidden' track 'Scared', play to that very frailty to achieve a mood of vulnerability and emotional realism. And his spirit was unquenched. 'New', the title track, might even be described as

Beatle-esque – all handclaps and harpsichord and the promise of endless summer.

Pop music, or rock, has been McCartney's lifetime calling. But his career cannot be defined by it. There has by now been a huge chunk of classical music also, which we'll explore shortly. And there was also film, whether movies or video. That is what we talked about next.

CHAPTER 13

That's a Great Idea, Eddie!

How the Beatles saved rock-and-roll movies and invented the pop video

He has pointed his talents at almost every sort of music, but McCartney has never seriously attempted acting. It's a move many rock stars have proved unable to resist, often with risible consequences.

Yet he has a decent catalogue of film and video appearances to his credit. Even the ventures that were not judged to be triumphs – *Magical Mystery Tour* and *Give My Regards to Broad Street* – are free of embarrassing misfires from McCartney himself. He is a fair actor and despite his disavowals a good dancer ('I can bop a bit' is as much as he will claim). Paul knows where the cameras are and treats them as his friends.

The videos he liked making most, he says, are those where he didn't appear, or simply played music: 'You'll find that with a lot of bands. I know guys who just won't do them. "Oh no, what, acting? Not doing that, you know, dressing up in soft gear." They prefer to just be a guy in a band.'

But he came close to a proper acting role in 1967:

> Old Franco Zeffirelli [the distinguished Italian film director] came over to London and offered me the lead in *Romeo and Juliet*. I said, 'I can't do it, man, you're kidding. I'm just a musician.' The one with Olivia Hussey. Leonard Whiting played it.

He said, 'No, I really know you could do this. You look absolutely how I see Romeo. It would be perfect. Come to Rome and we make a film, it will be beautiful.' I bottled out.

I took her out, Olivia Hussey – this was before I met Linda – took her out to a nightclub. I quite fancied her, she was gorgeous with long dark hair. I sent her a telegram, 'You're a beautiful Juliet.' She sent one back: 'You'd make a great Romeo.' It was all very . . . [*romantic swoon*]. You'd vomit now, I suppose. My kids wouldn't believe it: 'Oh Dad! You didn't do *that*, did you?'

In 1964 it was far cheaper to buy a cinema ticket than a long-playing record, and many Britons formed their first impression of the Beatles by watching the group's movie debut *A Hard Day's Night*. I was one of them; my mother took me to see it in a Merseyside picture house where the group had played live only three years previously. On that occasion, John and Paul unveiled the new 'Beatle haircuts' they'd just adopted in Paris, yet they were still a mere warm-up act for local comedian Ken Dodd.

The four boys' supposed personas were largely defined by *A Hard Day's Night*; to my mother, her sisters and friends, Paul was emerging as the charmer. They'd shyly confess that he was easy on the eye.

I asked McCartney how much of an education the film had been:

We were just so young and excited to be making a movie. We'd had a couple of offers, but they weren't very good and we stuck out. Rock-and-roll films were traditionally bad movies, like *Don't Knock the Rock*, but it's got the few guys you wanted to see. So we went to all those films: 'Hey, why don't we book Clyde McPhatter tonight?' 'That's a great idea, Eddie!' Alan

Freed or someone would be a DJ trying to act, and it was really bad.

We had this idea it would be great to be in something that was actually decent. We held out for someone good and Dick Lester's name came up. We said, 'Who is he?' They said, 'He's a TV director essentially, but he did make *The Running Jumping & Standing Still Film*, an early Goons film with Peter Sellers, Spike Milligan, Graham Stark, all of those guys.' It was surreal for its time, one of our cult films. 'Wow, that's great, that's a student's film, that is.' We were chuffed that he was interested.

Dick got Alun Owen, a Welsh playwright who knew Liverpool well – he'd written *No Trams to Lime Street*, a good TV play with Billie Whitelaw in it, quite well thought of. We met Alun, he hung out with us for a few days, and he got the sort of wacky humour that we'd got going: 'He's very clean, though, isn't he?' 'I fought for the likes of you in the war.'

This is the stuff you grew up with in post-war Liverpool. We'd all been asked to turn radios down on the train, so we'd tell him this and he'd say, 'Oh, that would make a good scene.' He made most of it up, but a lot of it was based on our anecdotes.

The waiting around was the staggering thing. Everything else was entertaining. But you were nearly all day waiting while they lit a shot and then you'd come in and go, 'He's clean, though,' and they go, 'Great, thanks, that's it.' You'd go, Bloody hell. You go home. But it worked and it became a cult film itself because of Dick being a good director, Alun being a good writer and us, being really up for it. There was no moodies.

The only one who wasn't quite so keen was George. I don't know if he was shy or just thought we should be making music. He wasn't keen on the acting thing. But Ringo took to it like a duck to water, there was no holding *him* back. He became the star of the film, in a way.

He did look like a natural performer on screen.

Yeah, he is. Ringo is a film star. He always was. He's got that in his personality. He's very contained, sort of content with himself, and they found that out when we were doing *Hard Day's Night*. Dick Lester wanted a scene with Ringo in it. Ringo had been out clubbing all night and he arrived on the set after virtually no sleep. And Dick just said, 'Well, you know, stick this hat on him and an old raincoat, and could you walk along the banks of this canal, please?' [It was the sequence by the Thames, in Kew.]

Ringo said, 'Yeah, OK.' So he started doing things, kicking cans, and a little boy comes up, but it's just Ringo's natural personality. He sees what's required of him and he can deliver it. He's natural, so he's good to have in a film.

John was very good, because he's very good anyway. We were OK, the four of us came off well, and it was a big hit. And what we liked was that it was a film, it wasn't just a vehicle for a rock-and-roll act. It captured our personalities.

They gave me Wilfrid Brambell as my supposed granddad. Who was 'very clean', and that was nice because people were always saying about old people, 'I'll bring him.' Oh *don't*. 'But he's clean.'

Was he already in Steptoe and Son *[the British TV comedy series] at that point? He was always being called a 'dirty old man' by his son.*

Dirty old man, that's right [*snaps fingers*]. Of course! It's as you say, he was Steptoe, a dirty old man. Anyway. We loved it and it was an exciting experience meeting all these actors, the kind of people you didn't normally meet.

So, through the movie, through Brian [Epstein], that was all part of the continuation of our education, really. We got to see how films were made, which was very important. So later on, we dared to do it ourselves.

A Hard Day's Night was black and white, which was great.

We were glad. It just seemed harder, more student-y – that's a bad word but you know what I mean. More artsy. We liked all that.

Because of its naïve energy – and, as Paul suspected, by the aesthetic prestige of black-and-white film – *A Hard Day's Night* still packs more punch than its slightly decadent successor from 1965, *Help!*

I like it now, it's got a lot of the fun quality of *A Hard Day's Night*. But for us it was a strange film, because it wasn't approached as seriously. With *A Hard Day's Night* we'd never done it before, so we let *them* do it. We were in awe. But once we'd done it: 'Hey, what's our follow-up, babe?' It was like that.

In fact one of the first conversations was, 'Can't we go somewhere sunny?' It was conceived in that frame of mind.

'Well sure, where?'

'Y'know, the Bahamas!'

'Sure, we could write a scene where you go to the Bahamas.'

'Great, thanks! Oh, and skiing? We'd like to go skiing. We've never been skiing.' It was like ordering up your holidays. And it was also for guys to pull chicks.

So it was, 'Where d'you wanna go? We'll write a film around it.' They tied it in with tax things too. Not many people know that. It was conceived from this funny angle, and I'm surprised it worked out. We were a bit blasé by that time. I'd certainly never read the script until the first day. Imagine the arrogance of not reading a script. I'd never do that now.

We were, 'Uh, what page is that on, Dick? Oh, seventy-nine?' It was naughty, a fairly laid-back approach. But it was fun. When we did go skiing, it was Austria, and we'd never been to snowy places, except when it had snowed in Liverpool. We knew we loved *that*, so we thought it must be good in those snowy places.

People always suspect you when you talk about the innocence: 'Come off it, you weren't *that* bloody innocent.' And in a way we weren't, either. But it really was pretty innocent stuff, it wasn't very serious.

They found Obertauern in Austria, which suited their purposes, and we went there. They said, for the insurance, 'Nobody must ski.' Films are all about insurance. You've got to take a medical before you make a film, did you know that? Cos if you die in the middle of a film they've got to pay. So they said, 'We can't have injuries, it'll hold up the schedule. You can *stand* on the skis, but don't go anywhere on them.'

We said, 'We can't ski anyway.' But you know, young guys, it's a challenge, and Are We Not Men? So it's 'C'mon, *I'm* gonna go!' There's a lot of that in the film – anywhere you see people skiing very slowly, it's us. And when they get really dynamite and fast, it's the stuntmen. There's a shot I love because we saw it happen. They were doing a bit with Ringo and somehow he got backwards with his skis downhill. He didn't mean to.

There was a lot of spontaneous stuff. They'd take a piano up this huge hill, we'd show up and they'd say, 'What shall we do?'

'Oh, I don't know, let's just lie under the piano, shall we?'

'Well, I'll lie *in it*.' Great!

We learned how to ski a bit by the end of that film, even though we were told not to. Nobody broke their necks, but it's surprising, actually. They put us on those little ski-bikes, and we just said 'Yeeaahh!' I came off one of those, nearly killed myself. But, young guys, you somehow manage not to kill yourself.

Then there was the Bahamas bit and again, you know: Bloody hell, the water's so clear, and blue! It was like that, tourists. They made up little vignettes. 'Another Girl', I'm carrying this girl, a very groovy-looking girl. Basically I was trying to get off with her. It's what we were trying to do, get on with our lives, but at the same time make a film. But our thing was pulling the girls, going to nice places.

Ah! The grilled cheese man!

As Paul's assistant John Hammel came in with toasted sandwiches, I postponed our chat about the next Beatle movie, *Magical Mystery Tour*, because I was wondering about the short promo-clips, forerunners of the all-conquering pop video, which the group now began making.

In 1966 there were 'Paperback Writer' and 'Rain', shot on location at Chiswick House by Michael Lindsay-Hogg. The musical sequences of *Help!* had been its most likeable elements, and these promo clips were similarly set up as band performances, with scant pretence to realism.

Soon afterwards, in the spirit of *Sgt. Pepper*, they dispensed with mimed instruments altogether; the video for 'Penny Lane' has the Beatles on horseback and 'Strawberry Fields Forever' is almost doggedly strange:

> 'Penny Lane', they gave us red hunting jackets and put us on white horses, and none of us could ride. Again, this was like the skiing thing. It's an actor's story: 'Can you ride?' 'Yeah!' And you can't.
>
> Well, they didn't even ask us.
>
> Ringo was petrified. He's got a thing about horses to this day. We got on, walked through the gate for the shot, and of course these horses pelted off. They saw this open field. I would never do that now, because I know they'd go, but then you didn't. 'Stop! Hey you, stop! Whaay!' We're galloping down, Ringo nearly fell off. It was all fairly hairy. 'Hey, hold them!'
>
> 'Strawberry Fields' is the one I really remember. We met this crazy Swedish guy [Peter Goldmann, a respected TV director]. Met him in a club and he was saying, 'Hey, you know, you guys are great, I wanna film you somewhere. Like Bergman. You guys could make a great video, crazy!'
>
> So we said, 'Yeah, well you should make it.' And a lot of people still like that. It was ahead of its time. We just showed up, and he had a piano: 'I want you to bash up the piano.'
>
> We said, 'Fair enough.' Cool, fairly simple assignment. 'Where's

the hammer?' And there was some food: 'Why don't you throw it at each other?' Another simple assignment.

'Hello, Goodbye', I got that one together. The only hang-up was unions, this idea of 'You've got to have a minimum twenty people'. Oh no, man, we only need two. 'No, sorry, the union manning laws here. Five grips.' So that put us off. We would have made more films had it not been for that.

By this point the Beatles had stopped touring, and the new complexity of their music would have made live performance difficult. A promo film of 'Hello, Goodbye' could be sent to Ed Sullivan's show and reach the entire United States. In 1968 the group unveiled 'Hey Jude' with a world premiere for David Frost's programme. The commercial argument for pop videos became compelling.

~

And so it remained throughout Paul's later career. Was that a thing he welcomed, or merely accepted?

The advent of the music video was a double-edged sword. In one way it was exciting, making a little film. In another way it was *not what we did*. So it was good and bad.

It spawned millions of young directors who have gone on to become film directors. It's a good learning ground for them. Keith MacMillan did a lot of stuff with me: 'Pipes of Peace', 'Ebony and Ivory', 'Coming Up'. A very enthusiastic guy, great to work with. We got the hang of it together.

For instance, 'Pipes of Peace' [the single and title track of 1983's album], I was sitting with Keith. Suddenly one of us came up with this idea: 'Remember that old film that they used to show on the BBC when on Christmas Day you got the German soldiers and the English soldiers all coming out of their trenches and they had a game of football?' OK, that's it, there's the idea.

I wanted an anti-war thing, because that's basically all the song is. Keith directed it great, we got freezing trenches and it was a real wintry morning. Looked fairly realistic for a video. They said, 'You can't look glamorous, man. You're either a soldier in the trenches or you're not. You're gonna have to *not* look like a rock star.'

I liked 'Coming Up' [the single from 1980's home-recorded album *McCartney II*], which again I did with Keith MacMillan. He said, 'How did you do the record?' I said it was one of those studio jobs where I played all the instruments. So we got some very sophisticated computer system, and I did the guy out of Sparks [Ron Mael], the keyboard player with the Hitler moustache. I did Hank Marvin [from the Shadows], which people thought was Buddy Holly. I did a Japanese rock player, which was no particular significance. I did a country bumpkin drummer, which was based on John Bonham.

Richly cinematic, the 1983 video for 'Say Say Say' is a reminder of happier times in Paul's acquaintance with Michael Jackson:

Out in the Santa Ynez Valley in California we worked up this story of Mac and Jack. I was a travelling medicine man who had a bit of a con, but the trick was that we gave it to the orphans' home. It was a cutesy, folksy little story but nice. And Michael being so hot, it was a peak period for him. LaToya [Jackson] appears in it, with my daughter, and Linda of course. LaToya plays Michael's girlfriend, it was a good experience.

Finally for now, if there is a more peculiar pop video than 1978's 'London Town' I have yet to see it. It's quite as surreal as the song itself, with pathos and humanity, and a great cameo from the actor Victor Spinetti, a well-known face in the Beatles' movies. But I can imagine a studio of people, not least Linda and Denny Laine, wondering what exactly their leader was thinking. There must have been other projects that were just as puzzling – *Magical Mystery Tour* and *Give My Regards to Broad Street* are two we've already mentioned – but those we saved for a later conversation.

Meanwhile there was another subject to discuss: classical music. Pop stars who hoped to be actors often came a cropper – just look at the Beatles' hero Elvis Presley. How would McCartney fare when his competition was Beethoven?

CHAPTER 14

British Light Music

McCartney revives a noble, forgotten form

Paul was one of those post-war working-class children who received a grammar school education, courtesy of the state. It was the implied mission of such places to instil respect for certain middle-class values and tastes. That worked for Paul as far as English literature was concerned.

But classical music? Not so much.

'Music lessons?' he shrugs. 'At that school, you would have just had to play one Elvis record and we would have been hooked. We'd have turned up in our droves to that lesson. Whereas in actual fact we turned the record off and played cards.'

Nor had his home life inspired much love for the classics:

> The radio was a big feature, the BBC mainly. The earliest memories would be *Listen with Mother*, which had the only classical music you heard. You got a very broad education, you'd hear light music, a bit of classical.
>
> But classical used to get switched off in our house, because me dad was a bit of a jazzer. If a symphony came on he'd turn it off. So I never really heard any classical music, it was all light music, mainly British.

British light music – an orchestral genre that flourished in the 1940s and 1950s – was, like his family singalongs and scratchy

78s, an influence McCartney absorbed as naturally as daylight. But parental efforts to formalise his piano playing came to nothing:

> I'm primitive on music. I don't want to learn music. It doesn't appeal to me, really. It's too serious, it's too like homework. That's what put me off learning the piano. The minute they gave me stuff to do at home, 'This is it, I'm jacking it in.' I hated homework. When the piano lady gave me some stuff, 'Go and learn these crotchets' and stuff, bloody hell, I hated that. I loved the music, I just couldn't get beyond those first few lessons.

Back in 1957 his attitude was probably summed up by Chuck Berry's 'Rock and Roll Music', later covered by the Beatles, wherein our Chuck declares unswerving love for the big beat – and contempt for anything that sounds 'just like a symphony'. At the same time, despite himself, Paul would have breathed a cultural atmosphere that still placed classical music at the apex of excellence. Indeed, he and George honed their novice guitar skills on Bach's Bourrée in E minor, whose influence resurfaced a decade later in 'Blackbird'. Essentially, McCartney's wide-open mind could never ignore anything for long.

Once he'd installed himself in London, especially as a house guest of the artistic Asher family, Paul was ready to look beyond rock. His taste for more formal music began to blossom and he's nurtured it ever since. Once, when I asked him about the records he most treasured in his collection, he cited an LP of the guitarist Julian Bream playing Vivaldi's Concerto for Lute and Strings, Rodrigo's Concierto de Aranjuez and Britten's The Courtly Dances from *Gloriana*, 'which I always thought was cool. Very nice.'

The Beatles were fortunate in becoming the protégés of George Martin – their producer was a commercial pop craftsman who also had deep understanding of classical forms. And of the four band members, Paul was the keenest to draw on this abundant source of expertise:

> It's always been good for me to have someone like George Martin, who actually knows music. In a way he's like a scribe, an elevated scribe like the Egyptians used to have: 'Take this down, scribe, get me thy papyrus, send a letter to Nefertiti, she's to come over at five o'clock.'
>
> It always seemed OK to us to have someone write it down, so long as they're a good mate and they understand you. There's no break of creativity. You're not handing it over to someone, they're just taking it down because you can't write that. Like translating it into another language so musicians can understand, trained musicians . . . What am *I* if not trained? But you know what I mean.

Martin's classical grounding enabled the graceful translation of raw compositions like 'Yesterday' and 'Eleanor Rigby' into works of orchestral sophistication, free of either saccharine or bombast. And he played a central part in Paul's first stab at extended composition, the 1966 film soundtrack for *The Family Way*.

Performed by an ensemble named the George Martin Orchestra, Paul's chief contribution to *The Family Way* was a wistful waltz tune, 'Love in the Open Air'. Martin took the composition through a series of elaborations, often arranged for brass band instruments to evoke the film's homely Northern setting. McCartney's own grandfather had played the E flat bass tuba in just such a band, so redolent of Edwardian Lancashire; it's somewhere in the genetic code of *Sgt. Pepper* too.

Paul himself did not appear on the *The Family Way*, though the sleeve placed his name as prominently as possible. Nor, in fact, is it really classical music at all. But it was a sign of one path that McCartney's extra-curricular work would eventually take.

Decades pass and the Beatles' music holds its own. Those scholarly comparisons to Schubert, seen as bizarre in the early Sixties, are no longer controversial. Many accept the group's best work is equal to anything made by the men in white wigs and frock-coats. But it was a long time before Paul himself would test those deep uncharted waters. The *Liverpool Oratorio* of 1991 was his first full-scale attempt at classical composition.

Partnered by the American conductor and composer Carl Davis, he accepted a commission to write something for the 150th anniversary of the Royal Liverpool Philharmonic Orchestra. The piece would be premiered in the city's vast Anglican cathedral, across the street from his old school playground. This was the very place where, as a boy, he'd been turned down for the choir. Now that same choir would join the orchestra in performing Paul's classical debut.

'It's exciting for me,' he told me, when he started work with Davis. 'It's something I've never done before. At the same time it's what I've *always* done, because it's still songs. But the nice thing is you don't have to go: intro/first verse/chorus/verse/middle eight/chorus/intro/two choruses/fade, like most pop songs. What's good is you can keep going. With serious music you never have to go back to the chorus if you don't want. The form is very exciting:

> I've always had my leanings that way. I've always liked the sound of a French horn, I've always liked a string quartet. 'Yesterday' and 'Eleanor Rigby', those kind of things, 'The Walrus' with John. We've dabbled with that enough to know what it's about. You meet musicians and know some little tricks and some little things that get orchestras 'at it'.

The *Oratorio* took a semi-autobiographical story, split into eight movements.

> It's loosely based on my upbringing in Liverpool. So it starts in the wartime with two parents in an air-raid shelter, and they're gonna have a baby – quite dramatic, having a baby in war. It's dramatic anyway, having a baby. But in wartime in Liverpool, that was definitely one of the places that got done in. My dad was like a fireman, trying to put out all these incendiary bombs.
>
> So the first movement is very chaotic, it's weird, almost avant-garde. Then in the middle there's a little ray of hope, a sort of a burst, this hope for the future. It's a moving idea that with all this shit going on they still dare to hope for the future.
>
> The next movement is school days, and after that it gets to teenage years. We're not going to do heavily the Beatles thing; it's overdone, that segment of my life. The other segments are just as interesting, particularly to me. Particularly Liverpool, it's so rich.
>
> School was some nuthouse, that was. Really. Throwing piss bombs. You get kids, 'Yeah! We throw water bombs, fill a balloon with water.' I hate to tell you what *we* filled it with, lads.
>
> I told Carl a few of these experiences. We used to 'sag off'. He said, 'What do you mean?' He's American. It's playing hooky, playing truant.
>
> We used to go in the cathedral graveyard, cos our school was there. Very irreligious, we'd take our shirts off and sunbathe on the gravestones. Not much respect for the dead, I must say, but it didn't occur to us. But Carl likes that, particularly as it's going to be performed in the cathedral.

Davis, like George Martin before him, turned Paul's ideas into fully scored reality. And in the course of their collaboration, the self-taught rock and roller, who never learned to read music, discovered the unfamiliar disciplines of classical practice:

For instance, I'll probably think of what key they're in. I never do that, I never take that care. Normally I do a record in the key I've written it. I just go in and scream it if I screamed it, or do it real low if it was a quiet night when I wrote it. I can never think of it in another key.

Now we're talking about a tenor range from there to there, or a mezzo-soprano's range. I realised that in rock and roll there's no such fucking thing. You don't even think about it. I'm doing [*high shriek*] '*Waahh!*' which just isn't on the page. And then I'm going [*low and mellow*] '*ba-ba-ba . . .*' So it's just ridiculous. Consequently it's easier to wipe yourself out. At least Beethoven or Mozart normally wrote for the guy, he never had to go 'Waahh!' It's not in any music. But *we* all do that shit. We'll do it just to introduce a solo.

What's interesting is the way you write it. Because it's all in manuscript you can actually see its structure. Like doing a painting, you can understand the song better when it's written out. For an orchestra to play it, you have to give them every clue.

With a band you say, 'It's in A, "Twenty Flight Rock",' and they're in, they do it. You can't do that with a cellist. *He* doesn't know what you want, whereas a guitarist does: A-chords, to the tune of 'Blue Suede Shoes', or whatever. But you've got to tell a cellist, and it's a nice discipline.

Structure is interesting. It reminds me of *Abbey Road* and *Pepper*, we kind of structured them. We knew what was gonna be coming here, knew what you needed here, knew that 'Day in the Life' had to go there.

There's suddenly a lot of opportunity with the orchestra. I call it the ultimate synth. I went to see the Proms last year, and it was like you're looking at the inside workings of a synth. The only difference is, there it is real.

There's a lot of physical work there. You have to do the whole eighty minutes writing out what the first violin's gonna play. Then you've got to do it all again for what the cellist's gonna play, then for the oboe. So the cello will have ten pages where he's not even in, but you've got to *say* he's not in for ten pages. There's a lot of paper to write for an orchestra. It's like a legal brief, millions of pages to get through.

In 1995 he told me about a second *opus* he'd agreed to write, this one for the hundredth anniversary of EMI: 'Yeah, in '97. Which in terms of lead times is suddenly looming. That's one of my little tricks, I've noticed. I accept things cos they're five years away.'

The result, *Standing Stone*, was McCartney's first full-length symphony. Hugely ambitious, its structure derived from a long poem Paul had written, 'in which I try to describe the way Celtic man might have wondered about the origins of life and the mystery of human existence.' This fascination with Celtic creation myths ran deep. He'd already been moved to write a piece called 'Spiral', on seeing the enigmatic patterns carved into Ireland's haunting prehistoric edifice at Newgrange.

And 'Spiral', which might well be his finest single work in this field, found its own release on a 1999 CD called *Working Classical*. That name, of course, was McCartney's wry subversion of the genre's bourgeois image. It was a born populist's reclamation of high art for the everyman.

His cause was helped by the album's format. Using an orchestra and a string quartet he combined new pieces with instrumental reworkings of numbers from his catalogue. Some of the old songs were quite obvious, others were less so, but there was usually an implied tribute to his late wife: 'My Love', 'Maybe I'm Amazed', 'Golden Earth Girl', 'She's My Baby' and, of course, 'The Lovely Linda'. Of the five classical pieces, two are as short and sweetly accessible as any pop tune; three longer compositions round out the set beautifully.

It's only right that *Working Classical* should feel so unified – McCartney's idea is that his work is all one. He approaches pop music or 'high art' in the same spirit, as an attempt to express universal feelings through melody and tempo. The differences in structure, orchestration and complexity are almost incidental. And it's telling that he released the album just a few weeks after its polar opposite, the primal rock rampage that was the album *Run Devil Run*.

Ecce Cor Meum ('Behold my heart') arose from another invitation, this time from Magdalen College, Oxford, who had a new concert hall to celebrate. The request was again for an oratorio, though its subject matter was up to Paul. Work was postponed by the death of Linda, but the piece was eventually performed in 2001, and after some revisions he recorded it in 2006. *Ecce Cor Meum*'s four movements, with an especially moving interlude, sound steeped in Christian musicology – its title came from the inscription Paul saw on a church statue of Jesus – but in fact they're resolutely non-doctrinal. Instead, the moods and message are of spiritual uplift. Like *Standing Stone*, this is a hymn to McCartney's hopeful faith in the power of human love, connecting to a larger, benevolent life-force.

I first heard about his next commission, *Ocean's Kingdom*, in 2010. Talking to Paul in his office at MPL, I was struck by a curious cabinet on a side table. 'D'you know Joseph Cornell? He does these boxes. I like the title, Hotel Neptune.' I learned that Cornell, who died in 1972, was an American artist known for 'assemblages' of found objects, arrayed in glass-fronted boxes.

'I've got a project on, to do with underwater and stuff. It's a ballet, would you believe – New York City Ballet. You can't keep me down, man!'

Ballet? Well, that's about the one thing you haven't done so far.

'I was looking for a title for it and I thought, Hotel Neptune, that's a damn good title. Like "Hotel California" but for a ballet.' By the night of the ballet's world premiere in late 2011, its name was *Ocean's Kingdom*. Through four purely orchestral movements, the dancers enact Paul's fairytale romance of star-crossed lovers: an earth-prince and a water-princess.

Even beyond these larger undertakings the McCartney *oeuvre* – and, yes, it's earned a word as grand as *oeuvre* by now – has expanded in more directions than any rock discography can accommodate. In 1989 he recorded a soundtrack for the short animated film, *Daumier's Law*; released in 1992, this was based on the work of the nineteenth century French artist Honoré Daumier. We've talked elsewhere of his work for the *Rupert* film, and that's not to mention more conventional songs for movie soundtracks such as *Spies Like Us*, a John Landis comedy in 1985. In 2014 McCartney wrote a score for the video game *Destiny*, including its Bond-like theme song 'Hope for the Future'.

As the man said, you can't keep him down.

Hour for hour, work in a classical vein has become a sizeable proportion of Paul McCartney's catalogue. His readiness to tackle almost any musical genre is not fired by vanity or cultural aspiration, but by an innocent optimism. He'll try anything, and if he tries hard enough, he thinks he'll probably produce something good.

The poet Adrian Mitchell, who edited Paul's own collection of verse, wrote that McCartney 'is not in the line of academic or modernist poets. He is a popular poet in the tradition of popular poetry.' Perhaps we can say something similar of his classical music. The tradition in which he stands is British light music, which wafted from every wireless set and picture house during the mid-twentieth century.

'Light' in this context suggested music that was always tuneful, but there was also sophistication and emotional range. The genre grew from classical music and came to sit somewhere close to pop, with healthy elements of both. We can trace its antecedents from Mozart and Haydn to Elgar, Gilbert and Sullivan and, ultimately, radio and cinema stalwarts like Edward Coates, Albert Ketèlbey and Richard Addinsell.

Then the remorseless advance of pop, led of course by the Beatles, pushed it aside, leaving its remnants to a middle-of-the-road style known as easy listening. But British light music of the golden age is by no means a genre to be despised. It seems, in fact, a form that McCartney was born for. We can hear him reviving the form at its best in certain passages of *Standing Stone*, *Working Classical* and *Ocean's Kingdom*.

Considered in that respect McCartney is not a classical lightweight, but a light music heavyweight. And that makes him the modern century's pre-eminent heir to a great lost art.

Which prompts our next question. What would John Lennon have made of all this?

CHAPTER 15

John

People sometimes see it as arch-rivalry. It wasn't

I sit with Paul as he completes a questionnaire for *MOJO* magazine's All-Time Heroes issue, in 2001:

Who is your hero?
John Lennon.
When did this person first have an impact on you?
At Woolton Village Fête in the year of Our Lord Whatever.
What is it that you admire in them?
Massive talent, great wit, courage and humour.
Have they had an influence upon you?
Very much so.
Have they ever disappointed you or has your admiration ever faded?
Yeah, from time to time, when we were having a barney. But only infrequently.

The world's most famous living Liverpudlian has grown more open about the world's most famous dead Liverpudlian. Unbidden references to John Lennon occur in almost every interview I've done with Paul McCartney. It's clear their complex partnership still stalks the halls of his memory.

Their talents, in the years they worked together, were not only complementary, they were equal. Each man had his precise counterweight in the other, and the fine adjustments of that balancing seemed to create a dialectic of genius. As fellow Beatles their relationship was both collaborative and competitive – whether writing alone or in a team, they raised the collective game.

Sgt. Pepper's crowning achievement 'A Day in the Life' might be the greatest instance of their chemistry: two independent efforts combining into a perfect whole. Paul's is rooted in the everyday, stoic optimism of his nature; John's is lost in abstraction and doubt; both are suffused with the same dreamlike wonder. A few months earlier, the pairing on one single of 'Penny Lane' and 'Strawberry Fields Forever' had much the same quality.

But I also love the subliminal contrast to be heard in the song 'A Hard Day's Night'. John's restless pushing at the boundaries of frustrated longing is suddenly, deliriously, rewarded by the soaring celebration of Paul's voice at the middle eight; 'When I'm *home* . . .' And everything seems to be right.

Even later, when fatigue and dispute were bringing the great Beatle adventure to its close, Lennon and McCartney could recover the unforced joy that had brought them together as young rock and rollers. One evening in spring 1969 – George and Ringo being absent – the two men went to Abbey Road and made 'The Ballad of John and Yoko'. Its name alone would have reminded Paul of the band's recent divisions, yet he steps up to the mark with bass, drumming and a background vocal that are thrillingly robust and wholehearted.

Looming so large in one another's lives, it's not surprising that Lennon and McCartney should appear in each other's songs. The pity is that John's 1971 song 'How Do You Sleep?' – as spiteful a put-down as anything in popular music – is the most vivid example from his side of the fence. Paul was known to snipe in less explicit ways, for example on his *Ram* LP, but his equivalent song to John from that period was the far more conciliatory 'Dear Friend'.

John Lennon's death in 1980 changed everything, of course. After that tragedy, Paul's every reference to his old partner was necessarily respectful. He wrote a poem called 'Jerk of All Jerks' (directed at the assassin, and published in his *Blackbird Singing* collection) to express the rage that mingled with his grief. But his feelings found sweeter expression in a song from 1982's *Tug of War*. He described it to me in 1989:

> I wrote 'Here Today' about John. It's just a song saying, you know, 'If you were here today you'd probably say what I'm doing is a load of crap. But you wouldn't mean it, cos you like me really, I know.' It's one of those 'Come out from behind your glasses, look at me,' things. It was a love song, really, not *to* John but a love song about John, about my relationship with him. I was trying to exorcise the demons in my own head.
>
> It's tough when you have someone like John slagging you off in public, cos he's a tough slagger-offer. So I wrote this song to try and come to terms with it. I thought I'd do that on stage but then someone suggested, 'Why don't you do one of John's? That would be poignant.' And it would, I don't know if I could even get through it – you've got to deal with the emotion of something like that. [A year later Paul did tackle some Lennon material in concert.] But it would be nice to make a nod or a wink to the lad, cos he was great. He was a major influence on my life, as I suppose I was on his.
>
> But the great thing about me and John is that it was *me and John*, end of story. Whereas everyone else can say 'Well you know, he did this and so-and-so and so-and-so.' The nice thing is that I can actually think, Come on, when we got in a little room it was *me and John* sitting down. It was me and him who wrote it, not these other people who think they all know about it. I must know better than them. I was the one in the room with him. But sometimes you don't believe it.

He developed this thought into a song, 'Early Days', on the 2013 album *New*: 'Everybody seems to have their own opinion,' he sings of all the commentary. 'But they can't take it from me, if they tried.' As if to underscore his own memories, he plays the double-bass once owned by Bill Black of Elvis Presley's group – a gut-raw element in those magical discs that first drew Paul and John together.

McCartney remembers Lennon as by far the more impulsive partner:

> John always wanted to jump over the cliff. He once said that to me. 'Have you ever thought of jumping?' I said, 'Fuck off. *You* jump, and tell me how it is.' That's basically the difference in our personalities. John is the guy who said, 'Why don't you try trepanning?' [Drilling a hole in the skull for medical or psychic benefits.]
>
> John picked up on all of this because Yoko would say, 'This is very good art, we must do this.' Whereas the people I was with: 'Well, that's a good laugh, Macca, but we can't do it.' She was like his Sergeant Pepper, she gave him the freedom to do all that.
>
> In fact she wanted more. 'Do more, do it double, be more daring, take all your clothes off.' She always pushed him, which he liked. Nobody had ever pushed him before.
>
> But he unfortunately went too far, into heroin and stuff – well crazy. He did masses of great stuff, but then he could let it all out, these bizarre sides to his character that he'd never dared let out before.

In the Beatles, genuine Lennon–McCartney collaborations grew rare as time passed, but the unspoken power of veto – and of its flipside, encouragement – remained in force.

Exactly. John would bring me 'Glass Onion'. I remember him in the garden in St John's Wood, saying, 'Here, what do you think of this?' We would just run it past it each other, like you would run it past a mate. He actually asked me, 'D'you think I should put in this line about the Walrus was Paul?' I said, 'Oh yeah! You're kidding? It's brilliant.'

I tended to agree with his stuff, and I must say he tended to agree with mine – like in 'Hey Jude', I was going to knock out that line about 'the movement you need is on your shoulder'. He said, 'You're not, you know. That's the best line in it.'

Often it wasn't so much negative as just bolstering each other up. I might go through the whole studio experience thinking this line's not right. But the minute he'd signed off on it, I thought, this line is ace! Similarly with him – he knew I liked the line 'the Walrus was Paul', and that was at least two of us in on it. It was the strength of unity.

From youthful escapades in Liverpool and Hamburg, to the giddy excess of global touring, Paul and John must have shared more experiences than even the vast body of Beatle books will ever record. But McCartney can also recall the moments when Lennon was not so cocksure.

On the final US trip, for example, reporters grilled him over that calamitous 'bigger than Jesus' comment. 'Well bloody hell,' says Paul. 'John just mouthed off, that's all. Isn't he allowed to make a mistake? He got the fear of God put into him, and if you've ever seen those interviews, if there was one point in John's life when he was nervous . . . I mean, we were *there*, you know? Try having the whole Bible Belt against you. It's not funny. We tried to laugh it off but it wasn't so funny.'

The thing I find myself doing, which is a pity, but it's because of the unfortunate circumstances, is trying to justify myself against John. I hate to do that. I never felt the need to do it, but because he got shot and is martyred . . . Certain people are starting to think, he *was* the Beatles, darling, there was nobody else. George just stood there with a plectrum waiting for his solo.'

Now that is not true. George did a lot more than sit and wait for a fucking solo. John would be the first to tell you that. But John has reached this plateau, where he's like a saint.

You can't blame people for feeling that way, cos it was a hell of a tragedy. I don't mind saying stuff that does redress the balance but I don't want to look like I'm justifying myself. It's a weedy position: 'No I really was OK! I did write quite a lot of the stuff! It wasn't John!' Anyway . . .

So it's a delicate area for McCartney. But Paul's work ethic was also a distinguishing factor, especially in John's last years when they were reconciled:

John had periods when he renounced the whole thing. I remember him phoning me and saying, 'Look man, it's the most difficult thing to renounce our fame. We're hooked on fame, but you should kick it over.' I'm going, Hmm, do tell me, what do you mean here? I listened to him, but after about a year of that he was back and what was his famous line? 'This housewife wants a job.' He'd done the role reversal bit. 'This housewife wants a job, love.'

That's what *I* find. I'd like less distractions, I'd like more time for what I do, but the minute you really listen to that philosophy, you've sort of got *too much* time . . .

A story Paul likes to tell is of his 1980 hit 'Coming Up'; the record came to Lennon's attention when he was gearing up to make what turned out to be his last album, *Double Fantasy*:

Apparently John heard it when he was in New York. I saw a John documentary and somebody was saying, 'I brought this record of Paul's to John and played it for him.' John went, 'Oh fuckin' hell, the bastard's done something good! I've gotta work!' I love the idea of forcing him up off his arse.

I like that, because we were always doing that with each other. I'd hear something and go, 'I've got to work!', which is a great thing. People sometimes see it as an arch-rivalry. It wasn't. It was a friendly competition that was actually very necessary. He'd do something and I'd go, 'Whoh! Now *I* must do something.' Similarly with him, so I'm proud of that one.

The irony of John's final five years, between the birth of his son Sean in 1975 and the events of 8 December, 1980, was that Lennon grew more domesticated. He expressed as much in several tracks on *Double Fantasy* and its posthumous sequel *Milk and Honey*. Given Paul's cosy image, this reversal of a long-standing stereotype is notable:

Yeah, it's lovely. You're right to say they were stereotypes – they were cultivated images. We were talking about John, how everyone thought he was the hard, working-class hero. As you know, he was actually the middle-class one, from Woolton. You look at his house and it's different. *We* were the scruffs, and he had the full *Works of Winston Churchill*; nobody any of us knew had that. And he'd read 'em, I think.

There were so many stereotypes of John. I love the fact that in the end – it's one of the blessings of my life – that during his last year, we made it up. Thank God for that, cos I would be so fucked up now, if I'd still been arguing with him and that had happened. It's bad enough what happened. It was cool that I'd started ringing him. We had the bread strike over here [in November 1978] and I rang him, saying, 'What are you doing?'

He says, 'I'm baking some bread.' 'Oh! *I've* been baking bread.' Imagine, with the stereotypes, John and Paul talking about baking bread. Cos he'd just had Sean, and he was talking about the cats, and padding round the apartment in his dressing gown, putting the cat out and changing the baby. I'd been doing all of that, and as you say, been stereotyped. Just cos I'd been open about it.

I loved that. It was really warm to be able to talk to him like that, finally. It was like we'd got back to where we'd been when we were kids. We could actually talk about stuff that didn't matter, but it *did* matter.

How far did John's murder inhibit Paul? Leaving aside his drug bust in Japan at the start of 1980, and the consequent binning of Wings' concert schedule, it's striking that he gave up touring for almost a decade. 'Yeah, it's something to do with John's thing,' he said, when we spoke in 1989:

But it's one of those. It's like Muhammad Ali said, 'When God calls me I'll go.' He's gonna get you one of these days, one way or another. We had a lot of scares like that with the Beatles, and yeah, I know on the eve of the tour I'll go, Dear me, am I kidding, going out on tour? But you've got to live your life.

It's like people used to say, 'Living in the shadow of the Bomb'. Well it's true, but what good does it do to think like that? You've got to get on with it. We're all in the shadow of something. And I'm not the only person out there who might get mugged or might get shot at. You've just got to cross your fingers, and touch a lot of wood.

Back in harness, Paul began a regime of live performance that has hardly stopped. Playing Liverpool in 1990, he sealed the occasion with a sequence of John Lennon numbers:

I didn't want to go crazy with it: 'Oh sacred memory of The Great Loved One.' I didn't want to get too precious. But I did feel good about copping a little medley, just nice songs to sing.

And the emotion of singing some John songs, for the first time in my life. It should be Liverpool; if I'm going to do it, that's the place.

He used to do 'Lucy in the Sky with Diamonds' – remember he did it with Elton, and his quote was he's 'finally got to do Paul's part'. And Elton did his [Lennon's] part. So he got to sing 'in the sky with diamonds' in the higher harmony.

[Lennon performed the song with Elton John at Madison Square Garden on 28 November 1974. The final song, John's last before a public audience, was Paul's 'I Saw Her Standing There'. He dedicated it to 'an old estranged fiancé of mine called Paul'.]

It was a bit the way I felt: I finally got to do John's part on 'Help!' and 'Give Peace a Chance'. Which, of course, I'd never done. And 'Strawberry Fields', a great song to sing. I always loved it, and thought, I won't get precious, won't think about it for hours. Originally I was just going to take an acoustic, stand there for quarter of an hour and totally get into a few John songs. But then it's 'McCartney Sings Lennon', all on me own, and it felt too precious.

So I thought, why don't we just learn these up with the band? It'll be part of the normal act, but we'll just stop a while and say, 'Here, a little tribute.'

If John had not met Paul, their lives would have been incalculably different. And so would ours. It is impossible to guess what the world might have become, probably it is pointless to try. But, of course, it is tempting. A magazine once asked me to make an attempt, and so I obliged:

One fateful day the fifteen-year-old Paul McCartney cycled over to Woolton and met an older teenager called John Lennon, who was playing in a skiffle band at the Summer Fête. What would have happened if they never met?

Suppose the Fête was rained off, or Paul had decided to go to the pictures instead? How different might human history have been? And would our world be a poorer place, or a better one? Let us try to picture it.

I see George Harrison, who has become a bus driver like his father before him. Twice a day he takes the Ribble route 311 *from Liverpool Skelhorne Street to Blackburn, Lancashire. 'Bloody road,' he moans. 'Must be four thousand holes in it.' Yet he is a philosophical cove. 'The farther one travels,' he says to Big-Nose Ritchie the bus conductor, 'the less one knows.'*

The stolid Ritchie nods, and drums a paradiddle on the canteen table. Life has been a mild disappointment for him since Rory Storm & The Hurricanes played their last Butlin's Summer Season in 1966.

Americans grew morbid after the killing of President Kennedy in 1963, *and nothing arrived out of the skies at JFK to cheer them up. Russia took down the Berlin Wall. 'Our young people visit the West,' said a Soviet spokesman, 'but it's so boring they always come home again.' The USSR will soon celebrate its* 100*th anniversary.*

Elvis Presley, the King of Rock and Roll, was never deposed. No upstarts ever challenged his supremacy and he lives a frugal, contented existence in Memphis. Rock in fact fizzled out, but there was a new golden era for professional songwriters: where would New York's Brill Building be without Simon & Zimmerman?

Up the road, in a bar on West 72*nd Street, a drunken Scouse seaman called Johnny Lennon swears contemptuously when the flickering TV shows images of the ever-popular Paul McCartney Dance Orchestra. He gets into a fight with a moody guy from the New Jersey haulage firm of Springsteen & Son, and both are evicted.*

'We coulda been contenders,' they mope at one another on the sidewalk. Lennon has broken his Buddy Holly glasses. A flyer in the gutter promotes the one-woman show by an obscure Japanese performance artist.

In London one David Jones, the odd-eyed chief of a Soho advertising agency, wishes he'd kept up his saxophone lessons. Who knows, he might have won a place in the Reg Dwight Big Band. What was it the Reverend Jagger said at Evensong last Sunday? 'You can't always get what you want.' How true that was. The fact is that British rock and roll had never really taken off.

If you were in the know there was always imported black music from the States. Soul and hip hop were the only vibrant sounds to be heard after 1963. *But even in America their appeal was limited by race. Nobody knew how to interest the white mass market in records from Detroit or Compton, LA.*

England's dreaming was undisturbed for 50 *years, and Elizabeth still reigned. 'Monarchy in the UK!' said the patriotic window display at McLaren's High Class Haberdashers,* 430 *King's Road.*

Except, of course, that this is not what happened at all. Paul McCartney did meet John Lennon at that Woolton Summer Fête. The butterfly flapped its wings and a distant mountain toppled over.

PART TWO

CHAPTER 16

Unfinished Business

The Beatles after the Beatles

Summer in an English garden, and shadows are lengthening across the lawn. Mugs of tea to hand, a trio of codgers shoot the breeze, chuckling with the gentle intimacy of men who have known each other for most of their lives. Every so often they pick up ukuleles and softly strum old Elvis tunes. They reminisce and fill the gaps in one another's memories. Occasionally they can't agree, but it doesn't matter. It's all done and dusted now.

This is Paul, George and Ringo in the Beatles' *Anthology* film, first screened in 1995, and we are watching what are almost their final hours together. A few years later, one of the three lay dying, with the others at his bedside. The scene is poignant for anyone whose life was entwined with theirs, or felt themselves enriched by the music they made.

The *Anthology* project, including a book and three CDs of that name, received its green light in 1989, when there was at last sufficient peace among the four main players – Yoko representing her late husband – to consider cooperation. Paul and George had discussed making background music for documentary footage collected by their assistant Neil Aspinall. In the end, the *Anthology* took in all these ventures, with two 'new' tracks, built on John's solo recordings 'Free as a Bird' and 'Real Love'. The core of the story is still the career of the Beatles, from the dance-halls of Liverpool to the law courts of London.

The finished documentary has no authorial voice-over, just a dazzling mass of footage and imagery – blurry backyard snapshots, Technicolor chronicles of world conquest, abundant interviews. Like the *Anthology* book, this film is essentially an autobiography, with all the benefits and the limitations that implies. There are no outsiders represented, only the four musicians with occasional contributions from their closest surviving allies, including George Martin, press man Derek Taylor and of course Neil Aspinall – the terse, black-hatted character who began as their roadie and became the head of Apple.

It goes without saying that the *Anthology*'s deepest flaw is John Lennon's absence. The one Beatle who was not around for its making was the one who might have brought the most in wit, subversion and bracing candour. He is represented as fully as the archive clips will allow. Interview snippets reveal him as whip-smart and funny, and it's frustrating to wonder how much his missing perspective might have shaped our modern sense of what the Beatles were about.

Paul, being Paul, is almost wholly upbeat and loyally supportive of the Beatles' achievements. It's clear that he resents the other three taking sides against him in the final disputes, and he cannot conceal the exasperation he felt when John brought Yoko inside the group's inner sanctum, the studio floor. McCartney is at pains, however, to make amends to George – he admits talking down to the guitarist on occasions. Perhaps he had lapsed back into his Liverpool role of older schoolboy on the bus.

But the *Anthology* took an age to come about. They'd kicked around the idea of an official documentary since the last days of the band: events, of course, put that idea in abeyance.

In spring 1989, I was wondering why Paul hadn't joined George and Ringo at the Rock and Roll Hall of Fame the previous year, when the Beatles were inducted. Was it due to that old stalwart, 'business differences'?

No, I hate that, don't you? Business differences. I'll tell you what it was. Apple still isn't sorted out. It's only twenty years later. We've all got our sides of the story. My story is, I just want us to divide it in four and then go home and be nice to each other. All the advisors say, 'It's not as simple as that.' So it goes on forever.

One of the levers they have against me in negotiations, George and Ringo, is there's a lawsuit about something I wasn't supposed to do, and I think I was allowed to do it. [There was a festering dispute over differential royalty payments; an agreement would be reached in November of that year.] It's just a difference of opinion. I rang them up. What happens with Apple is you do it all through Neil Aspinall, who's our guy. He used to drive us through the Mersey Tunnel in a little van.

So Neil is a very strong guy from the past. We haven't done his health any good, he had a heart attack last year. [Aspinall passed away in 2008.] I rang up and said, 'Look, I'd really like to come to the Rock and Roll Hall of Fame thing.' Cos we keep talking about a film we wanna do, *The Long and Winding Road*. I'd like to make it the definitive Beatles story, where we get our heads together and say, 'That was how it was.' Get it all in the real words.

But I keep saying to everyone, 'We've gotta sort out our problems. We can't move forward in harmony while you're suing me. We've got to get rid of this lawsuit to do the Beatles film.' I'm still hopeful we'll do it one of these days.

I wanted that to be the reunion night. If you can drop this lawsuit, guys, or show me something that you love me . . . Give me a sign, a wink, and I'll do it. It just went and went, and I kept ringing. George was in Hawaii and I got a message from him, 'Sit tight, don't rock the boat, don't worry.' But that was no good to me. I had to ring him up and say, 'I can't come to the Hall of Fame.' No way am I standing up on the stage going 'Yo! United!' when I know they're suing me.

So that became watered down as 'business differences'. But it's bloody embarrassing, cos I'd have liked to have gone along. My thinking was 'It'll be great, we could hold hands.' They'd take a picture which would go around the world, and we'd use that as a jumping-off point to do our movie. It made sense to me. But it just wasn't to be. I think some advisors kicked in somewhere.

Hopefully one of these years it'll get sorted. If we do, the film could be interesting, cos we've all got private footage. I've got some in Rishikesh, with us all being very Swami indeed. I've got some stuff from what was John's house, then Ringo's, Tittenhurst Park. We could extend the idea that we the Beatles try to set the record straight.

We could mess with the records, we could take orchestras off if we didn't want them, maybe 'Long and Winding Road', for instance – which is a bone of contention! That wouldn't be bad.

So that's the plan, get friendly, maybe do new songs. That's an interesting area we could get into. George has been writing with Jeff Lynne, I've been writing with Elvis Costello; it's natural for me to write with George, and we've never done it. It's only getting shit out of the way and getting a bit of sense happening.

Most of the business tensions were eventually resolved, although George felt the film should not be named after a Paul song. Thus *The Long and Winding Road* became the *Anthology*; its partner CDs of Beatle rarities were a revelation to all but the most ardent bootleggers, and the old-new Lennon songs were generally welcomed. In the Beatles' homeland, their release chimed nicely with the mid-Nineties emergence of retro-styled

'Britpop' bands, and the Beatle franchise proved more potent than ever.

As Paul told me in 1995, 'Timing's a bit like that, if you get it right.'

> I showed up at the War Child thing the other day for Paul Weller, his 'Come Together' session. [In Abbey Road, the two Pauls teamed with Noel Gallagher of Oasis; their cover of John's song raised funds for children caught up in wars.] And it was just like *then* – with the way they're all dressing now. It was a time-warp for me, the room's full of young people being Beatles, or Small Faces or whoever they're being. I've never seen so many Epiphones [the electric guitar played by the Beatles] together at one time.
>
> You see so many groups, *all* the new groups, and it's derivative. It's like old Pete Thingy's Family Trees [Pete Frame wrote meticulous genealogies of many bands' changing line-ups]. But there's also a *derivative* tree you can do, and a lot of it comes from the Beatles. He said, modestly. But it is true, I was listening to ELO the other day, you know, all their first great stuff, and some of it is spotting the riffs: [*gasps*] 'That's *us*!' Luckily we got in first.
>
> And the harmonies. George always said that about Queen: Can you hear the harmonies? It's the Beatles, ELO, Queen.

At Q magazine we'd dubbed the remaining trio of Beatles the 'Threetles'. And the *Anthology* CDs found McCartney quite at home with his heritage:

> It goes right back to 20 Forthlin Road, Allerton [Paul's childhood address]. Do you remember that place? Ha! It's good to have the old blues players' first twang. And they are a bit twangy. But there are some great things, they must have been done when I was a teenager in Liverpool when John and I first started writing.
>
> It's strange to be going back pre-Beatles, cos half the thing

you are, in my case, is the Beatles. So there's me and John kicking around and [*crooning*] 'Yeew'll be miiine, all the tiiime,' just goofing. It's mad shit that we did and never thought any more of. But since the Beatles thing has happened in the meantime, of course it makes that stuff more important.

Then you start getting the auditions, when we were turned down by Decca. You can see why . . . No! Not really. They should have snapped us up.

Do you think it sounds good, the Decca stuff?

You can't claim that it *sounds* good, cos technology's better, we can make better records now. But that early stuff is interesting. It's like seeing some artist's early sketches. It may not be as good as his later work, but you see the germs of it all.

It's a pity there aren't more tracks like 'Free as a Bird', but because of the tragedy occurring, there's only so much stuff that Yoko has of John's. She played us a couple of tracks and we chose them. The good thing about 'Free as a Bird' for us was that it was unfinished. So the middle eight didn't have all the words to it. That was like John bringing us a song and saying, 'Do you want to finish it?'

This opportunity came up with the *Anthology* to maybe have a go at one of John's songs. So I rang Yoko and asked if this would be on. I ended up going to her house after the Rock and Roll Hall of Fame dinner where I inducted John as a solo artist. I checked it out with Sean, because I didn't want him to have a problem with it. And I said to them both, 'If it doesn't work out, you can veto it.'

I said to Ringo, 'Let's pretend that we've nearly finished some recordings and John is going off to Spain on holiday. He's just rung up and said, "There's one more song I wouldn't mind getting on the album, but it's not finished. So if you're up for it, take it in the studio, do your stuff like you would normally do, have fun with it, and I trust you."' With that scenario in place, Ringo then said, 'Oh, this could even be joyous.'

And it was. We'd not met for a long time, we did it down in my studio, and the press didn't guess that we'd be down there. We had technical problems to overcome. But because we said, 'John's only left us this tape,' we could take the piss. That was our attitude, we were never reverent to each other.

What was the crack like between the three of you?

Really good. It was better when there was three of us than when Ringo left me and George to do it. Me and George, as artists, we had a little more tension, which I don't think is a bad thing. It was only like a Beatles session. You've got to reach a compromise.

We all turned out to be veggies. Ringo's walking around with a bag of seeds, and sunflower and nuts, it's all so healthy. Ringo is so healthy for a guy who's been in intensive care and nearly dying for most of his life. He was told he'd be dead when he was three [Ringo had been hospitalised as a child with appendicitis and peritonitis], and he confounded all those stories. Then he got into heavy drinking in Monaco, he was put on a life-support system with seven very nearly dead people in the room. He says, 'You're lying there, on the drip, and your heart thing is going *blip . . . blip . . . blip* . . . Suddenly you hear *durrr* and you look up to see if it's you!'

Ha! Only the boy could do that. Now he's completely sober and his head's very together, he will not put up with any shit.

George ended the record playing beautiful guitar. To tell you the truth, I was a bit worried. When Jeff suggested slide guitar, I thought it's gonna be 'My Sweet Lord' again, George's trademark slide. Maybe John might have vetoed that. But in fact he got a much more bluesy attitude, very minimal, and I think he plays a blinder.

There was another song that John had, called 'Real Love'.

That was good to do but it was a bit 'boiling your cabbages twice.' An old Liverpool expression you know, Paul, 'I don't boil me cabbages twice.' You do a thing that's so exciting, you do it again and the novelty's eroded.

That was with Jeff Lynne again?

Yeah. I was worried cos he was such a pal of George's. They'd done the Wilburys, and I was expecting him to lead it that way. I thought that him and George might create a wedge – 'We're doing it this way' – and I'd be pushed out. But he was really fair.

It's strange after all this time, to be still going in [to Abbey Road]. We're finding these takes that you couldn't use. One of them is 'And Your Bird Can Sing'. John and I have sung it, and we're going now for a double-track, but we start giggling. We could never have put it out, it would have been 'How indulgent of them, are they kidding?' It's not like that now, it just sounds like a hoot.

There's nice things like 'While My Guitar Gently Weeps', which is just George on acoustic, no Beatles, and no Clapton playing the lead. There's the first take of 'Yesterday' – turned out we only ever did two takes, and I was twenty-two. There's a big body of work there, and you can look at all the track sheets; you see exactly what day you did it on, exactly how old you were.

The strangest thing for *me*, it's like drowning, like your life flashing by in front of you.

There's a really nice song ['I'll Be Back' from *A Hard Day's Night*], 'You know, if you break my heart I'll go, but I'll be back again . . .' And that's in 4/4. But the original take, it turns out, was 3/4. God knows why. So it's like, 'You know, *chikka-chik*, if you *break* my heart . . .' But in the middle of it John goes, 'It's too hard to sing, I can't do it!' Then you hear the proper version. It's interesting the way we developed stuff. We were very free in the studio.

'Free as a Bird' is pretty emotional, I've played it to people who've cried. It's a good piece of music, and John's dead, and the combination of that can be emotional. But it's great, emotion. I love that, I don't have a problem when something so grabs you by the balls that you've gotta cry. I rather respect that. I'm not eighteen any more – you might have noticed. When we were eighteen I would have hated that to happen [*gruff macho mutter*]: 'I'm not fuckin' cryin'!'

Do you think John would have approved of the Anthology project?

I'm sure he would. He might have chosen some different takes. There's a few things of mine that I didn't want in there. I mean, at that time I was doing the kind of cabaret-stroke-Little Richard, that was my role. So I'd do the 'Till There Was You's and the 'Besame Mucho's. There's a couple of those that I wouldn't have minded removing. But it *is* my life, that's what I wanted to do. And it's only me who'll get really hung up about that stuff. I'll talk to somebody else about it and they'll say, 'We don't mind that about you, you've always done the odd ballad.' I don't like to admit to that: 'No. I'm R&B, in an R&B group.'

Now you and George have done this, might you do other things together?

We've been offered a humungous amount of money to tour, to just do ten dates in the States. But no way. I think that would be pushing it. I don't think it really works with three of us. At least with 'Free as a Bird', John's on it, so it's the Beatles.

I had a rather obnoxious customs man when I was going through New York. He was very serious, a pasty lad, who said, 'The project you're doing with the Beatles . . .' Yeah? 'I just want to tell you that I don't consider it the Beatles without John.'

I was in no mood after a plane flight, this guy's customs, I don't need this shit – I said, 'I don't *care* what you think, and it shows how much *you* know, cos John *is* fuckin' on it!'

The three of us touring, even for humungous money, doesn't make sense. You can't do it just for the money.

You know what people will say: Well what about a charity show, then?

Well OK, if you were going to take the money and give it to charity, that would be good. But the fact remains that the three of us would have to get up there and make a noise, without John. And that's not as easy as it might sound. To do that, we have to spoil something. If we went out on tour, what do you do? You get another singer? It's all of that shit. I can't see that happening.

Are you more relaxed about Beatle nostalgia now, now that you're so far away from it?

The scariest thing is seeing your life just laid out in front of you, it's like someone's written your memoirs. And I don't particularly want to write my memoirs.

I sat through the whole *Anthology* project, listening to these takes, praying I wouldn't make a mistake. It was like I was still doing it live. And there's another little person in your head saying, 'It's all over, mate, no need to worry! You've done it.'

You've passed the audition.

You've passed the audition. It's been nice to work with the guys. Cos you realise, we love each other. After all the bullshit, we've just known each other for so long. And we relate quite easily. We can put up with each other's bullshit. There was one nice moment when we were doing 'Real Love' down at my studio. I was trying to learn the piano bit and Ringo sat down at the drums. We don't play together any more, really. He was just jamming along and it totally reminded me of what we used to do. Like no one has been away.

The *Anthology*, which itself followed the fanfare of Beatle transfers to CD, presaged a new phase of authorised projects; these would include revisions of the *Yellow Submarine* and *Let It Be* albums, the *1* compilation of chart-toppers, a collection of remixed tracks called *Love* and even a Beatle video game. In 2003 I spoke to Paul about their new presentation of the band's awkward finale, now revamped as *Let It Be . . . Naked*:

I think Ringo came up with the idea of calling it *Naked*. Me and Ringo individually went to listen to it and were blown away. There's not an awful lot you can do – it's an engineering job, y'know, the record's been made. I said at the time, Winston Churchill's papers get browner and crinklier, and our recordings get more golden and shiny. And anyone who worries it should be as it was, well, get the original records. It's all still out there, it's not like it's gone away.

While the film of *Let It Be* has not yet been reissued, the *Let It Be . . . Naked* album was an interesting variant on the original record. Even its cover was a sort of remix: 'It's going to be similar to the old one,' said Paul, 'with the four photos in a square, which always reminded me of a tobacco box. Four Squares, d'you remember that one?' [Four Squares was a brand of pipe tobacco.].

George Harrison, sadly, had died in 2001. Even the Threetles were no more. So I asked Paul how the process now worked, with half of the band missing. He explained that their widows, Yoko and Olivia, simply took their place: 'They *are* John and George, it works exactly the same way, a four-way vote. The four of us have to agree, there's no three-to-one or two-to-two. Which is always the Beatles' thing.'

How involved was everybody in revisiting *Let It Be*?

We've had some input, but the truth is the Beatles have done with our career. We've been and done it. So you don't really find us getting too involved, except for the *Anthology*. The *Anthology* was, Well, everyone else has written so much about us, we should try and get it in our own words. Before our memories go on the blink, which is imminent. So we did that. To answer your question: All the ideas go into a melting pot, the best ideas come out and we all finally approve them, Yoko, Olivia, me and Ringo.

I love the idea that you do get a project like this and suddenly, John is in the room. It's exciting for me. Close your eyes and it's exactly like being in Abbey Road making those records. Only there's no hiss. And you can't argue with that, cos there wasn't any hiss when we made it, the room was quite clear. So it's taking it back to reality and I think it's exciting for that reason alone.

When we spoke there had recently been hit remixes of the Elvis Presley tracks 'A Little Less Conversation' and 'Rubberneckin''. After Michael Jackson's death in 2009 there were similar studio resurrections, notably 2014's *Xscape*. Could McCartney see his or the Beatles' catalogue receiving the same posthumous treatment?

I start off by digging my heels in and saying, 'Oh, you should never do that with Elvis or the Beatles or the Stones. They're pure and should remain like that.' But there is an argument that the young kids coming up, they'll hear it down a club and go, 'Who's that? It was Elvis? Who's he?' It sounds incredible but there are young people who don't know who Elvis is and who the Beatles are, even though they're historical figures. They also don't know who JFK is. They think it's a chicken restaurant. The point being, you could argue it's a good thing, just to get people introduced.

On a morbid note, how would you feel when you're not here any more, if somebody at Apple said, 'Let's go back and . . .'

You mean Yoko? Ha!

Well anyone. Whoever's looking after Apple in fifty years' time.

You know, I've become less strict about that stuff. We're not doing it now, because we think of the thing as pure. But I certainly wouldn't mind after I'm dead, cos I won't be thinking about things like that.

You won't be turning in your grave, going, 'Leave my stuff alone.'

No, I don't think I would be that fussed. When I heard that Elvis thing I thought *that's* cool, cos it was Elvis, and when I heard the backing was changed it was, well, I can get the old backing any time I want. This new one is probably better to dance to in a club. So that's the reason for it existing. You could certainly do it with the Beatles and I know a lot of people have done, sampling the *Sgt. Pepper* drums or 'Tomorrow Never Knows'.

You're kind of almost there. I don't want to be the one to say, 'Yeah, it's great, I approve of it.'

Your 'Come Together' bass line is another favourite.

I like that people like it enough to sample. To me it means they can't play anything better, which is a great tribute. I don't want to be the one to approve it, but I also don't want to be the old fuddy-duddy who says 'Ooh, music was much better in *our* day, Eminem's a terrible person.' I don't think that. It changes.

They were always trying to get us to say Benny Goodman was terrible, y'know? [Goodman had been a pre-eminent bandleader of the pre-rock era.] He started slagging us off, so we did go with that one. We started to say, 'Well, he's not so good anyway. What is he, a fucking clarinettist?'

People in the street are always doing this to me: 'Oh, I don't like all this rap stuff, it's not as good as *you*.' But it's a new generation, twenty-first century, you can't expect people to live in the past. And there is a reasonable case for that stuff because time is moving on. If somebody quotes our music in the future they've always got the opportunity to hear the pure version. I can go back and hear Beethoven's symphonies, but I can also hear the ELO version – *da-da da dummm* – that goes into 'Roll Over Beethoven'. I don't mind that, and I'm sure Beethoven doesn't mind. He'd probably think it's quite cool.

CHAPTER 17

Apollo C. Vermouth

I'm a pretty good foil. I Foil Fine

The young McCartney thought his future might lie in supplying songs for others to sing. In the great days of George Gershwin, after all, the whole system of popular music was founded on specialists – the jobs of composer and wordsmith were usually separate – who'd submit their work to publishers, for others to perform.

History had other plans. Ever since the Beatles and Bob Dylan, rock musicians have nearly always written their own material and few bands depend solely on outside sources. But Paul never lost his liking for that old romantic role of jobbing tunesmith.

Nor was he averse to striking up fresh relationships. Since John Lennon he's partnered with several other writers. He's also made duets, appeared as a guest player and done duty as a record producer. To list every one of his dalliances would require a book of its own, but some seem worthy of special mention – Michael Jackson, Stevie Wonder and Elvis Costello, for instance. There was even a legendary collaboration that never quite happened, with Frank Sinatra.

'I didn't flip out after John and I split up,' says Paul, 'because we did also write separately:

> Like, the words to 'In My Life' were done without me, then we got together and I helped with the tune. 'Yesterday', 'Michelle',

some of those very McCartney ones, I'd written on my own cos they'd come quickly. By the time I took them to John it might be one little word he'd wanna change.

But I did miss a collaborator. Even if you've written a thing on your own it's handy to take it along to someone. *You* must have it when you write an article – you show it to someone. And if it's someone you respect, and they go, 'Great, man!' you just feel good.

They only have to tell you it's great. Sometimes that's all the collaboration you need. Otherwise you're still wondering. It's always good to have that second opinion. I did miss it, obviously.

At first I thought the natural thing: 'I've collaborated with Lennon and anybody else will not be as good.' Which I still feel. If you've written with the best, who else is going to be as good? There were thoughts of people like Paul Simon. He's quite a friend, and I think we probably would do something serious together. But you just don't get round to it. I didn't want to ask him in case it all got too intense.

The British band 10cc were a quartet of writers whose wit and melodicism was often dubbed 'Beatle-esque'. Hopes were high when Paul announced he was writing with Eric Stewart of the band, for the 1986 album *Press to Play*. Alas, the magic was lacking: 'We did a couple of nice things, but it wasn't a very successful album. I thought it was OK, but again, John's a difficult act to follow for anyone.

'I feel sorry for *them*, really, because they're writing with me and they must think, the last guy you wrote with who was good was John Lennon. Holy shit, how am I gonna live up to that?'

There was more anticipation, though, when Paul teamed up with Elvis Costello – known for both his punk edge and his grasp of classic pop. And their collaboration was fruitful: after a 1987 B-side, 'Back on My Feet', came four tracks on Paul's 1989 album *Flowers in the Dirt*; a further few co-writes emerged on 1993's *Off the Ground*. Costello himself released two tracks apiece on his *Spike* and *Mighty Like a Rose* albums, followed by 'Shallow Grave' on 1996's *All This Useless Beauty*:

> Again, pressure on him, really. I felt he was the nearest to John and I get a lot of journalists asking me this. 'Yeah, there *are* similarities between them . . .' But I got pissed off after a while and I ended up answering, 'Yeah, they both wore glasses.' No matter how anyone reminds me of John, they're not John.
>
> We got these songs, a bit different for me, a little more wordy than if I'd written them. He's very much into words, Elvis. He's a good foil for me, and I think I'm a pretty good foil. I Foil Fine. I write something and he'll sort of edit it, and provided I don't mind, that goes OK.
>
> Occasionally he used too many chords, for my opinion. I've found in writing music over the years that it's often cool to cut your chords in half, and make do, leave all your melody the same, but really space out what's behind it. I remember doing that with Elvis, going, 'Look, if you just go from the C to A minor and lose all the passing chords in between, it'll be great.'
>
> So it was good, we kept buzzing off each other. I thought he was very opinionated. But I don't mind that, cos he's up-front.
>
> People have said that the hard edge is what I lack. It's not totally true. Anyone that knows my stuff, there are hard-edged things like 'Helter Skelter'. With Elvis, he did have a satirical edge to him, and his personality reminded me of John's – hard on the outside, soft on the inside. He's all right, is Elvis. It was good to collaborate with him.

And how was it for Elvis? I asked Costello in 1989. 'Inevitably there was a bit of, Fuckin' hell it's Paul McCartney,' he replied. 'He's written loads of famous songs. He's very practical about songwriting – very formal, funnily enough. People say he seems to dash them off, but that's not really true.

'If you don't like what he's singing about, if you think the sentiments are not tough enough, then that's a personal thing. I wouldn't say this holds true for every song he's ever written, but when we sat down together he wouldn't have any sloppy bits. That was interesting.

'I don't think he's sweetened up the songs. He has discipline and a good ear for melody, plus his playing as a bass player, of course. He has good instincts about music. And people are too concerned about who he is and what he represents, and what he's been and where he's going. That's an unreasonable demand to make on anybody.'

Being managed by Brian Epstein, the young Beatles belonged to a family of Liverpool acts. But their clear superiority as songwriters soon put them in a category of their own. In the early Sixties they obliged with a flow of Lennon and McCartney originals for local acts like Cilla Black, the Fourmost, and Billy J. Kramer.

Down in London, their new best friends the Rolling Stones were given 'I Wanna Be Your Man' before it appeared on *With the Beatles*. Another Decca band, the Applejacks, received an early Paul composition, 'Like Dreamers Do', after the two bands shared a TV rehearsal. In Paul's time with his girlfriend Jane Asher, he took an interest in her brother Peter's act, Peter and Gordon, steering hits in their direction that included 'A World Without Love' and 'Woman'.

Cliff Bennett and the Rebel Rousers were likewise signed to Epstein and toured with the Beatles in 1966. Paul not only offered them his new *Revolver* track, 'Got to Get You into My Life', but produced it for them too, yielding the biggest hit of their career.

In 1967 Cilla secured her own TV series and Macca was again on hand. 'When Paul rang,' she told me, 'I was literally on the floor playing tracks the BBC had sent me for an opening. It had to be all razzamatazz, a big opening, but Paul said, "You don't have that personality. You should be inviting people into *your* home rather than you going into theirs." He was so right, and hence "Step Inside Love".'

Then came Apple. The Beatles' own label was formed in 1968 with the noble intention of fostering other artists' careers. But in the vacuum that followed Brian Epstein's death the year before, and given the four Beatles' disinclination to run a proper business, Apple was nobody's idea of a well-oiled corporate machine. Still, Apple was above all a record label, and in that light it was an amazing success.

Paul was characteristically bountiful. He penned 'Thingummybob', a jaunty homage to his Northern roots, for Yorkshire's Black Dyke Mills Band. When Apple signed a Liverpool-Welsh band the Iveys, renaming them Badfinger, Paul subcontracted them to soundtrack a Peter Sellers/Ringo Starr movie, *The Magic Christian*. He supplied their biggest hit, 'Come and Get It'.

He found another protégée in the gifted Welsh teenager Mary Hopkin, whose chart career he launched with a rearranged Russian folk song, 'Those Were the Days', a UK number 1 in 1968; he wrote her hit follow-up 'Goodbye' and produced its parent album *Postcard*.

Paul worked too with his younger brother Mike, producing 'Liverpool Lou' – a 1974 hit for his band Scaffold – as well as helping out on solo albums. But the McCartney surname was naturally an obstacle for any artist seeking recognition in his own right, which is why the records were credited to Mike McGear.

This issue bothered other beneficiaries of Paul's assistance. The Bonzo Dog Doo-Dah Band appear in the Beatles' *Magical Mystery Tour* – they'd been recommended by Mike McCartney, in fact – where they perform a film noir spoof called 'Death Cab for Cutie'. The Fabs found a rapport with the Bonzos' anarchic genius Viv Stanshall and his musical partner Neil Innes, who later led those exemplary Beatles parodists the Rutles. The happy outcome on this occasion was the band's only sizeable hit, 'I'm the Urban Spaceman'.

'Viv and Paul got on well,' says Innes, the song's author. 'We wanted to do "Urban Spaceman", but our manager was keen on spending no more than two hours on a track. Viv was bemoaning this to Paul and Paul said he'd produce us.

'He came along and played the ukulele. Viv got out his garden hose with a trumpet mouthpiece and wanted to whirl it around his head. The engineer said, "You can't record that thing!" And Paul said, "Why not? Just put a microphone in each corner of the studio." It was wonderful to have the power he had over convention.

'But we said to Paul, "Well, we're certainly not going to do it on the back of *your* name. D'you mind if we call you Apollo C. Vermouth?" And Paul goes, "Sure, why not?" And the manager's going *What!?!*'

As a curious footnote, the single was actually finished off by a rising young producer named Gus Dudgeon. 'I'm the Urban Spaceman' began a trilogy of extraterrestrial hits for him, being followed by David Bowie's 'Space Oddity' and Elton John's 'Rocket Man'.

The prolific Mr Vermouth has mucked in with others ever since. As well as The Fireman there were recordings with everyone from Johnny Cash to Allen Ginsberg. In the rapprochement that followed the *Anthology*, he and Yoko made 'Hiroshima Sky Is Always Blue', a strange and emotional work for which they enlisted both their families. He's spent studio time with Lee Perry, Brian Wilson and many more.

And he still wrote 'on spec', as any Tin Pan Alley man would: 'Baby's Request' was conceived for the Mills Brothers, harmony stars of pre-war vintage. 'I was hoping they would do it,' says Paul. 'Something happened and they never did, but I offered it to them.' 'Baby's Request' has since turned up on *Back to the Egg* and the full edition of *Kisses on the Bottom*.

Other artistic connections range from the quietly obscure to the stunningly well-publicised. Into the former category we might drop 'Penina', written on holiday for a Portuguese hotel band, or 'Catcall', for the Chris Barber Band. By 2015 Paul was becoming known to post-millenarian music fans for his work on video games and singles with Kanye West and Rihanna.

Has any collaboration ever matched his own best work? Possibly not. But let's look at two of the most celebrated – Michael Jackson and Stevie Wonder.

McCartney's partnership with Michael Jackson began in bland amiability. There are photos of them at Paul's kitchen sink, doing the classic 'You wash, I'll dry' routine. It was destined to end badly, over Michael's 1985 buy-out of Lennon and McCartney's song catalogue – ironically, it was Paul who had once advised Jackson to invest in music publishing – for which Paul and Yoko had been planning a joint bid. Jackson died in 2009. For the moment, let's note the pair sparked each other artistically.

Paul's song 'Girlfriend' was a clever pick for Michael's groundbreaking *Off the Wall*; few had paid it much attention when it first appeared on Wings' *London Town*. 'Michael rang up,' says Paul, 'and said he wanted to work together.'

> I said, 'What do you mean?' He said, 'I wanna make some hits, you know?' I said, 'Sounds good.' So he came over.
>
> We sat around upstairs in my office in London, I grabbed a guitar and 'Say Say Say' came out of that. He helped with a lot of the words. It's not a very wordy song, but it was fun working with him because he's enthusiastic. But again it's nothing like

> working with John. At that stage with Michael, you weren't even talking about a writer, more just a vocalist and a dancer. But he said, 'Let's make a couple of hits,' and that's exactly what we did.

'Say Say Say' was an enormous success. The new pals also made 'The Man', which appeared on Paul's 1983 LP *Pipes of Peace*. Biggest of all, though, was their duet 'The Girl is Mine', a cute-cum-sappy number that found immortality through its inclusion on Michael Jackson's *Thriller* – one of the few albums to outpace *Sgt. Pepper* in long-term sales.

If Paul's friendship with Michael Jackson ended badly, his dealings with another Motown deity, Stevie Wonder, were merely a trial of patience. For 1982's *Tug of War*, Paul imagined a parable of racial harmony, like the black and white keys of a piano. Of course, he called it 'Ebony and Ivory'.

After its recording he rang Stevie about doing a video:

> He said, 'Sure man.' But he's his own man, Stevie. He rung up a few days before and said, 'I got this problem, man, I'm doing this record. I promised Motown, it's really getting nasty.'
>
> But he's a great guy, old Stevie, and he started coming in with, 'I'm not sure I'm gonna be there . . .' He was gonna be in [London] on Saturday, rest up Sunday. So I said, 'Well, no sweat, just come in on Sunday.'
>
> Then he rang the next day: 'Not sure I'm gonna be able to make the Sunday, man, I've got this heavy commitment.' Hmm, it's gonna be a bit tight, but come in on Monday. You have a certain reverence for someone like Stevie.
>
> Anyway, it turned out, 'I'm not coming.' I had the worst weekend on the phone, trying to pull this thing together. I was up all bloody night, cos it was LA.
>
> 'Er, could I speak to Stevie Wonder, please?'
>
> 'Who's that?' 'It's Paul McCartney, I've been working with him . . .' 'Oh, hi Paul, this is Mike, the roadie.' 'Hi, Mike, could

I speak to Stevie please?' 'He's in the studio, man.' 'I'll hang on ten minutes, if he's got a tape going?'

'Ah, no. You better call back.'

You were given a major runaround. It was getting real crazy.

Finally his director Keith MacMillan suggested they revisit a technique used for the 'Coming Up' video, whereby Paul and Stevie would be filmed separately and the results spliced together. MacMillan accordingly flew to LA to complete the film with Stevie's performance:

The funny thing was Keith had said to me, 'OK, you turn to Stevie [*mimes big smile and a wink*].' Then in LA he said, 'And now, Stevie, at this point Paul looks at you and gives you a smile. I'd like you to look back and give him a little wink.' And Stevie says, 'No, man, we gotta do it the other way round. I'll have to wink *first*, and then Paul will have to respond. Cos I couldn't *see* him.'

Very good point. Which we'd missed completely.

Not for the first time, one of McCartney's biggest hits would go down in media lore as an artistic misfire. He begs to differ:

They didn't like 'Ebony and Ivory', the critics. I can see what they're talking about, but I think it was good. A black sax player, Ernie Watts, who plays for the Stones, he thanked me in LA: 'Hey Paul, that song? I've got a white girlfriend, it really helped.' Now, why am I gonna listen to some critic after that? I don't care if they don't like it, it sold OK. I got to sing with Stevie.

It wasn't the greatest coming together of me and Stevie. Cos he's a giant, and I can be fairly gigantic, and the *two* of us could have been mega giants . . . But for Christ's sake it was number one, you know? It did *something*. You find yourself justifying your successes. It's a funny state of affairs.

Possibly the oddest collaboration that Paul ever planned, however, never quite came to pass.

'D'you ever remember,' he asked me, 'on the *McCartney* album, there's one little fragment. We just found the full track, and it's *cool*, man, I love it. People over the years were going, "What *was* that?" It was this song I'd had forever, since I was about sixteen. I had my dad's old piano, that I used to tinker about on when there was no one in the house.'

The song was called 'Suicide' and, bizarrely, he had once intended it for Frank Sinatra:

> My feelings were that if you were ever going to be a songwriter, the height of it all was Sinatra. A bit before rock and roll, you were thinking of standards and things. So around that time I wrote 'When I'm 64' and this other thing, which I thought would be a bit Rat Pack, smoochy, with words like [*clicks his fingers in a swing rhythm*], 'When she tries to, run away, uh-huh . . .' *Boom!* And stabs from the band, y'know?
>
> I remember being in bed, and getting ideas for lyrics. That's probably why they're so bad! I kept a paper and pencil by my bed, I'd lean out and try and not wake up, try and write it down. The rhymes are painful but I used to do it as a joke: [*in cabaret crooner voice*] 'When she tries to . . . Good evening ladies'n'gentlemen! Bop-bee-bop yeah! Welcome to Las Vegas!' That kind of thing.
>
> Like I'd do 'Michelle': ''Ello [*comic French accent*], welcome to mah French clurb . . .' You had a few party pieces and 'Suicide' was the Rat Pack one. I never did anything with it. But then I actually got a request from Sinatra for a song.
>
> I spoke to him on the phone and told him about it: 'Great, Paul, send it along.' Thank you, Frank! So I got that out of it. I did a demo, sent it to him and he thought I was taking the

piss. He really did. 'Is this guy kidding?' You know, sending Sinatra a song called 'Suicide'? He did not get it.

I did think, Oh God, maybe I should have changed it a bit.

But around the time of *McCartney* I was goofing around on piano and there was a bit of tape left, so I used that fragment at the end of 'Glasses'. It's actually quite a funky version, though I say it myself. Over the years people have said to me, 'You know that little fragment that gets faded out? What *was* that?'

The paper and pencil by the bedside . . . The land between sleep and dreams and wakefulness . . . It's time to explore the biggest subject of all – how does Paul McCartney write a song?

CHAPTER 18

A Pot of Gold

McCartney on songwriting

Paul can show a little reluctance when he's quizzed about the act of creating songs. It's not that he doesn't want to share the secrets of his trade; insofar as he does have tips and tricks, he will happily pass them on. But I think he respects the mystery of it all. He is wary of letting too much light in on the magic.

Songwriting is an art that he has mastered without consciously understanding.

'That's the trouble about analysing all this,' he says. 'You start to feel like you're on a psychiatrist's couch . . . Some people know about it and analyse songwriting. I've never known about it. It's fingers crossed, every single time I sit down to do it. But I think that keeps you in love with it. That's my theory. I never do warm-ups, I just dive right in and hope for the best. And it seems to work.'

I've never met a songwriter who really enjoys describing the process. In Paul's case, too, there is a fear of rendering the mysteries banal. On one occasion we were doing a track-by-track interview for the press kit of a new album: 'I was thinking about this the other day,' he said. 'Talking about songs is always difficult, because it's *listening* to songs that's important. When I listen to them I think, *this* is giving me more information than hearing how it was written. I can talk about how they were written, sure. But sometimes it gives too much info. And I was thinking, if I didn't know anything about "Jailhouse Rock" I'd be happy. I don't need to know who the eff wrote it and how he did it.'

Still, the PR trouper in him came through and we dutifully did our track-by-track. For a hackneyed formula, it can yield good results. Reading my transcript back the next day, though, his misgivings remained: 'If I listen to the record when I'm going home, a two-hour drive and I'm having a little drink in the car because I've finished work, I'm like *in a world*. I see what this song means. But the minute I try and analyse it, it's, "Well, I wrote this on a boat." [*Mimes apathetic response*] "Yeah?" And it doesn't make it as *big* as I think it is. Or as readers think it is when they listen to it.

'I'm telling them what it is, when actually they might have thought it was something much groovier. It would be like Elvis going, "I just went in the studio and sang and it's called 'Jailhouse Rock'." And you go, "No you didn't! It's fucking *phenomenal*, man!"'

The way McCartney describes it, his songwriting sounds like a private and even lonely process; as he says, he used to favour toilets. Perhaps he doesn't regard a song as truly existing until he has shared it with someone else? Or does the mere act of creation serve some purpose for its creator?

> Writing music in the beginning was just a way to avoid covers, because all the other bands knew all the other songs, and we wanted something individual. That's what started Lennon and McCartney. Then it became a way to earn a living. It wasn't some hugely artistic motive. Pretty mundane motives really, just to have songs the other bands couldn't sing before we went on; and then to get a swimming pool, get a car. Very shallow motives.
>
> Then you started to realise that there was more to it. One

of the things I realised was that it was therapeutic. If you were feeling bad, that was a good moment to go off somewhere secret, the furthest corner of the house you could find – which in our council house was the toilet. When I write I often hide myself away in the deepest corner, a cupboard or a toilet or somewhere no one goes. It's the best place to write.

You start telling yourself tales, pulling in stuff that you were thinking and putting it somewhere, rather than just in your mind. And that has been a great thing as I've gone on. It is actually like having a psychiatric session.

Writing 'Jenny Wren', for instance [from *Chaos and Creation in the Backyard,* 2005], I just went off in my car, by this canyon where I didn't think anyone would find me, and started playing the guitar. This whole idea of letting it come to you, a bird that had a broken heart, which eventually was a girl who had a broken heart. And who lost her voice because of it. You're putting probably quite a deep psychological thing, if it was to be analysed, that you might not be able to verbalise.

You put them down into a song with symbolism attached, and suddenly it's dreamlike. You've framed your thoughts in a way that you can look at them better; like a painting or a photograph, you can be detached from it, you've got something physical, a song. Something's come through, and you've captured something that wasn't there before. That's the therapeutic idea.

Was that the answer to the question?

How do you feel when the moment arrives, and you can play a song to someone?

It's a good moment . . . I haven't become jaded. And in a way I'm surprised, because you'd think I'd be fed up with going into the studio, a bit fed up with playing the guitar, and the same old chords. But you discover one new chord in the middle of them all and you remember why you're doing it.

He describes his writing method as a case of 'anything and everything'. Part of McCartney's admiration for the Belgian painter Magritte lay in that artist's way of working – a quietly methodical, daily routine that was quite unlike the bohemian chaos we imagine a painter's life to be. I asked him if Magritte's approach resembled his own. It turns out that while McCartney certainly puts in the hours, his days are much less structured.

'Sometimes you've only got an airline sickbag to write it on, hotel notepaper, backs of envelopes, toilet paper. It's been done on everything, y'know? But normally I've got a piece of paper and a pencil to hand. It's an adventure every time I do it. In these promotion things I do, they ask, "Paul, why do you do it? It can't be the money, it can't be the fame?" And it's just that each time you do it there's some kind of mystery, as to whether you're going to pull it off.'

Most often, with McCartney, spontaneity trumps deliberate craftsmanship:

> There's not much that takes years and years. If it takes that long I normally abort it . . . The best songs are usually just written in one go. They're just done, inspiration just comes quickly, it falls in place. Something like 'Yesterday', I dreamed it, you know? Just woke up with this tune that had been at the end of my dream, and I thought, what's that? It sounds good, on a piano there.
>
> 'Put It There' [from *Flowers in the Dirt,* 1989] was done very quickly while I was on holiday. I don't like sweating over stuff, I really don't. Nearly always a sign that it's not good.
>
> The only Beatle song I can remember we got stuck on – though it still only took an afternoon – it's just we got stuck on this thing, 'Baby I can give you golden rings, I can give you anything, Baby I love you.' It was 'Drive My Car'. And I hated this, 'I can give you golden rings,' sounds like curtain rings or something. We just couldn't get past it.
>
> And finally we just got manic, 'Oh, let's forget it, let's just do

the next bit.' We moved off the block and somehow I thought, 'Drive my car, great, that's great!' And that was the whole idea then. Oh, you could be my chauffeur! As if you were talking to a girl, or Zsa Zsa Gabor was talking to a toy boy. And then of course, the little twist we were into at that period, like in 'Norwegian Wood.' he burns her place down after having talked about how wonderful all the wood is. He burns it because she wouldn't let him have it. That was the little twist of that. And 'Drive My Car' is that he hasn't actually got a car. One of these days I'll have one and then you can drive it.

So that was all right. Once we got that idea, drive my car, got it away from golden rings it went really quick, and then the 'beep-beep beep-beep yeah!' It all came in. Once you have a good idea it's easy to run with it. Normally I don't have to struggle too much.

'Yesterday', I did the tune easily and then the words took about two weeks, because it was all 'scrambled eggs, baby I love your legs' for a while. Then I thought, No, it's too beautiful a tune, can't have scrambled eggs. We never seriously intended to.

But it gets you over the hump: 'Bugger it, we'll call it "Scrambled Eggs".' You stop being too intense and it allows a bit of light in your brain. I hate getting too stressed out on a thing, cos you think, this is music, it's supposed to be fun.

Another example was one of his finest latter-day ballads, 'From a Lover to a Friend', off *Driving Rain*:

I had some words on this demo that didn't make any sense. So I suddenly decided that they *did*, and just stuck to them. And it's my favourite track. I began to realise, this is actually a cool idea. Who says words have to make sense? Certainly not poets. There is this thing called surrealism and many of us love it.

Brian Eno has a line like 'Honour your mistakes': they're your unintended intentions.

There's so much of that. It's like dreams, we're all so boxed in: 'This is life, this is real, that isn't.' There's so much in the unintended. 'Mumbo' [off *Wild Life*] was an early version of that.

I'm inclined to wonder if the lyrical effort was slightly lacking in 'From a Lover to a Friend', a beautiful tune that's somewhat stuck at the scrambled eggs stage. But McCartney is unrepentant:

I seriously have no idea what that's about. Written very late at night, a rather drunken demo, that was. And there's lyrics in it that aren't lyrics: 'Despite too easy ride to see' is my favourite line.

Is that it? I was wishing I had a lyric sheet when I heard it.

No, I'll tell you how that happened. When you write a song, if you write them like I do, you sort of just block 'em in. Rather than go 'Vah-zee-wah-day-say-ooh-wah-ay', you start to hear words. You start to find a meaning out of the sounds of the words. So I had, [*murmuring*] 'ooh-yah can't find a way . . .' I didn't really think too hard what it meant. But the interesting thing is that it always *does* mean something.

Arriving, as it did, not long after Linda's passing, I suggested that the song's refrain of 'Let me love again' would sound like a very personal statement:

Well that's right. And psychologically, I think you may do those things when you're writing songs. But I didn't do it consciously. I think probably 'Yesterday' was about the death of my mother: 'Why she had to go I don't know.' But it was only twenty years later when someone made that suggestion that I thought, Oh yeah, possibly a young guy might psychologically have been going there. It's a bit like that, undeniably. But I didn't write it as a 'Let me love again' song. It just came out as words.

It's been a standard opinion of McCartney's writing that he avoids the directly autobiographical, certainly in comparison with Lennon's frequent bursts of brutally confessional candour. As these examples show, Paul himself is not so sure:

> I'm always about half and half. 'Lonely Road' [also from *Driving Rain*] was written in India, and that's a bit . . . I don't really know what I'm doing, just blues longing. I say I tried to go somewhere 'old', that's India. 'To search for my pot of gold', well I wasn't, I was on holiday. So it's half imagination, half reality. If I'm looking for a rhyme for old, and pot of gold comes into my mind, then I don't resist. 'I try to go somewhere old cos I *no longer* need a pot of gold?' Fuck that. Let's go somewhere old to search for a pot of gold seems more like a song.
>
> When I write, I'm just writing a song, but I think themes do come up. You can't help it. Whatever's important to you finds its way in. I saw someone writing about an artist, a painter and he says, 'Every painting a person does is of themselves.' Even though it's a portrait of his wife. Himself gets in it. You really can't help it, cos it's you making all the marks on it.
>
> I think it's similar with songwriting. Whether you like it or not, even if you're trying to write a song for a James Bond film, something of what you feel always ends up in it.

You're not that precious about what people draw from your songs, are you? I've talked to songwriters who say, 'This is what I meant, and if people don't think that then they're wrong.' Whereas with you, as long as it's not completely wackoid, you're quite content.

Mm. I've seen this happen a lot of times, where people have reflected back to me a meaning they've seen in it. And even though it's not *my* meaning, it's quite interesting. And rather than say, 'No, that's wrong,' I'll say, 'That's great, that's your interpretation.' Again it's like looking at a painting, particularly an abstract painting. The very first time I ever saw paintings with Willem de Kooning [he and the artist were friends], he said, 'Looks like a couch.' I said, 'Well it looks like a purple mountain to me.'

It's the same with songs. You can see something deep in a song that I didn't mean as a deep thing. That's happened a lot. I had someone who said to me, [*sings a few lines of* 'You Never Give Me Your Money']: 'Oh, that magic feeling, nowhere to go.' He said, 'Wow!' And I go, 'Yeah, it's nice, but . . .' and he goes, 'No, deep stuff, man.' So I say, 'Yeah, OK.' I can see there are two ways you can take it. Just, you don't have to be anywhere this afternoon, or in *life* there's nowhere to go. It's pretty Zen if you look at it that way.

That's why I like to not get too precious. I'm often educated by other people's views of my songs. And if I just said, 'No', then I cut out that aspect of life.

It's like the song on Let It Be, *'Two of Us'. People often took it as being about your friendship with John. But it could equally be about Linda?*

All my songs, I often do that, so they can be taken more than one way. Even though I was married and in love with Linda, I've never written a song, [*improvises*] 'Me and Linda, going out driving . . .' It's awkward, I don't think it works. So I'd be happier to go 'two of us,' and it becomes a bit of a mystery: 'Which two did you mean?'

Linda used to drive out of London and liked to try and get lost. I remember we went out west one day until we hit countryside, the buildings went away, we'd park up and go into the woods and fields. I've got photos that Linda took of me sitting on the car with my guitar, doing that song. So it was that idea of two of us going nowhere. I don't know what 'spending someone's hard-earned pay' is, it's just a line, doesn't particularly mean anything to me. Or 'burning matches, lifting latches', there weren't any matches or latches. It was just, 'two of us doing stuff', you could call that song.

Because John and I sang it, obviously then the interpretation would be, 'Oh, *those* are the two of us.' It was basically about me and Linda. But when I sang it with John, it becomes about me and John.

I like that. I could write a song saying, 'I really love being in this room with you,' and the great thing is it really works now. Cos you'd be going, [*dreamily*] ''E really luvs me . . .' It will apply here now. But what's great is when you get it to the session and you're looking at the drummer: 'I love being in this room with you.' It's a magic thing about songs, they will translate. Then someone gets it on their CD at home, they're with their bird and looking at her, and it goes, 'I really love being in this room with you.'

I love that reinterpretation that songs do. It's magical.

Such reinterpretations, or alternative meanings, are plentiful in McCartney's work. 'Venus and Mars' was taken to be a code for Linda and Paul, though he has always denied it. It still works, anyhow. There's even a certain ambivalence in 'Let It Be': does it mean, 'It'll be all right, don't worry too much', as he told his interviewer Barry Miles in *Many Years from Now*; or has it the prayerful sense of 'May it be, let this come to pass', as he has implied elsewhere, discussing the song's performance at Live Aid? Reassurance, from a dream of his mother, or a global call to action? Every heart has its own response.

To Paul McCartney, that is 'magical'. It's the word he returns to every time. When I first met him, in 1979, he explained the songwriting impulse in this way: 'When I was a kid and you'd get into an argument with somebody, and feel a bit down, you go away and get your guitar. It's like a dummy, or a release, it's like a crutch. It still makes me feel good to write songs. The whole thing about it, it's magic.'

And it surely brought him his pot of gold. Let us now look at this magic in more detail.

CHAPTER 19

This Magic Experiment

Further confessions of a songwriter

The Lennon and McCartney partnership may have been the engine room of the Beatles' success, but it wasn't what got them signed to a record label. It's a touching detail of their story that Brian Epstein showed such faith in them when they'd written barely a handful of songs, and those were by no means classics. EMI's George Martin took them on, too, with no premonition of their potential to generate original material of epoch-making quality.

Yet they had a commercial instinct from the start. When Paul was mugged in Nigeria, in 1973, he lost his demo cassettes of songs intended for *Band on the Run*. While the incident was a nightmare, it did prompt Paul to recall an early virtue of his songwriting practice. To create music that people remembered, he should first find it memorable himself:

> I had to remind myself that when John and I first started writing, there weren't such things as cassette recorders. There were great big jolly green giants with a winking eye, but we didn't have one. So we had to remember everything that we wrote. This is staggering to me, these days. We used to say to ourselves: 'What if we forget it?' And the only answer was, 'Well, we won't, will we?'
>
> And the theory became, 'If *we* can't remember it, how do

> we expect anyone else to?' So we had to write stuff that we would remember. If you think about it, that would have a big effect on your writing. You couldn't throw in stuff that was impossible to remember.

His gradual uncoupling from John as a writing partner was partly a question of logistics. As their Beatle lives developed they were no longer in each other's company every day. Listeners learned to distinguish a 'John song' from a 'Paul song', not only from the lead vocal, but by the track's very character. As already noted, the separation of powers was shown to brilliant effect on 'A Day in the Life'.

That track also hinted at a taste for the fragmentary in Paul's work, whether in the form of abandoned scraps or more considered medleys. He recalls being impressed by Keith West's 1967 single 'Excerpt from a Teenage Opera', which shifts in mood and tempo like a pop precursor of Queen's 'Bohemian Rhapsody'. The famous *Abbey Road* sequence, superbly crafted from intriguing half-songs, was followed by many examples, the most fully realised being 'Live and Let Die' and *Band on the Run*'s title track. *Ram* abounds with tunes that are dropped in a moment, as if the recording could not keep pace with the joyful rush of his writing.

Whatever the structure, the outcome is seldom premeditated. When he describes the act of writing, Paul often sounds like a surprised spectator at the inception of his own music.

When we discussed the tracks of his 2005 album *Chaos and Creation in the Backyard*, each example served to point up some aspect of his writing in general. Of one track, 'Anyway', he says it was 'a little song that became a bigger song. The thoughts in it are quite little, but somehow when you set it down as a song it becomes bigger. And those kind of surprises are what I do music for.'

On the same occasion we were discussing themes for his next American tour magazine; we planned to make some interplay of U.S. and the pronoun 'us'. I suggested that 'Anyway' struck me as a real McCartney 'us' song: 'We can cure each other's sorrow.' When two people become one, they are suddenly more than the sum of those parts:

> I don't quite know where I'm going, because I make it all up. I haven't really had any lessons – except lessons of life, lessons of being in the Beatles and my life since then. But there is this magic thing. You have a little idea, you put some chords to it and it becomes *grander*.
>
> It's lovely to put stuff down not quite knowing what you're doing, but at the same time governing yourself to *know* what you're doing. It's a very fine line. You're in a limbo area and I find that exciting.
>
> I feel lucky. We always used to say, 'If your job could be something you like doing . . .' and a few of us have managed that. I feel lucky, number one that I've been able to be in music and be with the Beatles, and be with Wings, and do what I do now with the band. But number two, to be involved in this magic experiment of putting a few little words together and suddenly . . . As you say, you pick out a line that I hadn't remembered was in there. And I go, 'Ah, that's right.'

'At the Mercy', from that album, began at a piano, playing 'slightly darker chords than I would normally come up with.' From his subconscious came a vaguely unsettling line, 'at the mercy of a busy road':

> It was a case of just letting it come into me. I still don't know what I was trying to get at. But I don't mind that in a song. I like that because the audience can decide. 'We can watch the universe explode.' It means everything without meaning anything. You know what it means. 'At the mercy of a busy day . . .'

Paul in sessions for the *Ram* album at A&R Studios in New York, 1970.

The first touring line-up of Wings, 1972 – plus the ghost of Eddie Cochran.
From left: Henry McCullough, Denny Laine, Denny Seiwell, Linda and Paul.

John at the time of his *Imagine* album, when relations with Paul were at their lowest: 'It's tough when you have someone like John slagging you off in public, cos he's a tough slagger-offer.'

Finally vindicated by the success of *Band on the Run*, the defiant McCartneys enjoy a taste of freedom in Nashville, July 1974.

On stage with Wings in Philadelphia, 1976: 'I've seen some mighty stuff on tours. You see stuff that you didn't know about your work.'

The flight cases are ready for Wings Over America, 1976. Joining Paul and Linda are, from left: Joe English, Jimmy McCulloch, Denny Laine. 'We broke our own record. That was a big pay-off after all that terror, post-Beatles.'

Paul and Linda with Michael Jackson in 1983. 'Michael rang up and said "Let's make a couple of hits." And that's exactly what we did.'

With Stevie Wonder at the Rock and Roll Hall of Fame in Cleveland, 2015. 'I don't care if the critics don't like "Ebony and Ivory". It sold OK. I got to sing with Stevie.'

Elvis Costello at Paul's office in 1995. In March of that year they played the Royal College of Music together: 'He's a good foil for me. I Foil Fine.'

A photo commissioned for the artwork of 2007 album *Memory Almost Full*.

Paul and Youth – collectively The Fireman – preparing artwork at Central St Martins college for their 2008 album *Electric Arguments*.

Paul's contemporary touring band – the most enduring of his career – prepare for Sprint Center, Kansas City on 16 July 2014. From left: Wix, Brian Ray, Paul, Rusty Anderson, Abe Laboriel Jr.

Paul at Dodger Stadium, Los Angeles, 10 August 2014. It's a long way from the Cavern, but in some ways nothing has changed. 'It's never the last tour as far as I'm concerned. I've always said I'll be wheeled on when I'm 90.'

> I like to be on the cusp of meaning. I'm not quite sure what it means, but I really *know* what it means. That's an interesting area.

I asked him about his compositional technique and 'English Tea' was an illuminating instance: 'Descending lines are very common in music. Like Procol Harum, "Whiter Shade of Pale", or Bach's Air on a G String. Millions of hits are made on that descending bass line. If you ever want to write a hit, don't feel ashamed, do a descending bass line. There's a hint for everyone, it works every time. It's amazing: a chord C, then just do a B, an A, a G. You're in wonderland already.'

There was an echo of Bach in one other song:

> 'Jenny Wren' was 'daughter of Blackbird'. I love little guitar harmonic phrases. It happens a lot through my career, and John's. 'Julia' is a good example in John's case; in my case 'Blackbird' and a number of other songs that have these little progressions. I've always credited 'Blackbird' to a Bach thing which George and I used to play when we were kids [Bourrée in E minor, learned from Chet Atkins' version]. There's a bass thing that goes with it, and those progressions I always loved. I made 'Blackbird' out of that, in my mind, though other people say it's nothing like it.
>
> And it isn't. That's the lovely thing when you copy, it ends up nothing like it. You play those two records together you go, 'No, sorry' – but it's how you get there. This was along that same vibe, going back to Bach.

The wish to uplift is a perennial aspect of McCartney's writing, and exceptions are rare. One of them is 'Maxwell's Silver Hammer', which he described to Barry Miles as 'my analogy for when things go wrong out of the blue.' Ironically, this somewhat menacing song is often heard as evidence of Paul's facile breeziness. If *Chaos and Creation* has one track with a negative atmosphere it is 'Riding to Vanity Fair': 'about when you're looking for friendship, and someone else isn't. It can be a difficult time in your life.'

It's the only song here that mentions a trouble not overcome.

Yeah, an own-up song. Now it's become more elegant, but it's still a pissed-off song. When you're trying to reach out to someone, and it's rejected, that's a hurtful thing. That happened to me at a particular point. It wasn't Heather [his wife at that time]. It was about some other relationship that I had, and this was my therapeutic way of releasing myself.

More in sorrow than in anger?

That's it. You know me. I'm generally trying to reach out in my songs. And when it doesn't happen, it *is* more sorrow than anger.

Another track, 'Too Much Rain', began with a song by someone else altogether. Charlie Chaplin composed 'Smile' for his 1936 film *Modern Times* (its lyrics were added by other writers, later). Paul most probably loved the Nat King Cole version, though by 2005 it was in Michael Jackson's repertoire also.

'Too Much Rain' is about anyone who's had problems in their lives, and I know a lot of people who have. Including me. Life throws problems at you. It's like sympathising with everybody who's had all the shit thrown at them, and saying I know what you're going through. I can relate to it.

Its inspiration, I must admit, is Charlie Chaplin's 'Smile': 'Smile, though your heart is aching.' That was at the back of my mind, one of my favourite songs. That was just one geezer, Chaplin. Not only was he funny, he wrote 'Smile'. It's like he wrote 'Yesterday'. A classic song. So that was it. If there's too much rain, what are you going to do about it? You're gonna laugh, you're gonna sigh, but you've got to get on with it, and tell yourself it's not going to happen again.

I *do* those. I'm interested in 'Get over it' songs, I do a good line in those – he said modestly – because I'm interested in that idea. Because I know lots of songs have helped me, like 'Smile', or some Fred Astaire stuff: 'There may be troubles ahead.' Fucking right. That should be the backing: 'Fucking right.'

Remember when that came on in *Pennies from Heaven* with Bob Hoskins? [The 1978 BBC TV series featured actors miming to vintage recordings.] 'Let's face the music and dance.' I have a deep history of that stuff, you know that, through my dad, through my own personal likes and listening to Fred Astaire and stuff.

You suddenly realise the songs I've heard that are very encouraging, that have inspired me so much . . . and then people have fed back to me: 'I was going through school and having the worst time of my life, but *you saved me*.' 'I was going through chemotherapy but I listened to your stuff and *it saved me*.' And I go, Whoah, excuse me! Power. And it has become an important part of what I do.

From 'Eleanor Rigby' and all its lonely people, to 'Mr Bellamy' (the 2007 tale of a would-be suicide) a strand in Paul's story songs has been the everyday outsider, trapped in the social margins. The quietly compassionate 'Footprints', on *Press to Play*, personifies another stubborn loner, as invisible to society as the lives of quiet desperation he enacts in 'Teddy Boy' or 'Another Day'. You can hear the same well of fellow-feeling being tapped in 'Treat Her Gently/Lonely Old People' from *Venus and Mars* – an intelligent sympathy for the forgotten. If McCartney could be said to have a signature song, it could perhaps be 'With a Little Luck': the gentle optimism that seeks no higher (or lower) purpose than to help us all along.

⁓

> When I'm asked which is my favourite song it's always a difficult question. I sometimes say 'Yesterday' because it's been covered by so many people. But more often I say 'Here There and Everywhere'. It makes it on a number of levels. If it were someone else's song it would be one of my favourites.

As we've seen, McCartney's deepest roots are not in 1950s rock, but in the popular songs that preceded it. Historians tend to depict rock's arrival as a kind of overnight cataclysm, occurring around 1955. But in reality it all sits in a continuum. The blues, which had been around for many decades, gave early rock its structure and attack; then the mainstream songwriters of the early twentieth century taught it melodic variety and lyrical guile.

Like his contemporaries Smokey Robinson and Brian Wilson, McCartney carried such influences into the brash new youth music now arising. Traces of that education were always evident in his Beatles work – subtly, in his approach to composition generally, or humorously in pastiche tracks like 'Honey Pie' and 'Your Mother Should Know'.

In the same way, Paul's notorious 'versatility' – that blithe ability to skip from dive-bar stompers to supper-club serenades, which is so annoying to a certain sort of critic – also echoes old-time show business. In those days the sensible aim was to prove yourself an 'all-round entertainer'. The Beatles' immediate predecessors, from Elvis Presley in America to Tommy Steele and Cliff Richard in Britain, were readily steered in that direction. It may be that the Beatles demolished Tin Pan Alley, but there is a part of Paul that somehow never left it.

Speaking to him for the liner notes of *Kisses on the Bottom*, the 2012 collection of homages to a vanished era, I asked him more about those now-celebrated family parties. Had his understanding of song construction begun by learning old songs on his father's piano?

> No, I never learned to play them. All I ever did was sing them. At the family sing-songs, I'd sing along with everyone. But I still couldn't play them; they're quite complicated, the chords and things. I'd have a bash at them. I did eventually become the sort of family piano player, at the New Year's, as my dad got older and I got more capable. But I was always busking it – *he* knew the real chords. But it was good enough for the family sing-song.

On the other hand:

> If you think about it, a lot of these old songs had what they called a 'verse', anyone else would call it an introduction. It's always the bit that you never knew.

You do it here [on Kisses on the Bottom*] in 'Bye Bye Blackbird'.*

> Yeah. Then it goes, 'Pack up all my cares and woe' and you go, Oh, I know this song! You finally recognise it.
>
> 'Cheek to Cheek' [written by Irving Berlin, recorded by Fred Astaire] was always one of my favourite songs. I love the way it returns to its opening, it goes through the whole song: 'Heaven . . . I'm in heaven'. It comes back. Wow. It's a simple little trick, but as a writer I loved that. I kind of did that in 'Here There and Everywhere'. So all these influences have always been there.
>
> Unless you actually analyse the whole thing you wouldn't know it, but they [the preamble 'verses'] were definitely in a lot of what we did in the Beatles. John and I liked that. We used to talk about that as one of the things it would be good if we could do. 'To lead a better life, I need my love to be

here . . .' Whereas in the old days they would have extended that: 'She was here, and I was there, and I think she's everywhere. *Here . . .*'

Another song to use that trick [though probably John's initially] was 'Do You Want to Know a Secret': 'You'll never know how much I really love you . . .' It would seem that older influences still lingered in what was considered brand-new music.

That's right. That was where all that came from. A lot of the songs that we were trying to write, even though we were now living in the rock-and-roll era, and influenced by it . . . But when you say rock and roll, there's Elvis Presley doing 'Love Me Tender', which is an old song, way older than Elvis. So these songs lived in the rock-and-roll era as well, and it was good to have that mix.

It's an era you've revisited throughout your career: 'Honey Pie', 'You Gave Me the Answer', the Thrillington stuff; you've always kept it in your range of styles.

It's a style that appeals to me. People often say to me what songs do you like, or favourite composers, and I say Cole Porter, and people like that, because the songs are very skilled. The Gershwin brothers, they're very skilful songs. It's like if you're a furniture maker, you might talk about Chippendale, because even though he's not your era, it's still very skilful chair-making.

In 2001, I asked him to cite some of the songs that had meant the most to him. Was there, I began, a contemporary piece of work?

Sting, 'Fields of Gold'. I really like that. People used to say to me, 'Is there a song you wish you'd written?' And I used to say Billy Joel, 'Don't Go Changing' ['Just the Way You Are'], because I thought that was nifty. But 'Fields of Gold' is a great song, man, it's now become The One That I Wish I'd Written. And Eva Cassidy does a really cool version of it. That and 'Somewhere Over the Rainbow'.

I like 'Somewhere Over the Rainbow' a lot. It's such a song of hope, of belief. After all the cynical Seventies, the aching Eighties, and the Nineties, 'Somewhere Over the Rainbow' is still there. 'I'll make it one day!' It's such a great song. Hope is always out there somewhere. It's really soppy and possibly a bit of a fantasy, but I don't mind that.

And Marvin Gaye! Man, I'm major league into Marvin. And he did 'Yesterday'. 'Yesterday' won one of these MTV things and Geoff [Baker, Paul's PR at the time] says to me, 'You know who's recorded it, don't you? Everyone. Sinatra. Elvis Presley. Marvin Gaye. Ray Charles.' So we got our New York office to get them. And Marvin's version of 'Yesterday' is my favourite, even beyond mine. Just so cool.

And the flakiest version is Elvis. He doesn't know the words. I love Elvis to death but it's flaky. It's a live version and the pianist is trying to intro him, and Elvis is [*silence*] . . . then finally the drugs give him a moment's relief and he comes to.

[*Mimes Elvis as a drunk pub singer*]: 'Yezzurday, love was such an easy game to play . . .' Then he forgets, and it's 'Now it looks as though they're here to stay.' Which doesn't actually make sense. But I love him. [To be fair to the King, the error may stem from a rehearsal version of the song, released on a Special Edition soundtrack CD of the documentary *That's the Way It Is*.]

I love Nat King Cole. I've taken to playing him now. I loved him when I was a kid, I remember being in the kitchen of Forthlin Road listening to him on the radio: 'When I fall in love . . .' thinking he's a good singer, that's a good song. Now

I just think he's the best. I love his stuff and I love that era of songs.

I'm listening to a lot more jazz than I ever listened to. Miles Davis, Chet Baker, I love those guys. We weren't great jazzers in the Beatles, but I love that now. I heard a Duke Ellington and Louis Armstrong record the other day, called 'Duke's Place'. It's like one note: down-to-Duke's-Place. Louis is singing and he goes 'take it, Duke!'

Duke's on the piano, and the cheek of him, he goes *dn-dn-dn-dn* on one finger. Next verse comes around, you expect him to go [*mimes flourish of triplets*], but it's *dn-dn-dn-dn*. It's almost embarrassing, except it's just so ballsy. That is *good*.

I always liked McCartney's willingness to talk about other people's music – not all stars are like that. But it was time to return to the man himself. Is there, I wondered, a 'real' Paul McCartney?

CHAPTER 20

Beyond the Smile

Who does Paul McCartney think he is?

When people are famous enough to be written about in the media, they develop two selves. One is the self they possess, the other is the hologram that they read about. For more than half a century, Paul McCartney has read about himself as if there were a separate, fictional character with the same name.

When I met him one afternoon in 1989, he had just received a new biography of himself. It left him perplexed:

> I've read a bit this morning, someone sent me one to autograph. And it's this silly book. Why should I endorse it with my signature? It's like signing a bootleg. It's funny. How do you explain to people who you are? If someone says I'm a megalomaniac . . . you know? I think, I bet I'm not.
>
> Like those stories about me trying to get Stuart [Sutcliffe] out of the group, to become bass player. I got *lumbered* with bass player. I had to ring George up and say, 'Hey George, what do *you* remember, did I push Stu out of the group?' He says, 'No, you got lumbered, you were the only one who'd do it.' Ah, that's what I thought it was.
>
> You're constantly trying to remember if you're OK or not. I hate justifying myself. I remember looking at George Martin once: 'George, are we really gonna have to keep justifying

ourselves?' He said, 'Yeah. Forever.' You can never rest on your laurels. And it's just as well really. I don't particularly want to rest on them. It's probably why I'm touring, making new albums.

I don't actually *want* to be a living legend. I came in this to get out of having a job. And to pull birds. And I pulled quite a few birds, and got out of having a job, so you know, that's where I am still. It's turned out to be very much a job, a bloody hard job the way I do it, running a company and all this sort of stuff, but I love it, that's all you can say about it. If people think I'm a megalomaniac, and people think I'm mean, it's difficult to know what to do about that. I just say, Well *I* know what I'm about.

It's odd to watch Paul in crowded places. He will inevitably be the centre of attention wherever he goes. At a music business event, where nobody wants to seem uncool, they tend to fall silent as he passes – careful not to stare, yet plainly conscious of his presence. Surrounded by fans, on the other hand, something in him feels compelled to acknowledge them – the much-satirised 'thumbs-up' gesture is an efficient way of doing it.

McCartney is good with people, and especially good with children. He told me how Lennon watched wistfully while he played happily with John's young son Julian; the senior Beatle asked him, forlornly, 'How do you *do* that?'

I once took my eleven-year-old son along to a private screening for *Paul McCartney in Red Square*, a documentary about the Russian leg of the latest world tour. I thought my boy might meet him and, perhaps someday in the far-off future, he would mention it to wide-eyed youngsters. They in turn – well into the twenty-second century – might be telling another generation how they once met an old man who'd met one of the Beatles.

After that screening I did what fathers do with young sons and made him go for a wee before we left. Opening the washroom door we ran straight into Paul, drying his hands on a paper napkin. I introduced my lad and McCartney gripped his hand for a full minute, in a comic routine he must have done a hundred times before: 'C'mon mate, let go! Let go, will yer?'

Out in the world at large, it's different again. He was chatting to my wife one day and described going into TJ Hughes, the Liverpool department store, to buy some decorations for a relative's wedding car. 'How do you manage in a crowded shop like that?' she asked. 'You just keep moving,' he replied. 'Smile, and just keep moving.'

McCartney has put up with being photographed ever since *Please Please Me*. The paparazzi were often intrusive, but the modern ubiquity of mobile phones has taken things to a new extreme. The soft snap and flutter of infinite camera shutters grows inescapable. Constant photography becomes a sort of tax on his existence.

He offers a relevant soundbite on his collaboration with Nitin Sawhney in 2008's *London Undersound*: 'Nowadays you can get the attention of the paparazzi, and you don't want them to take a picture, you don't even necessarily know they're there. It suddenly reminds me of the whole idea that the Africans thought – they were stealing your soul. So, yeah, they steal your soul.'

'McCartney's experience was as valid as anyone else's,' Nitin told me later. 'It's his take on things, feeling invaded. He's still a human being, no matter how celebrated he is or how much money he makes. We are all human beings.'

And what about security? I told Paul how surprised I was to find him sauntering alone through the streets of Soho. (I couldn't dispel the memory of John Lennon's demise.)

He explained, 'I'm fairly sort of whatever the word is, what's the word, I can't think of the right word . . .

Fatalistic?

> Yes, fatalistic. I don't think it's a good idea to hide away. I've never been a great one for that. I'll go on the bus or I'll go shopping in London, and people say, 'You're mad! Walkin' round on your own in London? What are you doing? I expected you to have five bodyguards.' Yeah, but I'd be walkin' round with five bodyguards then, wouldn't I? *Lots* of fun, you know? You've got to make that choice. Sometimes you have to have that security thing, and on tour it'll be fairly tight I would think. Which I won't be pleased with, but you know, it's the realities of the modern day.

Waiting for Paul to arrive at a magazine shoot, I am helping my photographer. I stand before the camera while he adjusts the angles, backdrop and lighting. Suddenly Paul joins us in person, and taking my place he glides smoothly into a repertoire of poses.

'Wacky-mister-thumbs-aloft-perpetuation-of-image' he says to me out the side of his mouth. His shoulders hunch, the legs turn in like Elvis Presley at a microphone, then out like John Wayne on a horse. The eyebrows arch in mock surprise, the forehead frowns and the finger points. 'I've done this before,' he murmurs drily.

Aspects of this persona were frozen as early as *A Hard Day's Night* – the smoothie, the sentimentalist, the charmer. These were accentuated by people's need to define him against John Lennon, who was thought to be none of the above.

'It's funny,' he says. 'I've come out with the safe image. People don't look beyond the smile. They look at the thumbs-up and they think it's a safe image. It isn't. Beyond the thumbs-up, there's more to it than all that. Which I know about, obviously, because I lived the fucking shit.'

How, then, does *Paul McCartney* see Paul McCartney?

For all his extraordinary wealth, it seems important to him that he keeps a grounded attitude to money.

By repute you don't live in great luxury.

I'm not impressed with luxury, really. I think luxury is a transition phase, between not having much money and having a bit of money. The first thing you do is get luxury – get a big car, cos everyone's into that, so you get a Roller. After a while you find yourself getting seasick going round bends, and you think, I'm not into this car, I like me Ford Classic. That's going back a bit, my first car . . .

The great luxury I used to have was a chauffeur. Bloody hell, that's a *real* bum deal, especially if you like driving. It's insane, you let someone drive your car and he wrecks it for you. And you actually want to be driving it. I've tried a lot of luxuries, I've tried live-in couples, hated it. I tried the big house in London, didn't hate it but grew out of it.

So I'm not that keen on luxury. But I like comforts. I take luxurious holidays, cos I do like that. But I'm not that into luxury. I think it's where I'm from. They were always suspicious of too much: [*cautious parental voice*] 'Too far, too soon, son . . . Keep yer head on yer shoulders, moderation in all things.' My dad was always like that.

You've got to remember that when I first got money, with the Beatles, it was a long time ago. So I've had time to adjust, and pace myself, and get sensible with it. This is what I think is a sensible way to live with money, not have it rule you but really take full advantage of it. It comes in handy if anyone gets ill, for instance. You're not one of those people who says, 'I'm waiting for me hip replacement.' So there's instances with friends and relatives and people who work in the company, where I'm able to say, 'No sweat, let me treat you.' I like *that* aspect of money.

What sums it up for me is John. When we first got loaded

he moved out to St George's Hill in Weybridge, which is near a golf club, very much the landed gentry. And you could have anything you'd ever wanted, kind of, in the first flush of success. He went mad on Jaffa Cakes, went insane about them: 'Gimme gimme!' [*mouth full noise*]. About a week later he couldn't look at one, and he never looked at one the rest of his life. 'Oh, don't talk to me about Jaffa Cakes.'

I think that's why I don't like too much luxury. And if you can understand that you're a better man than I am. But you know what I'm saying.

Charity presents him with a sort of double bind. Keep your generosity off the radar and you're thought to be mean. Make it public and you look crass. McCartney's acts of private kindness are real enough and I can attest to a few of them. But the dilemma is real:

I've had people talk about charity. 'Why don't you do more charity?' I say, I *do*. But when I was in school, I think it was in the Bible: 'Don't shout about it.' I got the idea from somewhere that you should be modest about stuff like that.

And your children went to ordinary schools?

State schools. Yeah. [*Plain-spoken Northerner*]: 'If it was good enough for me it's good enough for them.' I always feared the day they'd come back from a posh school, saying, 'Hello pater, how are you?' and start to look down on me. Which I've seen happen. Working-class parents who make good, the first thing they say – and you can't blame 'em, you know, God love them – they say, ''E's gonna 'ave everything I never 'ad.'

I still know millions of public schoolkids, who wanna slum, they wanna groove, they wanna 'get their feet on the ground, man'. They suddenly realise that's what's important in life. To be solid with a few mates, or to care, deeply, about anything.

And that's what we learned anyway, just from being knocked about.

I've always thought, if they're really smart they can get to universities from state schools. So that's what we've done, roughly. We've had a little flirtation into the other. But generally they've all gone through state schools, and seem OK for it. It seemed important to me to keep their feet on the ground.

The term ordinary people crops up in a few of your songs . . .

Yeah. What *are* ordinary people?

It does beg that question.

What is ordinary, you mean? What is normal? Well, you really know. We know. Ordinary people? It's all those people out there. All those people who just do ordinary things. I sometimes hear myself in interviews, going, 'I'm just an ordinary guy, really.' And I think they go away and think, did he really say he was an ordinary guy? Cos there's a lot of evidence to the contrary. No ordinary guy is as famous as I am. Or has the money I've got. So, difficult to claim you're ordinary.

But *inside* I feel ordinary, and inside is where I come from. It's what's speaking. It's what's in here, not the exterior. I go back to Liverpool, I really like the earthiness: 'A'right Paul? I don't like that jacket, where d'yer get that? Fuckin' 'ell!' I just go, 'Yeahhh, fuck off.' I'm *comfortable* there, I'm not as happy when it's [*well-bred voice*]: 'Hello Paul, really super jacket. From Paul Smith's?' I just don't seem to get on as well with those people.

So that's this obsession with ordinary. It's just that I've never really found anything much better. I've looked, believe me.

McCartney spurns the Tortured Artist routine, perhaps at the cost of some charisma. He lacks that manic, dark other-worldliness that people have read into stars like David Bowie, Jim Morrison, or Kurt Cobain. But the policy has paid dividends in terms of his personal equilibrium.

The young Beatles may have looked funny and talked in a strange accent. They may have been extravagantly talented. Yet they were always the boys next door. Nothing about their astonishing rise to global fame could quite dent our faith that they were authentically Of The People. It was their role to be human, not mythic.

No matter how strange their art became in the haze of psychedelia, they never entirely disappeared into the counter culture. In the small print of its sleeve note, the *Sgt. Pepper* album guaranteed a splendid time for all – and made good on its promise. Even George's 'Within You Without You' – a daunting track in 1967 – ends by lifting its mystic veil with a peal of sarcastic laughter. The *Magical Mystery Tour* found them on a working-class charabanc, and the esoteric eggmen of 'I Am the Walrus' are balanced by the suburban ballroom dancers of 'Your Mother Should Know'. When 'Hey Jude' was presented on film for the world, passers-by were rounded up from neighbouring streets to clamber aboard the Beatles' soundstage.

McCartney has never lost this inclination to identify with the mass of humanity. Of his 1990 tour, he said to me: 'We put Pittsburgh specially on the itinerary, cos it's a working town, like Glasgow, Liverpool, Newcastle . . .

> I like those people. I do, actually. I'm always more comfortable with that crowd, cos I feel like I know 'em. If it's very rich – New York yuppies – I'm not sure I know 'em or what they're thinking. So I'm not too comfortable. Though you still just go and play your gig.
>
> New York is a rich town. You tend to get people with shirts

and ties. Much as I like a nice shirt and tie, I don't like to see them at concerts – unless it's the Liverpool football team. They showed up on one of the Wings tours and that was cool, that great suit they used to wear with the red ties. That's all right, that's The Boys. I can handle that.

The rough, democratic spirit of his home town has remained a kind of guiding principle:

I was the kid in Liverpool who went on a bus to the next stop, down to Penny Lane and just looked around. 'Who lives there?' Then go back up on the bus. I still like that, it's in my personality, just go somewhere and watch people. Last night I took the tube home, we went to the theatre, couldn't get a taxi anywhere in the West End. I really get a charge off that.

George never used to. His dad was a bus driver. I'd say to him, even when we were famous, I love getting on a bus. He'd say [*astonished*], 'Why? The bus? You've got a car, man!'

But I love getting the bus, cos you're just with people. A little voyeuristic. And now of course, with fame, they're looking at *me* a bit. There's one or two on the tube last night, cracking up laughing. The guy in the baseball cap decides he's got to cool himself out, pull it together, got off at the same stop: 'Al'right mate? Good luck!' And it's cool.

I enjoy going on the tube. I don't have a problem with that. It's refreshing and I think it's good for you. It's unhealthy to really think you're the big cheese all the time. Within the Beatles, we each reminded each other that we weren't, from time to time. I think there is a big risk with stardom.

You can get a table in any restaurant. I'd ring up and say, 'Have you got a table?'

'Sorry sir, we're fully booked.'

'It's Paul McCartney here.'

'Oh! Certainly! Mr McCartney, please! Come at eight o'clock!'

You get used to that, and I've never been comfortable with

it. Oh yeah? You'll let me in *now*, will yer? Bastard. I don't like that.

And yet this determined everyman can roam the outermost fringes of popular taste. McCartney's commercial instincts are sound, for he has enough gold discs to line the Great Wall of China. But his music has *led* that popular taste more often than followed it. He's proud to have been avant-garde, to experiment in forms – from techno to ballet – unlikely to find much mainstream favour.

He seems sweetly pleased by the hip recognition that has occasionally come his way; he tells me that 'Temporary Secretary', a lightweight slice of 1980 electro-pop, 'got picked up a couple of years ago by a DJ in Brighton. So that became a sensation, going mad in all the clubs. I love that.' Perhaps he shouldn't care, but for him it was a welcome counterweight to those idle jibes about the syrupy balladeer who built his home in the middle of the road.

Paul signed up to rock and roll in the mid-1950s, when it was the very essence of rebellion. It's a romantic conception he can never completely leave behind. I was at an MPL party in 2011 when I learned that his next album, a collection of vintage standards, was to be called *Kisses on the Bottom*. It shook me, somewhat, and I gather his own team had questioned its wisdom. But Paul fought his corner:

'Nobody liked the Beatles' name, either,' he shrugged. 'And they all told me, "You can't call a record *Sgt. Pepper's Lonely Hearts Club Band*." And anyway, it's not too bad. I could have called it —' And he offered a suggestion that makes *Never Mind the Bollocks* sound prudish.

McCartney has grown used to fame. But sometimes you wonder if that awareness has ever completely penetrated. He can even be starstruck himself. I would often feel like saying to him, when he described with apparent excitement how he had 'met' such-and-such: 'But Paul, you didn't meet *them*. Surely they met *you*.'

Looking back on another huge world tour, he remembered his initial trepidation at seeing Madonna's success:

> It makes me realise how people are affected by media. While you're looking at her, from your little lowly room, on your little telly, you think she's a goddess. You *give* her all of that. She doesn't even ask for it.
>
> Once she's on tour, she's selling out thirty thousand, she's a goddess. 'Look at the clothes she wears. No wonder. It's because she's better than us. We are only mortal, we've got tellies, and I bet she never sits and watches telly.' When you get out on tour, you're a fellow god. And suddenly you're on that level.

The touching thing is how he'll sometimes pause in mid-interview, and shake his head in mute wonder, as if he cannot quite believe the life he's had. Did these things *really* happen to him? Or was it someone else? Or was it a dream? The song called 'That Was Me', from *Memory Almost Full* in 2007, allows a crowd of early memories to waltz across his brain: 'When I think that all this stuff can make a life, it's pretty hard to take it in.' He sounds like he's trying to convince himself, rather than us.

'I've led a sailor's life,' he said to me one day. 'It really is. Talk about a rich tapestry. So much has happened.' In 1990 the four Beatles each had an asteroid named after them. The news left Paul incredulous: 'Imagine being at school, and they tell you one day there'll be this thing up there in outer space, with your name on it.' He looked sincerely spooked.

And in 2002: 'I was on Concorde on one of its last flights and I was asked to show my guitar to the pilot, did I ever tell you that? Cos he was a fan and had a band. So at Mach 2 – he was on autopilot, thank God – I lent my guitar to the pilot and he's sitting there, with his tongue between his teeth in concentration, playing a bass blues riff on my guitar.

'And I go, if you'd told me this when I was a kid, that I'd be flying at twice the speed of sound and the pilot would have my guitar . . . You wouldn't credit, that's a dream, you'd laugh at it. But here it is, all come true.'

Back down on the ground, Paul McCartney is a businessman as well as artist, with a whole company to run. So far as I know he is a good employer, though I've noticed that when he arrives for work, news of his mood is spread about the building like the day's weather report. It's hardly the court of Genghis Khan, but nobody likes to present the boss with fresh problems, and some days are going to be worse than others. While I have personally never seen McCartney in a rage, he knows how to give what staff call 'a bollocking'.

Imperial opulence is not his style. One day on the top floor at MPL I saw a famous painting of Liverpool's waterfront, by the Victorian artist Atkinson Grimshaw. This was startling, as one sees copies of it in a thousand Liverpool homes. Peering more closely, I saw it was not the original, just a humble reproduction.

I guess we are either enchanted, or disillusioned, that Paul would hang a cheap print up there. To me it's of a piece with his practical nature – a man more at home with casual comforts than conspicuous consumption.

Does he ever get the feeling, I asked, that people are disappointed when they meet him?

'Yeah.'

There's a tradition that stars . . .

. . . Shouldn't drive ordinary cars to premieres, you should dress up. But, you know, I'm not living my life for other people. This is what it's all to do with. I'm *tempted*, cos it's how we all live: 'What shall we wear? What are you wearing? Is it tuxedos? Oh, I'd better dress up.' But the truth of what the Beatles and all that shit was about, what people *liked* about that, was this refreshing honesty – 'I don't like your tie.'

CHAPTER 21

Living is Easy with Nice Clothes

On his personal style

Opposite Liverpool Town Hall, from whose balcony the Beatles waved to surging crowds in 1964, there is a quaint arcade of Victorian shops, almost hidden from view. Exploring it one day I found an old-fashioned tailor's: 'Our boast Savile Row at a Liverpool price'. I went in on a whim and came out with a suit on order. To my delight, I discovered I had just been measured by Brian Epstein's original tailor, Walter Smith – the man who made the Beatles' first set of suits.

I learned from Walter that many years before, he had been apprenticed to a tailor across the River Mersey. Among their customers in 1961 was the dapper young businessman Brian Epstein, who would visit on Wednesday afternoons when his NEMS store was closed. The staff had been surprised when Brian announced he was managing a rock band. It seemed an uncouth thing to do in those days. And the name – which Walter took to be 'Beetles' – was simply squalid.

However, the group were due to make their first appearance on TV and Mr Epstein wanted them in suits. He negotiated the price of each suit down from twenty-eight guineas to twenty-five. (A cynic might say it was the last bargain he struck on their behalf.) Walter's memory of the fittings is that the band used shockingly bad language; Brian was taken aside and asked to remind his boys that this was a respectable establishment.

They complied. But also, in trying on their narrow-cut trousers they removed their boots, which had likely been worn at a long hot Cavern session. The smell was so rank that the shop had to be fumigated.

It later became a commonplace that Brian 'neutered' the group by taking them out of rock-and-roll leathers. But as Paul McCartney often says, Epstein was not so much a manager as a theatrical director. He steered them away from the dated greaser look of the 1950s, towards a crisp modern style for the new decade. After Walter Smith, the Beatles used several tailors, from Dougie Millings to the partnership of Tommy Nutter and Edward Sexton. And, as a glance at the cover of *Abbey Road* will confirm, they were partial to a good suit long after Brian was around to nag them.

It's 2002. Paul is rummaging through a heap of clothes in the makeshift dressing room of a west London studio. He is deciding what to wear for that day's video shoot. A lot of his clothes, he says, arrive that way – chosen by someone else for him to approve or send back. You can't knock it, he tells me, but he hasn't forgotten the pleasure of finding a style for himself. 'You know my favourite misquote of all time?' he laughs. 'It was Elvis Costello's manager, Jake Riviera. He told me he used to think that line of John's in "Strawberry Fields" ['Living is easy with eyes closed'], sounded like, "Living is easy with nice clothes".

'I've always loved that. Living *is* easy with nice clothes.'

It's seldom remarked how well the Beatles usually dressed. Clothes are not important to many rock critics – and it shows – but I find the look as interesting as the music. And of the four, especially after they stopped wearing identical stage costumes, it was McCartney's style that impressed me the most. If I had to wear the same thing every day of my life, I'd probably copy the dark suit and light shirt he wore on the Apple rooftop for *Get Back*.

We rarely discussed fashion, as such, but a lot of Paul's snapshot recollections took clothing as a reference. He talked for example about a beat-group package show in London, back in September 1963:

> I remember this one golden morning. A Sunday morning, I think, by the steps at the back of the Albert Hall. At the top of those steps we all gathered. A summer's sunny morning and it was Mick, Keith, all the Beatles, Yardbirds, Gerry and the Pacemakers – a moment in time. And we were absolutely at our youthful peak. We were feeling really cool about ourselves. If you'd been in the clouds and seen that, it was a golden moment.
>
> The gig was OK, the acoustics in the Albert Hall were terrible – hence the mushrooms that they grow along the ceiling now. But that moment before the gig is always a golden memory. It was 'us guys' and we were all dressed great, button-down shirts, checking each other's gear: 'Where d'you get that?' Cecil Gee. 'Right. Kings Road?' Very friendly, no rivalry. I remember that as great.

Before the music press became too solemn, he told me, there was a more innocent mode of pop coverage. Best of all, the papers might supply you with cool gear to pose in:

> Then it was fun, we went down to the offices. We got photographed in [the teen magazine] *Fab* 208, buildings in Fleet Street. It was exciting, the first time you'd ever had your photograph taken in colour. It had always been school photos or your own roll. You never had them taken professionally, really, what for? There was no call for it. But it was suddenly this big coloured background.
>
> You got to try on these clothes. We'd do modelling sessions

for the *Daily Express* on some roof somewhere. Basically anything to get in the newspapers. If it was a fashion spread they'd say, 'We've got this year's good stuff. Cecil Gee.' Cool button-down shirts? Oh I'll do it! No problem there. Cos you were awfully young and groovy, and we really fancied our chances. And why not? We were pretty together dudes.

When did the collarless jacket appear?

That was Pierre Cardin. It was just a modern fashion, his collections one year, and we nicked it. A straight nick, cos we liked how it looked. We just had it made. That was a big thing for us. You never bought clothes, really, your stage clothes were always made.

You'd get these Soho guys, showbiz tailors, 'Dougie Millings: Tailor to the Stars.' You go round their rooms and he'd have little messages from Sammy Davis: 'Thanks Dougie, great fit!' Ha! This is it, man! Actually having a suit made. I'd had one made in Liverpool, cos you had to have a suit out of a proper gentlemen's tailors.

Dougie did it with vents, really tight trousers. He was a great laugh, he appeared in *Hard Day's Night*. He had fake telegrams sent to himself, which he put up: 'Dougie. Great work on the film. Cecil B. De Mille.' 'Thanks for the costumes, love.' And he was a poet, he wrote a beautiful poem which he sent to me after John died, no great literature, but felt. Nice guy.

And you'd go back to Liverpool and they'd go, 'What have you been doing?' Well, you know, went out with an actress, went to Dougie Millings. 'Wow, look at the jacket, great trousers!' *Sound!* Everyone was so impressed, cos you had millions of stories to tell. That was the fun, actually. Going home and telling them your exploits.

I asked Paul about their first Shea Stadium show, in 1965, and again it was the outfits that sprang to his mind:

We get changed into our beige epaulette jackets and suddenly we're *the four-headed monster*. It was always a great moment for me, cos we weren't just individuals any more. You were a group. You were part of this team that looked alike, in your uniform. It was one of my thrills with the Beatles.

And it had gone back to a Butlin's camp I was at when I was eleven in Pwllheli, in North Wales, where I'd seen this singing act that would win the talent show that week. I'm sure I've told you this, they all came out in tartan 'twat hats', as we used to call them [*small flat caps*]. Grey crew-neck pullovers, tartan shorts, and a towel under each arm. And they just walked on. That was why, for me, I was always keen that the Beatles had uniforms. It was just 'Yes! That is so cool!' We didn't look like any four guys, it was a unit.

On yet another video shoot, this time for 'This One' in 1989, he'd been in discussion with its director Dean Chamberlain. The question of costumes had put him in mind of the firm who made the matching frock-coats for *Sgt. Pepper*:

It's a theatrical thing. If you're going to be in *Nicholas Nickleby* your agent will say, 'Be at Berman's, ten-thirty in the morning. You'll be met by a Miss Shingleberry.' So you go and sit in Berman's lobby. 'Hello, Mr McCartney? About the *Nicholas*, come this way.' And they take you through this huge clothing store. You go past, you know, American Civil War, Horatio Hornblower, *Blackadder*, funny hats! Your imagination goes wild. For *A Hard Day's Night* and stuff we'd seen a lot of that.

By the time of the Beatles' first success, McCartney was still described as cherubic, but his face was acquiring a strong adult structure. The young group's signature hairstyle sat happily on his head – and he stayed closest to it. Unlike George and John, he avoided a total hippy look, employing the chic London hairdresser Leslie Cavendish well into the 1970s. He's seldom gone for anything eccentric.

He was fortunate also in not going bald; it's hard to imagine a Macca without a mop. It's notoriously true that he has dyed his hair for many years. I defend him because, since 1989, he has been a regular player on the stages of vast arenas. With his still-trim physique, his physical perkiness and the violin-bass guitar, he can give the masses what they crave – a living glimpse of Beatle Paul. It's show business, and McCartney has never denied he was in show business.

Clothes and fashion always mattered to him. In the 1950s he'd tried to become a teddy boy by narrowing his trousers in stages too gradual for his father's disapproving eye. But there's a conservatism in his dress that spared him the worst aspects of psychedelia or glam rock. His style anticipated the British designer Paul Smith's policy of 'classic with a twist' – the comfortable suits whose navy blue orthodoxy was subverted by orange socks, or later by the vegan's leather-free training shoes. There was junk-shop nostalgia in his big tweedy coats and the little Fair Isle pullovers, alongside novelty and idiosyncrasy. But there was usually a shrewd self-possession.

The ageing process is seldom kind to anyone, and it must be harder when the world is stocked with images of yourself from decades ago, at the peak of your beauty. The Beatles in particular had an uncanny ability to photograph well – in any situation, not one tongue of the four was lolling out, not one eye of the eight was half-closed.

'A state-of-the-art fashion photographer was asking me about that photo the other day,' he said of *With the Beatles*, where their faces are suspended in blackness like white half-moons. 'And he said, "That was a montage, wasn't it?" But it wasn't. The great reality was that it was one hour in a hotel, it was all we had to spare the guy [Robert Freeman]. He found the end of a corridor, a little window where natural light spilled in at about eleven o'clock. And he just sat us, "You sit in front there . . ." Now it's become legendary and they like to think, Oh, montage, couldn't have got all four faces looking that good. Cos we do all look fairly legendary.'

In the photo sessions I've attended he shows an educated awareness of the angles and lighting that will work for him, but he is not especially vain by the standards of his trade.

'There's an edge to youth that you can't deny,' he told me. 'But there's a double-edged sword because there's also an ignorance to youth. We used to say, "I'd love to be eighteen." But then you thought about it and said, "Not mentally. Just physically." I wouldn't want to go back to what I thought at eighteen. No way. The insecurities of being eighteen? No thanks. I'd like to look young and beautiful, but not if that's the price.'

CHAPTER 22

Heaven and Earth

Life, the universe and 'repairing this brave old world'

What does Paul McCartney believe in?

His 1972 single 'Give Ireland Back to the Irish' (an emotionally charged response to bloody events in Derry that year) remains unusual in his catalogue for its unvarnished anger. It's true that he's supported various causes like Adopt-a-Minefield, Friends of the Earth and Live Aid, and he led the pop world in rallying behind New York after 9/11. In each case, though, the essential impulse looked more humanitarian than ideological. McCartney's politics are in general not explicit. He strikes me as a small-c conservative by temperament, an easy-going liberal by conviction and only a radical in terms of his artistic curiosity.

Whenever his talk turned to religion, I took his position to be roughly agnostic with spiritual inclinations:

'I wouldn't become a Buddhist or a Hindu or something, but I get interested in the philosophy and the imagery and the spirituality of it. But not so much *being* one. I'm not a great "becomer". I try and stay myself, but listen to what everyone else has to say.'

In faith terms, his precise beliefs are as hard to pin down as his football allegiance: is he Liverpool or Everton? All the Beatles were vague about football, which set them apart from nearly every male in the city. Like John and George he came from a nominally Christian background – Paul's was half-Catholic and half-Protestant – but their families had outgrown Liverpool's old-time sectarianism, the legacy of massive Irish immigration into the city. The Beatles joined a general drift away from organised religion.

In 1989 we were talking about his song 'Motor of Love' and its line, 'Heavenly father, look down from above . . .' Like the lyric of 'Let It Be', it suggested church imagery and the memory of a much-missed parent. He thought about it for a moment;

> Heavenly father . . . That's either my dad, or God, you know? When I'm dealing in that area I don't want to be specific. I'm not really religious. Some guy who used to be on the Pier Head [the waterfront plaza of Liverpool] . . . there used to be all these preachers there: 'The Catholic faith is the only true faith!' And then, 'The Protestant faith is the only true faith, don't listen to him, brothers.' You'd go, Hmm, bloody hell, I wonder if any of them know, you know?
>
> But with life, and the stuff I've been through, I do have a belief in, I don't know . . . in goodness, in a good spirit, as opposed to messing round with evil.
>
> I think people have personified good and evil. So good has become God with an 'o' out, and evil has become the Devil with a 'd' added. That's my theory. Don't get me started on religion. God, it's terrible, I waffle on for hours. That is my theory. That people have personified it – if you don't behave, there's this guy who's gonna get you. And we go: 'Ooh, we better listen, there's actually a big fella with a beard in the sky, maybe the priests know something we don't know.' Whereas if you say [*in Eastern guru voice*], 'No, it's the spirit of goodness, my son,' it's 'Oh, piss off.' They won't go for that.
>
> I'm not very big into religion, so 'heavenly father' is like 'Mother Mary': my mother was called Mary. 'Let It Be' was 'Mother Mary comes to me'. That was true, I was going through my dark hour, a fairly trippy period. There was a lot going on and it was a bit

strange occasionally. 'Woo-oo-oo, what's going on?' And there was a lot of drugs about, too.

I'd say 'I had a dream about my mum, and it was very comforting.' She died when I was fourteen, she'd sort of come to me: 'Hello son, how are you?' 'Oh, you're there! Bloody hell, I thought you'd died!' That terrible one. I don't know if your parents are still alive, but mine aren't, so you get a bit of that. And my dad, too: 'Heavenly father, look down from above' at this love thing. And it could be God as well.

In 2004 I joined Paul at the Millennium Dome in London, where he was rehearsing for a tour. The arena (now The O2) at that time stood empty and vast, and McCartney took me for a spin around it in the golf cart they used to reach the sound-stage. The tour was essentially a warm-up for his appearance at the Glastonbury Festival – a hippy invention with deeper roots in British mythology – and he asked me to do a tour magazine with mystic imagery.

The night before, he'd rung me when I was in a restaurant with my wife. I took my phone outside as Paul outlined his current thinking; he wanted ideas, designs, themes, that might include the Zodiac or the Tarot, and would echo the line from Shakespeare's *Hamlet*, 'There are more things in heaven and earth, Horatio/ Than are dreamt of in your philosophy'.

Dismounting from the golf cart this afternoon, though, he found a manicurist waiting for him. Thus our discussion of the universe and its imponderable questions was mingled with close attention to fingernails.

His style of 'flicking' the guitar strings, he explained – especially on 'Blackbird' – was damaging his nails to the point of drawing blood. 'I don't have a correct finger style, where you actually just pick; John learned it for "Julia", but I never did. A lot of the guys learned the folky thing, and it's lovely, but I never had the discipline. So I did "Blackbird" and it sounds all right, but it's a bit of a cheap imitation.

'So for the first time in my life I'm going to nail parlours. And it's brilliant.'

He turns solicitously to the young white-coated woman who sits between us. 'You know your job. If you need to talk, just interrupt us . . .'

Glastonbury being the hippy festival that started in the Sixties, when we were getting into that, I suppose it affected Michael Eavis [the festival's founder] in the same way it affected all our generation: 'Yeah man, it's on the ley lines . . . Wow!' We all talked about that stuff. And I think it is fascinating, like the earth having acupuncture points. I don't see that as being a far-out idea. I mean, *we've* got 'em. The kind of things people see as far-out, like the moon having an effect on us . . . The moon affects tides, which is a huge body of water, so I can't see why it wouldn't affect us. Like we're exempt?

I'm fascinated by it. I remember Glastonbury when it started, unlike most people on the planet. Just to think of it brings back memories of the Fool design team, all our hippy mates, how we used to dress, the Tarot, I-Ching, meditation, joss sticks, it's all tinged with that.

We spoke last night about that Shakespeare line, 'More things in heaven and earth . . .'

I always liked that. At school you may hate doing Shakespeare because it's school. But there's stuff that lodges in your brain. Things I probably had to learn for exams have stayed with me, and gained significance as you grow and experience more in life. You go around the world with the Beatles and you realise there really *are* more things in heaven and earth. And that quote is a brilliant way to say it: 'There's a lot out there, mate, believe me.' But that's not as cool a way of saying it as old Willie's way.

In interviews I was always asked, 'What's your great advice, what are your mottos?' And I remembered, 'To thine own self be true,' [also from *Hamlet*] and that was always one of my quotes when I had to dredge up some motto. That seemed like a great one because it was very Beatles. We were certainly to our own selves true, and that was half the success of the Beatles.

The heaven-and-earth line is also open-ended: you don't necessarily know what the 'more things' are, but you believe in something beyond the here and now . . .

Exactly.

Beyond what we can see and touch. Would that sum up your view? Not specifically a believer in this or that, but open to the possibilities?

Yeah, that's a good point. I can't say I'm a believer in this or that religion: 'This is how it is'. But I like some stuff in Christian religion, some stuff in Buddhist religion and Hindu religion. I suppose I'm a magpie, I pick up various bits that seem to work for me. I think I've seen enough, I've been to enough places, and I've seen enough so-called coincidences to know there's more to it.

A lot of that happens to me. Just waking up one morning and dreaming the tune of 'Yesterday'. It's made me a successful songwriter, but that wasn't a conscious move on my part. I certainly have to believe that in your head there is something going on that I don't know about. I remember going to the doctor's and him saying you've got two breathing systems, so if you faint your body keeps going. There's an autonomous system, and if you get knocked out you don't just die because you forget to breathe. Your body's much cooler than that.

It's like that old comic strip, the Nutties or whatever. [Probably the Numskulls, from children's comic *The Beezer*.]

Yes, or Georgie's Germs, all these little fellas running around inside you. [Georgie's Germs were in the comic Wham.*]*

Yeah. So you just learn these little snippets of information, 'Wow, that is amazing.' George's beliefs, for instance . . . [He is interrupted by the manicurist.] That's looking good. Lovely. And have you got time to do a couple of the guys in the band? Am I done?

Manicurist: 'Is it smooth enough on the edge?'

I think it is, darlin'. That's classic, thank you.

I went to this nail parlour in LA and I thought, Ooh, no, us blokes from the North don't do this. Then the drummer Abe said he could have a pedicure, for his feet, you know? In drumming, you've got to keep your feet right for the bass drum. So we all went for a pedicure and a manicure – got in touch with our feminine side. A good laugh, a very bonding session for the band.

We spoke no more about philosophy that session.

His talk of the Devil put me in mind of something else he'd brought up once. In 1993, he played in Chile, at the Coliseo Nacional in Santiago:

It was the stadium where fellow-me-lad – was it Pinochet? [Chilean dictator General Augusto Pinochet] – put, you know . . . It was chilling, being in the dressing room where they'd shot his poets and his artists. I got that feeling of having to exorcise the Devil. There's a place in Frankfurt [Festhalle] where Hitler had spoken, and when you know Pinochet or

> Hitler's been there and done dirty work, there is a sort of blessing about coming in and singing your peaceful songs. I feel particularly good doing 'Let It Be' at those gigs. Chile was a particularly good show, great crowd. But that dressing room is what sticks in my mind.

Describing an earlier tour, Paul admitted the nightly repetition of songs on a long tour could get boring, which sometimes led him to think more closely about their content: 'You don't normally, you're on autopilot. But when you've done them a lot you start listening. "What am I saying to them? I hope it's good."'

> Without getting too smug, I was pleased. If you have to go around the world saying stuff to people, most of the songs seemed like a reasonable message. 'Fool on the Hill', I think, still applies in modern situations. 'Let It Be', Iraq [this was during the First Gulf War], whatever, they carry some kind of message and it's reasonably positive. I could either do that or totally go the other way, totally get down and it's 'Helter Skelter' all the way.

McCartney, then, sees the message in most of his and the Beatles' music as one of universal values – honesty, optimism, largeness of spirit – rather than in statements of specific views. That's not to say that he's a man without opinions, or that he's above feeling indignation or sheer exasperation. But overt protest is not his favourite mode of songwriting.

'I've Had Enough', from 1978's *London Town*, has an echo of the period's punk rock in its hard, impatient edge, though it's really about the complaints of a put-upon everyman, nagged, harassed and taxed. 'The First Stone', a 1989 B-side written with Hamish Stuart, aims its ire at the hypocrisy of TV evangelists.

'Big Boys Bickering' (1992) deploys a sweet arrangement to attack political leaders, 'fucking it up for everyone', as he puts it, in a rare resort to expletives.

As a public figure he's more forthright on the topic of animal rights, and his vegetarianism is well-known. 'Looking for Changes' (1993) is a lyrically blunt denunciation of animal experiments. But his 2014 campaign song for Meat-Free Mondays is more typical – let the Monday be a 'fun day', he sings. Paul is seldom hectoring or strident, even on the subject that engages him most strongly. His instincts, ever populist, favour gentle encouragement. On tour, one soon accepted there would be no beefburgers in Macca's backstage hospitality, and that was more or less that.

As a writer he says that feminism – or at least an instinctively pro-woman stance – is recurrent in his work. He cites with some pride his 1979 track 'Daytime Nighttime Suffering', one of several songs to adopt a female character's viewpoint:

> Somebody in a *Billboard* interview said to me about women's songs and that's one of those. I don't do it on purpose, I suppose I just have sympathy. I'm one of those guys who likes women. For various reasons. But I do. You know, like civil rights, you stick up for people whose rights have been diminished. It's maybe a Sixties thing, or it's maybe a Me thing. There are certain people who like to defend people who've had a raw deal. So I like to see women coming through.
>
> And it's been a long theme of mine. 'Daytime Nighttime Suffering' is a song I liked and I think it comes over. I remember Linda loving that one.
>
> A lady film director [Allison Anders] once pointed out how many pro-women songs I'd done. I didn't think I'd done any, but she pulled out about fifteen. It's true, I am pro-woman and I've always been like that. I'm pro-fairness. I'm pro-liberty, pro-freedom, so therefore I'm pro-woman.

He once mentioned how much he'd been enjoying 'Stan', the 2000 hit by Eminem, and expressed his pleasure that Elton John had recently joined the rap star on stage, which was broadly taken as exonerating Eminem from accusations of homophobia:

> So I guess that put that down. Which is good, because it *is* only showbiz. Even Eminem is only showbiz.
>
> It's good to remember that, otherwise you think, what the fuck's happening in the world? My son was the first in our family to get into rap, and there'd be these lyrics like 'slap my bitch', denigrating women. I'd have to say, 'Are you sure about that?' And he says, 'It's only a song, Dad.'
>
> It reminded you that we had all of that with rock and roll; Elvis isn't trying to shag anyone, he's just moving his hips. Whereas all our parents went, 'Oh! The state of him!' We never saw it until they said it. I think it's all the same again.

Sometimes, the enormity of events compels even the most cautious of performers to take a public stance. As an entertainer, Paul had accidentally played a large role in transforming twentieth century American culture; now he was eyewitness to the country's most traumatic moment of the twenty-first. In 2001, seven weeks after 9/11, we met in MPL where Paul described his own experience, and his efforts to help New York in the aftermath, both in concert and through the song 'Freedom':

> I was just taking off from JFK, after a trip to New York. There were a few planes ahead of us, we were taxiing out. It was quarter to nine when the pilot said, 'There's been a terrible accident in New York, and you can see from the right-hand side of the aeroplane.' We looked out. You could see the one of the Twin Towers burning. Oh my God. And as it all unfolded,

the horror . . . first of all thinking it's an accident, then, 'Oh, it's no accident.'

I was unable to leave the States, because they closed the airports for about four or five days. I had to stay around, but it wasn't a bad thing. I felt OK to be there while it was all unfolding. You got to hear the whole debate, to see the heroism of the firemen. And it reminded me that my dad had been a firefighter [during the German blitz of Liverpool in the Second World War]. By the time I was growing up he wasn't a firefighter, he was a cotton salesman. To me it was just some story he told. I heard words like 'incendiary bombs'.

This all brought it home to me. I thought of him going in buildings. And when we went to see the guys, the firemen, they were saying, 'Wow, those guys in England in the war. They fought all that stuff with a hose, the whole block with just one hose.'

I wanted to do something, and there was nothing you *could* do. Like a lot of people I felt helpless. I'm not a firefighter. So I started to work up a song. 'Freedom' was what Bush and Giuliani had been talking about – this being an attack on America's freedom, freedom of choice, freedom for women to have equal rights, these things were all mentioned. So this idea of being free in a free country, unlike repressive regimes, became important to me. I thought, I'll try to write some anthemic thing, do a concert.

The televised Concert for New York City was held at Madison Square Garden on 20 October 2001. And 'Freedom' became its emblematic performance, though not without some opposition beforehand . . .

When we came to rehearse, a few people were nervous about me doing a new song. They said, 'Well, you could do "Let It Be".' They were more comfortable with that idea. Give 'em a nice safe ending and then, if there was time, we could try my new song. But I just had a hunch it would work. Only half a hunch; I don't relish the thought of introducing new material in concerts. Because they want 'Penny Lane', we all know that.

They said, 'You and Mick [Jagger] and Pete [Townshend] should discuss the idea.' So I went in and was trying to sell it, had to play it on a backward guitar [i.e. right-handed], the only one I could grab. This was terrifying: 'This is my right, *chink chink chink* . . . Freedom!' And Mick's going [*Cockney accent*]: 'Nah, Paul, I dunno mate. People don't like new songs. Stick to the old stuff.' And Pete's going, 'Hmm, well . . .'

And Pete was funny, he said, 'Paul, you're a brave man. D'you mean you're gonna workshop a new song in front of a hundred million people?' I said, 'Ah, if you put it like that, Pete, I do see the insanity of it now.'

And it went great. Everyone joined in, stomped their feet and clapped. That was exactly what I wanted to happen.

I was at a Yankees baseball game the next day: 'Yeah! We gotta go.' Cos I'm a bit of a fan. And in New York – it was like if Liverpool had been bombed, you know the football team would be almighty – and the Yankees were like that.

We showed up and the most gratifying thing was people saying, 'That was a great thing you did for the city, Paul.' It did occur, 'Here's me who was really just some little Liverpool lad, and God, I'm helping New Yorkers with their confidence.' If we'd thought of that when we were eleven . . . well, it would have been unthinkable.

I was having to come up with the brave wartime spirit, that I'd seen our folks do in Liverpool: [*sings*] 'Hitler has only got one ball.' I was having to retrieve all that knowledge. You've got to keep going now, keep the humour. There was a lot of that needed to be done.

McCartney will often place his personal brand of idealism in the context of what he calls 'our lot', the generation of the 1960s. 'Somehow since the Sixties, there's been a social conscience within all this. There has perhaps been a greater idea tying it all together, which to some degree has worked and to some degree is in the process of working. But it's a cool idea. Because now a lot of *us* from the Sixties are older than the Prime Minister or the President of America or the President of Russia, which is quite a trippy feeling.

'We talked about it in the Sixties: "Y'know, one day, man, our generation will be in power and that'll be interesting." Then you think of [Tony] Blair having a Fender, a Stratocaster. That's quite amazing.'

Once, describing his 2005 song 'Promise to You Girl', he called it 'basically, "Hey, you and me, girl, we're gonna take on the world and sort it all out."'

> A massively optimistic song, talking about the time it takes to repair this brave old world, because it really is a brave old world. It's this idea, this crazy Live Aid, Beatles thing, that we *can* do something, we can contribute.
>
> People say, 'No you can't, you're just pop people.' But you look at Bangladesh [for which George Harrison staged benefit shows in 1971], 'Give Peace a Chance', you look at Live Aid, and way beyond that, and there is a power that is indisputable. Even if you want to dispute it, and many people will. People have said to me, 'Do you really think music can change the world?' I said, Yeah.
>
> Cos you bloody know it can. On a heart level it certainly can, but even on a political level. We can change things. All the people listening to this record can do something, and me and my girl can do something and you and your girl or your fella can do something. There's something that can be done about this brave old world.

CHAPTER 23

Punks and Rivals

What am I doing, worrying about dancing like Michael Jackson?

McCartney has rarely been combative in his public pronouncements about other musicians. His inclination is to praise more than attack. The few spats that he had – with John and Yoko, with Phil Spector, and to some extent with Michael Jackson – were not agreeable to his nature. But while he has avoided confrontation, he is certainly competitive.

From the first Liverpool talent shows, to the jostling for status in London's pop scrum, to proving his supremacy in global arena rock, he has never stopped playing to win.

Sales statistics might suggest that punk rock, in the late 1970s, never came close to toppling McCartney and his ilk. But I doubt that he ever felt complacent. In his homeland at least, punk challenged the pop aristocracy that he symbolised. I've never met a single star of his generation who did not feel some degree of existential threat in that period of spiky-haired iconoclasts.

We know the Ramones had taken their very name from McCartney's fleeting stage name Paul Ramon. Yet he was more closely identified with rock and roll's old guard than John Lennon, whose rebel credentials still held sway, and far more so than David Bowie or Bruce Springsteen. Punk was the first time in pop history when the very attributes of wealth and fame – hitherto seen as the laurels of success, even by hippy artists – were denounced as antithetical to the music's nature and purpose. It was a challenge he took seriously.

I asked him in 1989: 'When punk came along in 1976 did you think, there's a big divide now and I'm on the wrong side of it?'

The whole thing was boring old farts. That was the expression. Obviously there was the age difference. They were doing what we'd done ten or twelve years before. That gave them the edge that *we'd* had. Youth. That was the first impression: Oh God, they've got it over us. But then you saw drummers like Rat Scabies [of the Damned] and you thought, it's only Keith Moon, and we were doing that years before. It's just a bit faster. They used to do twenty-minute sets. Well, that's what the Beatles used to do.

There was a divide around that time. Strangely enough the only record I had out was 'Mull of Kintyre'. So it certainly was not a question of competing on their level. I must say I thought, we are kidding, aren't we? Releasing a Scottish waltz in the face of all this furious spitting and gobbing. And Heather, my eldest daughter, was well into punk. She knew too many of them for my liking. She went out with Billy Idol. Just what a father needs!

But she was knowledgeable about the punk scene. I'd check it out with her. She said she had this punk mate who was putting 'Mull of Kintyre' on the jukebox.

So things are never clear-cut. Whereas you think 'Mull of Kintyre versus punk', it wasn't quite like that. I like that things aren't cut and dried. If they were, we'd be slashing our wrists, cos it can look so dark sometimes, so gloomy. It's always good to think, you know, this might not be how it seems, this moment.

So that turned out to be a bigger record than any of the punk records. Once you've thought, well, we did 'Helter Skelter', for Christ's sake. We did 'I'm Down', all the Little Richard stuff that's screamy and manic. And 'She's So Heavy', a lot of John's stuff. So I don't think I ever felt they've done stuff that we could never do. I know people like Keith Moon were not so much threatened, as just pissed off, that the people who were emulating his drum style were calling him a boring old fart. All they had was youth, just the innocence of it all.

It was good, it was the broom, it needed sweeping. It was all a bit Rod Stewart in LA at that time, getting decadent. But like anything it went too far. 'Pretty Vacant' [the Sex Pistols' third single] was my favourite. And we used to like the Damned. But it was fairly short-lived for me, all bashing and clattering, and spitting. It was fine if you want to go down and speed, to an all-nighter, just jive out your skull. But at that point I was married so I wasn't into all-nighters any more.

It was kind of threatening at first. But I'll tell you what was threatening at first: Alice Cooper. This is what time does, gives you a perspective. At that point [1972], Alice Cooper was threatening, it was like the Dark Side was creeping in. Of course once you *met* Alice Cooper, he was a real sweetie. It's just image. He was doing songs like 'No More Mr. Nice Guy', which were pretty threatening to me. Cos I took it seriously for a month: 'Oh my God, maybe the world *is* swinging toward a darker, more violent . . .' It appeared like it was going to go overnight then.

You'd think, when did I last feel threatened? Oh yeah, Dave Clark Five. And it's all in proportion then, it all settles. And the time before that? Oh yeah, Gerry and the Pacemakers. That was the other big threat. And you realise, Oh come on, we outlived that. So maybe there's hope. And we ended up outliving punk. And most of them mellowed. You either burn yourself out or you find somewhere to settle.

Thank God. I'd just hate to be speeding round those clubs still. I got knackered with all that shit. I'm glad I did it, so I can talk about it now, but no way would I want to be still at it.

Let's note in passing that 'Mull of Kintyre' was not, in fact, the only record Paul released at that time. There was also a semi-anonymous LP called *Thrillington*, which was even less like punk. The supposed 'Percy Thrillington' put out an all-instrumental version of the *Ram* album, in part like a 1930s dance orchestra, in part like one of the 1960s' easy-listening records that were issued for mums and dads. Paul had actually made it back in 1971, straight after *Ram* itself. Delaying its release until 1977 was among the more inscrutable decisions of his long and strange career.

The project was shrouded in secrecy, with a larky press scam that featured cryptic classified ads and coy public denials. Like *Pepper* before it and the Fireman records after, *Thrillington* was an instance of Paul disguising his more left-field ambitions by pretending to be someone else entirely. The arrangements were by Richard Hewson, whose other credits included some of *Let It Be* and 1973's 'My Love', with session guests who ranged from Herbie Flowers to the Mike Sammes Singers. By the time of its CD remastering in 1995, when the author's true identity was no longer concealed, *Thrillington* found a receptive cult audience among a generation open to retro-lounge conceits, and nowadays takes its place in McCartney's catalogue of category-defying delights.

Following the success of his 1990 world tour Paul confessed to some relief. He can be frank in recognising that his art must always operate in a marketplace. 'I'll tell you what was really good,' he said. 'Looking at the *Billboard* charts. For years I would look at those, and if you don't go live you never feature. But if you're in it, then it's work talk. It's shop. Brilliant to see *your* figures when you're playing sixty thousand, in a stadium, a hundred per cent sell-out. You'll see these other big stars that you're in awe of before you started touring . . .'

Imagine looking at Michael Jackson, from my perspective as an older rocker. There's Michael, the hottest little thing since sliced toast. And he's just done *his* tour.

You have to look at how Michael Jackson does it, and instead of it being a big mystical thing – [*again, awestruck*]: 'Seen him do that dance he does? That Moonwalk?' – it's, 'Well I can't do the Moonwalk but I can certainly play, and I can sing, and I can play guitar solos and he can't.' You start actually daring to think of yourself in the same breath as the big stars.

The athlete who doesn't go to the Olympics for eight years, he's looking at the swimmers there and thinks, I won ten gold medals. I bet I could beat those kids, one more time. Instead of just sitting at home going, 'No, I'm no good any more, I'm older now . . .' It's daring to have a look. To see if you can do it.

Suddenly there was a pile of us back on the road. The Stones, daring to come out of mothballs. The Who were doing it. Grateful Dead were basically my inspiration for going on tour, just seeing Jerry [Garcia] up there – if he can come out of a coma and tour [the singer's health problems had included a diabetic coma in 1986] . . .

Instead of imagining there's this marvellous showbiz mystique . . . You look at *The Chart Show*: 'God! Everyone can dance so good! They're marvellous. They've all got number ones.' You start to get it in perspective: 'Well, that's their only hit, so don't go crazy about *them*. They're not going to intimidate you.' Michael Jackson's going to out-dance you, I know that much, but I don't dance anyway. So what am I doing, worrying about dancing like Michael Jackson? My thing's another thing.

As the band got tighter, and better, all the nice things kicked in. I kept saying to the band, if ever there was a problem: 'Gentlemen, guys, remember, we are the dudes now. We're on tour. *We're* the pinnacle of the mountain now.'

He'd felt the same way with Wings, whose unique predicament had been to follow the Beatles:

In a way it wasn't too bad, it gave us something to aim for. So by the time we got to the '76 tour, *we* were top of the pile that year. And it's happened ever since. The last tour in the Nineties, it was Madonna I was worried about. If you're in any way competitive it's what you do. You look at the charts, see what they've sold. Well let's try and sell some more. It's just life.

I'm sometimes struck by how un-blasé you sound. By your excitement about ticket sales, say.

I never take anything for granted. At any minute it can all change. I had a meeting with a promoter today: 'Have we sold out? Oh *yeah*!' To me that's great. To me it means people want to see me. It really helps, to go into a hall and think, all you people really tried to get here, you made an effort. It's not a school function that you've got to attend.

I wouldn't want to get blasé about that. I think it's cool.

How reliable are your commercial instincts? Do you tend to know, for example, if a new record will sell?

Not really. You listen to people's reactions. And then you've got sales. I always think it's funny, people who say, 'Oh, it doesn't matter if it sells, we don't look at that aspect.' I think that's what *does* matter, really. The people out there with their pennies, going to the shop and spending them, when they don't really want to spend them. That tends to be what I look at, that people will buy it. Some people think that's crass commercialism. But I don't. I think it's the public's vote.

CHAPTER 24

If I Were Not Upon the Stage

Paul McCartney on the road

'People say, "Aren't you bored? Don't you get fed up?" And I say, "No, I really don't."' McCartney looks at live performance in the same way as songwriting – it's best when it doesn't feel like work.

'Do I get fed up touring? No. We don't work, we *play* music. It's simplistic but it's true. How lucky to be *playing* with this whole thing.'

As Paul has already recollected, of the bickering that marked the Beatles' last years, his undiminished appetite for road-work drove a wedge between him and the other three. Once he'd assembled Wings he was free to indulge that idea of a travelling band, which had been frustrated at the time of *Let It Be*. 'Yes,' he says of the now-fabled university tour with his new group. 'Finally got to do my little dream . . .'

> It seemed to me that for a band it's essential to go on the road. We'd given it up in '67 with *Sgt. Pepper* – our new decree was: 'The record will go on tour and we won't. We'll make a great record and send that out.' After that we made some good records, but missed the stimulus of going back out on the road. Seeing the whites of their eyes, getting a reality check: 'They liked that one, they didn't like that one.' And we hadn't done it for so long that my choice was either give up music, or continue to

make it. If you continued to make it you wanted to go out as a live band.

But the 1980s, post-Wings, saw a ten-year pause in his touring habit. Was this a reluctance to appear in public after John's assassination?

'That must have had something to do with it. But it was mainly after my bust in Japan, was what really put the kybosh on it. I just thought I'd rather stay at home. And you'll find a million people will sympathise with that. If you didn't have to go out and work, you could just hang around at home, dig the kids. A lot of people would go for that, and I'm tempted, too.'

Still, his deeper instincts were not to be denied. In 1989 he put together a new line-up and became a born-again gigging musician. Why was that? 'I was up for it,' he says, simply. 'There was this decision: "Do you want to do it?" But you look at the alternative, which is you *don't* tour. "You're not gonna tour again?" And I don't like that idea.'

The live ensemble took shape during sessions for *Flowers in the Dirt*. Joining Paul and Linda were the keyboard player Paul 'Wix' Wickens, drummer Chris Whitten, and the guitarists Hamish Stuart and Robbie McIntosh, previously well-known from the Average White Band and the Pretenders, respectively. By the tour's end in summer 1990, they'd played 102 dates that included a record-breaking attendance at the Maracanã Stadium in Rio and a huge waterfront show in Liverpool.

Fired up by the success of it all, McCartney spent most of 1993 on his New World Tour, with Blair Cunningham replacing Chris Whitten on drums. In between these epic journeys there were intimate 'Unplugged' nights, promoting the album made for MTV's acoustic-only series.

The next decade was active but less frenetic, marked by occasional benefit shows for assorted causes and a 1999 return to the Cavern with his *Run Devil Run* line-up. The catalyst for his next band was another album, *Driving Rain*, which introduced him to a couple of American players: drummer Abe Laboriel Jr and guitarist Rusty Anderson. They were soon joined by another seasoned guitarist, Brian Ray. Still on hand was Wix, from the last band, who came to assume the role of musical director. This team became the Paul McCartney touring band from that time onwards.

The trend since then has been for shorter but more frequent tours, interspersed with numerous one-off appearances, and the effect has been to give McCartney a near-constant media presence. There was the Queen's Golden Jubilee at Buckingham Palace and a memorial for George Harrison at the Royal Albert Hall (both in 2002), Live 8 in London in 2005, the Queen's Diamond Jubilee and the Olympic opening ceremony (in 2012), not to mention a few Super Bowls along the way.

McCartney's discography has been expanded by several live albums: *Tripping the Live Fantastic*, *Paul is Live*, *Back in the US*, *iTunes Festival* and *Amoeba's Secret*. As well as songs of the Beatles, Wings and solo periods we find abundant rarities: anything from the formative favourites 'Blue Moon of Kentucky' and 'Hi-Heel Sneakers', and music hall jokes like the British holiday camp stalwart 'If I Were Not Upon the Stage', to random covers such as 'Ain't No Sunshine', and things that he's written and never got around to recording, including 'A Fine Day' and 'Inner City Madness'. Best of all, perhaps, is the tribute to George Harrison, a ukulele-driven 'Something' that has tugged at heartstrings everywhere.

Is McCartney a sort of performance junkie? After all, he scarcely *needs* to tour:

> You could say that nobody has ever needed to perform, really. I could have done a job in a factory. I had a perfectly good job

in a coil-winding factory at Massey and Coggins. So it's not like I *needed* to. It's just for the love of it.

Someone asked Ringo why he was going out on tour, and he said, 'It's what I do.' And that's exactly right. It's what you do. It's what I've practised enough, it's what I love doing.

What I suppose people mean is, they wouldn't go out unless it was for the money. But they're not artists who say that. I don't need to go out for the money or the fame, but that's not why I ever went out. I only went out cos I love it. Now it's the same. However, I always talk to the promoter and say, 'Does the audience want it?' And we put a few tickets on sale. And as long as they get some good results, then we'll go out.

It's not a need, it's a desire. Anyone like yourself who gets involved and sees what goes on, will know. It's cool to come to work in the morning with this lot. I get to talk about great production and where we're gonna put the speakers and how high this is gonna be and chat to a great team. I love being part of this kind of project.

Being Paul McCartney, his stage-struck enthusiasm is tempered by commercial sense. Having established the likely demand for another set of shows, he begins to plan their content: 'My first thought,' he says, 'is always, what would the audience like to see and hear?'

If I go to see the Stones, I really hope they're going to do 'Satisfaction' and 'Honky Tonk Women' and 'Jumping Jack Flash', songs I'd be disappointed if they left out. With me that means doing some Beatles, some Wings, some recent stuff and the new album. It's representative of the whole span. It's what I think an audience would basically want.

It's kind of what I fancy. I like doing numbers that go down. I don't like struggling. I have this nightmare – I particularly used to get it in the Beatles – where I'm playing to an audience and they start walking out. And I'm going, 'Do "Long Tall

Sally"!' And they're still walking out. 'Yesterday!' And they're still walking out in droves. I wake up in a cold sweat, it's a performer's nightmare.

I don't have to do the same numbers every night. But I do get set in a pattern because I look to see what goes down well. I'm the opposite of Dylan. I heard that one night Dylan was told by some guy, 'Oh, "Mr Tambourine Man" went down great tonight.' And Dylan said, 'Right, we'll cut it tomorrow night.' I love the courage of that, but it's not me. I tend to go, 'Right, keep it in.'

Are you interested in reinventing the old songs? Or do you think you've pretty much set them in stone?

I'm interested. I'm ambivalent about whether the audience wants me to do it. Dylan reinvents them every night, and it probably keeps him interested. I tend to do them like the record. The Beatles always tried to do them like the record, assuming that people would say, 'I love that one, but they did it funny.' I try to please the average punter. But I've got a fancy for 'Hello, Goodbye', it's got a modern beat. 'Coming Up' could be updated. There's certain ones that could take it.

His first Wings tours were caught in a bind; on the one hand he wished to avoid the Beatles, but on the other, there simply wasn't much solo material in existence:

I used to be shy of doing Beatles songs. I thought, I can't keep harking back to my past. This is a new band. But as time went by you started to think, I like these Beatles songs, the people in the audience like them and now I've established Wings. We've had hits like 'Band on the Run' and 'Live and Let Die'. I can loosen up a bit. So I started to include a lot of Beatles songs.

How did audience reaction vary between the new songs and the golden oldies?

In New York it was investment bankers. In Milan it was the designers, the head of Fiat showed up – Agnelli and Armani, this was their town. Suits were going round like Kleenex. 'D'you wanna suit? We're in Milan.' 'Yeah! I'll have it, man!' There's a bit of that. The promoters in New York and Milan, where they figure they've got an important crowd, that's what you'd get. Those people like the Beatles tunes, and tended to wander off for a beer during 'Put it There'. Which is all right.

You've got to train an audience, that's something I realised on tour. And they know they've got to be trained. I saw a video of Queen and it's 'We-will-rock-you-we-are-the-champions'. If you see them before the stadiums they're just a little Seventies group, then somebody caught on, and suddenly it's anthemic. Rod Stewart knows that too. It's a whole other ball-game; you're not playing an intimate theatre any more.

On a majority vote, the old numbers are the most popular. I have to admit, 'Let It Be' is a better song than 'My Brave Face'. It just is, that's fairly obvious.

Everyone who has ever played on stage knows it's difficult when you're foisting your new material on the audience. If it's me or the Stones or the Beatles, when you've got a back catalogue, people want to hear some of that. With me, people would probably be disappointed if they didn't hear 'Get Back' or 'Let It Be'. If you ask people what they want me to do, 'Maybe I'm Amazed' will probably be in there.

I would love to do my whole new album, but I'm aware that it might not be the favourite show for the people who pay the money. So I take that into account.

I've never been on tour without a contemporary album. I think people would have me out on tour these days even if I didn't have a contemporary album. They say, 'Well you can do your old stuff.' And there is a lot of material to choose from. But I wouldn't feel the same. I'd feel like I was doing a Sinatra farewell tour if it was just my old stuff.

I've got to feel there's something contemporary there that

> I'm interested in. I actually like the old songs, I like the material, but if I'm *just* doing that I feel like a has-been. And I don't want to feel like that.

McCartney can draw on decades of stagecraft. He'll pace the set so that new and unfamiliar songs do not obstruct the overall dynamic of the night. Even so, there is a special *frisson* from the big numbers that tap into a crowd's collective memories. 'Get Back' or 'Jet' will carry the people forward on waves of elation; a quiet moment for 'Yesterday' will induce a low moan of awe and surrender.

Most intriguing are those that have never been played on a public stage. My own proudest moment came before a 2004 summer tour when I persuaded him to introduce 'I'll Follow the Sun', that beautiful track from *Beatles for Sale*. Audience reaction to such numbers has been pent up – something seen most acutely in the emotional crowd for his show at Red Square, Moscow, after long decades of Cold War.

'It's been bottled up,' he nods. 'I hadn't thought of it like that. But there was a feeling of that. People would have signs: "I waited twenty years for this."'

'Before you go out on tour,' he told me after the 1993 shows, 'you dread hard questions from interviewers. You dread *weather*, in the stadiums; you dread all the dread things, the audiences not liking it.

'At the end of the tour, you're like an Olympic athlete, you've totally remembered how to do it. For me it was like being a Beatle, everything was the same, the press conferences, I didn't mind.'

Apart from the performing, how does he view the actual process of taking a tour around the globe?

The worst moment is when you're in a hotel that's not really brilliant. You're bored and you're thinking, I've got horses at home, I love going in the woods on them. What the fuck am I doing here? But everyone gets that. That's touring. We try to have enough days off to enjoy it. I don't work like I used to. With the Beatles it used to be every day of the year. But now you can do the leisurely things and keep an interest in gigging.

Artists complain about the grind of it all. Except for the time on stage, it's the travelling, endless hotels, the waiting around in lobbies. How do you deal with that?

Our luxuries aren't tons of vodka backstage, cos I don't do any of that. I can't. I won't remember the words if I get smashed. There isn't a huge banquet backstage where all the money goes. In fact, the money goes on our travel. We'll get a base where we can stay and then fly in and out. We don't actually stay at that many hotels. It's really not bad at all. If you're somewhere like Miami, on a day off I'd do something like hire a sailboat.

They're good hotels, out of the city, nearly always with a lake or some sporting gear handy, so it's like being on holiday. And then you just appear at the gig.

The gig itself is your machine. You know everyone, a big family machine. You say *Bonsoir* to the French guys, ask how the romance is going. It's like being in *Coronation Street*, it's a big soap. The only thing I used to like about going to school was the social, seeing the mates: 'Eh, did you see that last night? Eh, look what I've got! Zippo lighter!' All of the interplay that you get off people, I'm big on all that.

As a band we feel a kinship on tour – at the end of the night, it's just us that take the bow. And then there's the crew. It's roughly a hundred and forty people, like circus folk setting up the Big Top every night. You come for a soundcheck: 'Hey, how're you doing?' There's a camaraderie that I like in the team feeling.

But what about the travelling?

Having travelled so much since I was a kid, I don't mind it like some people do. On this tour [2004] we're going to Prague, a couple of places I've never been to. Most people *pay* to go to these places. It doesn't upset me to check into a hotel. I think for people who don't travel, it's a major upheaval. I've got friends who go to America and spend three months getting over it: 'Oh, I'm poorly this week.' What's wrong? 'I've just come back from America!' Yeah? A bit of jet-lag I can understand . . .

Do you see much of these places?

I get to see more than I ever did. We nearly always have a day off after a show. Unless we're running home for anything we'll actually stay and have a look around. In Japan we'd get bikes and go riding around Tokyo. You don't get too bothered, because if anyone does bother you, you're on a bike and they're not! Ha! So it's like: 'Yeah, great to see you!' *Pedal-pedal* . . .

I was in Paris and I'd been reading *The Da Vinci Code* like everyone else. A friend on holiday – it was Terry Venables [the football manager] – he'd been reading it and said, 'I can't put this book down.' So I read it and I went to the location in the book, where there is this famous 'rose line', the meridian. I went into [the Church of] Saint-Sulpice, which I'd only seen in my mind, in the book, before. And it's a trip, you know?

Actually it was better than the book, because there was a service on. There was this French priest with a really nice voice [*performs a sort of Gregorian chant in a French accent*] and the congregation are singing. It wasn't [*plodding hymn style*] 'duh-duh de-duh', like we get. So it was a great experience. And there was a big guy in the congregation who took his hankie out and wiped away a tear. I love all that. It's like I'm in a film or a book.

That's great, seeing some famous cathedral, some famous

museum, some famous river. Like most people I love that. I've been to places recently where we went with the Beatles, and I never saw any of them. You go back and stay, instead of just running through.

But even Paul McCartney can't tour forever. As far back as 1989, when he still had decades of live shows ahead of him, it was the question most often asked.

Everyone said, 'Is this your last tour, Paul?' I said, 'Look guys, just cos we're at this great "venereal age" as my dad used to say, this venerable age . . .' They naturally think it's my last tour, it's the Stones' last tour, it's the Who's last tour. 'How much longer can they keep going?' In fact, I did have an inkling of that before the tour. But as it went on I thought, Jesus, I'm feeling better and better each day. Your stamina improves, you've gotta do two hours' workout every night, so you don't have to jog. You're physically working, there's no doubt about that. And when we got the pacing right, it actually seemed easier to do.

People say to me I'm foolhardy sometimes: 'Why are you going on the road? You've got all that Beatles reputation, why fuck it up? Just leave it, man. Retire, fuck off somewhere.' But I like it too much. I find myself risking for the fun of it.

It's never the last tour as far as I'm concerned. It's tempting to say Yeah, and get them all to come, like a lot of people do. But I never think it's my last tour. I've always said I'll be wheeled on when I'm ninety. And that might be a dreadful prediction that comes true.

You age, but you don't think you do. I certainly don't. I'm still enthusiastic and very energetic. Thank God. It's a blessing that I still fancy it and I'm still able to do it. The first number I did at the Concert for New York was 'I'm Down' and I didn't think about it. It was only afterwards that I thought that was thirty years, if it's a day, when I recorded that – and I did it in the same key! At the same speed! I mean, you'd think you'd say to yourself, 'No, no, no – slower, and lower.'

I just expect to be able to do it. That might be a bit of a secret. They do say about the power of positive thought. I may be just stupid in thinking I can do it, but I don't knock that.

CHAPTER 25

Another Wide Prairie

The day the nerves go, man, you might as well give up

Another night in a new town, another wide prairie of waving arms, swept by floodlights; and the roar of a thousand throats in happy accord. Paul McCartney has taken the stage.

Maybe *all* his world's a stage:

> I always feel like I'm out playing live, even if I'm making a record. To me, it's kind of the same thing. I don't make that distinction between live, and record, video, playing music of any kind.
>
> I always like playing to an audience, there's no substitute for it. It's the feedback, the applause, the acceptance of your peers and all of that stuff, you know? And the little things – if you say a joke, and they get it. With Beatle fans you can say something obscure and they get it: 'Cranberry sauce . . .' [a murmured Lennon line in 'Strawberry Fields Forever'] and they go 'Heyyy!' Whereas somewhere else you'd have to make sense.
>
> There is a bond between the band and the audience, if you're lucky. And I'm often lucky that way, since the earliest days of the Beatles. Once we'd got over the teddy boys throwing coins at us. We just picked them up, and that stopped it.

He's played the biggest venues on earth. But for McCartney it's essentially the same trade he once learned in small Northern clubs: 'Aye, you're a grand bunch in here tonight,' he will say to a roaring Midwestern stadium – as if it were a Lancashire Royal British Legion Club in 1953.

There are people in every one of his audiences who can scarcely believe tonight is happening. But they are not alone. Paul's own impressions reflect the wide-eyed child who stands to one side of his adult mind, gawping in wonder at this improbable future. Here he is, playing for the Queen at Buckingham Palace, or serenading moist-eyed Russians in Red Square. At times he imagines if he'd tried to tell his dad all this, way back then.

The secret of a successful touring set-up is that it's the same at every show, no matter where in the world. Each night the stage will ideally feel as familiar as your own living room. Paul's assistant John Hammell will place a red cough sweet on the speaker, then busy himself retuning those guitars.

The soundcheck, beforehand, can be a performance in its own right. Backstage, afterwards, there is often a parade of famous faces: Sting, Sylvester Stallone, Brian Wilson, Kevin Spacey, Bill Clinton, Demi Moore, Ozzy Osbourne . . . Paul McCartney is in town and diaries are magically cleared.

Just as an audience watches the stage, so performers watch the audience. McCartney, though, does not see a single, undifferentiated mass. In the same way that his songs so often celebrate the human individual, his stage nights are an opportunity to pick out vignettes of real life. 'I've seen some mighty stuff on tours,' he says:

> In Helsinki I was singing 'You Won't See Me', and there was an older lady and her husband, a tall guy. She was just leaning back on his chest, he had his arm around her. She had her eyes closed, totally loving it. I saw him looking down at her. Whew . . .

I had to draw my breath in. The trouble is I'm singing a song, I'm not supposed to be voyeuristic here. But I'm starting to well up: 'Oh God, I can see she's from the Sixties, this is one of her favourites, he loves her . . .' And I find it very touching.

I've seen a lot of that. It happens more as time goes by, there are more memories. Now you see it across generations, children with their mum, the twenty-five-year-old, and her parents the fifty-year-olds, and sometimes their parents too. All these generations in my audience. I like that, being very family-orientated.

You see stuff that you didn't know about your work. You see a reflection of how important your work can be. You're just going, 'I hope this works, I hope this is important to someone.' Then you take it out on tour, and you see that it is.

I've a clear recollection of a guy in the crowd with a black beard, and his daughter with long black hair. He had his arm around her, and the pair of them were crying during 'Let It Be'. It's pretty moving. And seeing people bopping, I like that.

I saw this nice couple in Scandinavia. She was a beautiful blonde, he was a swarthy-looking guy, and you're looking at them as if you're in a bus queue. Just people-watching. You're doing your song but you're on autopilot and all these things are happening. She'd just been holding her lighter up, and to hold a lighter for the length of a song, it's not easy, that thing gets hot. And she burned her finger.

So I'm doing 'Fool on the Hill', and her boyfriend's licking it, kissing it better, and they're necking.

And again in Europe, an old-ish guy, he looked great, like Neptune with a big curly beard. And *man* he was *cryin'*. It totally touched a nerve in him. Whoah, it's bit of a choker. 'Hey Jude . . .' Hmm, don't look at this, better look at someone who's laughing. Oh Robbie [the guitarist] is laughing. Ha ha! Get trivial.

Sometimes it goes right through you. This man with his lovely daughter. You know instantly that he's brought her to say, '*This* is what I was doing in the Sixties.'

Even this born performer has known a few instances of stage fright, especially when he was starting out – fluffing his guitar part with the Quarrymen, or at the Beatles' Decca audition, or the band's first session for EMI. I've watched him in dressing rooms and leading his band along those corridors to the auditorium. He looks upbeat – and as a bandleader it's part of his job to project some confidence – but he's doing more than going through the motions.

What he's praying for is that state of automatic competence, when the inner mind has quietened and a sort of muscle-memory takes over:

> A friend of mine, John Hurt, said about first nights, those terrible nerves that happen: 'First night, nobody plays it. Second night, somebody else plays it. The third night, *you* play it.' It's like that. First night, it's just [*in a daze*] 'Ah, hello . . .' Everyone comes round later and says, 'Great, man, fabulous.'
>
> 'Was it? Oh. I wasn't there.' You just learn to go with the flow. 'Thanks. I'll have a drink now.'
>
> But that's showbiz. At every level, that happens. People get disappointed with me: 'I'd hoped the stage you'd got to, you wouldn't get nerves.' But Sammy Davis Jr said, 'The day the nerves go, man, you might as well give up.'
>
> On our '76 tour in America, Linda used to say it was easier to do the show than to be in life. Because once you get the hang of the show it's really like clockwork, a beautiful experience. You know how it goes and it happens the same every night.
>
> It's like having a wonderful bath and a massage. Cos there's nothing to worry about. In life it's, 'One of the kids has got the flu, oh my God.' Things keep happening at random. Whereas the show locks in; it's not random any more, it's lovely. But that takes a couple of weeks.

Then there are the physical mechanics of playing live. 'The bassline and the vocal are two separate lines of research,' he says, pointing to the left and right sides of his head. 'It's quite an interesting thing, how you play when you're singing live. Something funny happens to you, you have to split your whole being in two.'

Performing the *Sgt. Pepper* song 'Fixing a Hole' was especially challenging: 'The bass is 3/4 or something, dunno what it is, and the vocal's 4/4' – he rotates his right hand above his head, his left around his stomach, to show the coordination problem. 'You have to get that mathematics right in your head somehow. But suddenly it happens and it's great.'

A show is new for the audience every night, but not for the touring performer. A tour may take a little while to reach that welcome stage of being in a groove, but how do you stop it getting in a rut? McCartney likes to surprise his team – which includes many more people than the actual band. The lighting crew, for example, are tracking the set list through a computer plot, but during the 1990 tour they were taught the importance of staying awake:

> I had a thing where I would say, 'Tonight we're going to do something *different*.' And that really was talking to the crew. Everything goes to manual: 'Shit! Panic. Jeezus, what you doing here, man?' But they like it, it breaks it up for them. One of the laser guys used to sit there and do my lines with me. Good job I didn't see him. I was going, 'When I went to New Orleans, I met Fats Domino,' and he would be saying it, just before I said it, to tell everyone around how predictable this was.
>
> So I would change it every night, just cos I knew this guy was out there, repeating it. 'Well, when I went down to a little place, called New Orleans, I happened, maybe perchance, to meet this fat chap . . .'

I wondered whether McCartney feels a song has not reached its full height until he's played it to a live audience?

'It can reach its full height on a record, but the feedback from an audience is great. When you do anything, it's lovely for someone to say that was great. Even if you cook a meal, it encourages you. So does playing it live and seeing people crying to one of your songs. You think, Wow, I really should stick at this.'

So your audience is effectively a part of the performance?

Instead of just sitting at home and writing a song, then going in another little room, the studio, and recording it . . . You're now actually facing the people who buy it. That's a total buzz. Just doing 'Got to Get You into My Life' and they hit the ceiling: 'God, they really like this!' Or you see 'Pepper' through their eyes. You see *their* perception: 'He's come to our town, the guy who wrote that big hit in the Sixties, that mysterious anthem from the psychedelic time, the golden years, and here he is singing for us. Cor, this is better than the record.'

I'd been to see Dustin Hoffman in *Merchant of Venice*. I know him a bit, and when he came on stage, I got a powerful feeling of, like, 'I'm in the same room as Dustin!' I got the feeling I could go, 'Oy! Dustin!' I was that close to him.

If this was a film I was watching, it would have made no sense to go 'Oy, Tootsie!' If it's a record or a video, you can't do that. You don't feel in the same room as them.

So that became one of the things I used to say to the audience: 'Great to be in the same room as you tonight.' And we were. There was fifty thousand of us, but still it was 'We're all in the same room.' I think that's exciting. That's what live is. Anything can happen. There's no guarantee that's it's going to go right, or he's going to remember the words.

And indeed it *can* go wrong. Paul's landmark performance at one of rock's defining events – Live Aid, in London, in 1985 – was also among his worst onstage experiences.

He'd been without a live band for six years. It was his longest lay-off since the Beatles stopped touring in 1966. Right up until the moment he stepped out for the show's finale there had been rumours of a partial Beatles reunion. In fact that was never going to happen, but the Wembley stage suddenly felt like a very lonely place:

> Live Aid was a nightmare for me, personally, because my mike went down, and I didn't really know it had. Originally Bob Geldof had rung me up, [*brusque Irish voice*]: 'We're doing this thing called Live Aid, and we want you to be on it.' I said, 'Ah, come on, man, I haven't got a band, I'd love to but I can't.'
>
> He says, 'Fuck the band, just come on your own with a piano, that'll be enough, do "Let It Be".' OK, he's a fairly forceful gent, young Robert. Anyway, the cause was so major – you were seeing that horrific footage from Ethiopia – that you just wanted to do something.
>
> I agreed, and as it got nearer I thought, I've never been on stage in my life on my own, with a piano, what the hell am I doing? Well, it's a favour for Bob, and it's more of a favour for the people in Ethiopia, yeah that's right, don't worry.
>
> It was a great day, a huge national day. I started watching it on telly at home, then drove into Wembley, started to see the crowds like in a football match. Went backstage and then I watched from the wings. Personally experiencing it was the final trip. This is not media any more, this is me. This body was gonna now experience it live, with this huge sea of faces.
>
> And I suddenly realised I couldn't hear my monitors. I thought, well it's OK, they're plugging them in. It turned out it was Queen's roadies. Freddie Mercury and Brian May had done their number just before I went on, their roadies had pulled what they thought were their jackplugs, and pulled

mine as well. I wasn't there with anyone, didn't have a road crew.

So there I was, on world telly and I couldn't hear the piano. My mind was saying, Wait a minute, this is a BBC programme, probably we haven't got the monitors, but I bet the sound is great on telly. Cos that often happens. So my mind goes, Just shut up, get on with it. 'When I find myself in time of trouble . . .' It's not going down *that* well but maybe they'll warm up as I go along. Then suddenly I just could hear [*muffled voices of technicians panicking*], 'You've got the wrong plug! That's not my plug!' Oh dear, I wonder if *that's* coming over on the BBC?

Meantime, half of me is singing 'Let It Be', trying to remember the words. And this other side of me is going, Don't worry, it's OK. I went, 'There will be an answer . . .' Then it suddenly started to feed back, which is another nightmare. My brain was arguing with itself and at the same time singing this bloody song.

Anyway, about halfway through the sound came on and the audience started to sing it.

We'd arranged that Geldof, Bowie, Alison Moyet and Townshend were gonna come on and sing the last chorus. But by this time I had no idea where I was. Nobody came in on the chorus, I thought, right, repeat the chorus. By that time I sneaked a look, and they were there. But it was dramatic. Paranoia City.

When we got home, I looked at it and went, Bloody hell, disastrous . . .

But it had been a great day. The truth was that this guy Geldof had set out to raise money for people who were dying, and it didn't really matter if my mike went out. Nothing compared to their problems.

These nightmares happen at every stage in your career. The first time I ever played it happened. With the Beatles it happened once or twice. And you just die, that's all it is. You go very white. You get a very funny feeling.

In the end it was more than all right on the night. The microphone malfunction simply added another human touch, a grace note of creative chaos, to an event that always teetered on the edge. 'Let It Be' was not so much a performance as a global campfire singalong. Live Aid brought rock and roll into the cultural mainstream and defined its hierarchy. Paul's position as the top act on the bill, bringing all the other stars together to sing his song, was confirmation of his and the Beatles' place at the pinnacle.

CHAPTER 26

More Cowbell

Bands and bass guitars, studios and producers. McCartney on making music

He does like a band. Only two of Paul's albums were literally solo records: the aptly named *McCartney* and *McCartney II*. They were made without guest musicians or a producer, and being a consummate all-rounder he could play the studio hermit forever, if he wished. But then, there is always the call of the open road. And as a musician he is happiest in a gang.

It's striking that *McCartney* and *McCartney II* were both made when his bands of the time – the Beatles and Wings respectively – were in the process of falling apart.

'Yeah. It seems to be what I do,' he nods. 'When the band splits up, go in a room.'

But isolation brings challenges. In making *McCartney II*, up at his windswept Gaelic retreat, he experienced the loneliness of the long-distance cowbell player:

> So that was the thing. Scotland . . . I shut myself up, and felt like the nutty professor in his laboratory. Some of the tracks, 'Secret Friend' was one, and 'Blue Sway' was another, they go on for ten minutes. I just got into it.
>
> That's all very well when you're doing your first take, but then you've got to put a cowbell on it. And I would sit there in real time for ten minutes, glancing at my watch. And I've

got five more minutes to go: *dink-dink, dinka dink-dink* . . . I'd think, are you kidding me? You're really gonna stand here and do this? Why don't you just do the cowbell on *that* bit? No, I'll mix it out later. Right, now we'll do maracas! *Ch-ch-ch-ch*, looking at the watch again. Did the whole song, just standing there. Quite weird.

I did think, I've got to get a band. This is *not* going to work.

So, no more cowbell. Paul can play the solitary boffin, but he's most himself when he's not alone. There is a pre-war photo of Paul's father, Jim, surrounded by the massed ranks of bow-tied band members and their friends; it was perhaps a forerunner of the *Sgt. Pepper* sleeve. Paul understood the romance of lonely writers in garrets, but his own vision of artistry tends to involve collaborators.

They need not be numerous. Speaking of his 1990 tour, he was proud of that band, his own small platoon:

Six people, the band on stage for two hours. At the end, just six people took a bow and I was chuffed. Everybody else, it seems, took out the thirteen or fourteen-piece thing. People were saying, 'Are you going to take horns? If you do "Got to Get You into My Life"?' And it was a big decision: Should we take a security blanket? What if our voices just go? Then you've got three backup singers. Horns can do a thing. You've got extra keyboard players, or tape.

And those six people in a new band, there was no guarantee we were gonna gel, or not fall out. But we ballsed it out. During the tour I would think, it's still not over, might totally fuck up on the last night.

But we didn't. It was, 'OK guys, there's just going to be six of us, and we're gonna cover the whole thing.' We had to be a bit courageous. I'll pat myself on the back for that one. I think we took the right decision.

I watched him rehearse his 1989 band. Their camaraderie shone forth. But they were still a band with no name. Why not?

> The current favourite is Lumpy Trousers. It's been everything. 'Bucket of Water.' Hamish [Stuart, guitarist] had a dream: 'Hey, Paul said to me in the dream, the group's called Bucket of Water.' So it was called that for a while. We haven't got a name, really. We thought of a few, but it gets to be a joke session.
>
> I feel pretty good about it. I feel amazed that I can still sing. Cos you know, I'm forty-six. I never expected to be doing this at forty-six. We thought twenty-five was the end of the line, forty-six is fairly far-out. But I get off on doing it.
>
> I *really* get off on jamming. That's the thing I love. The problem is we won't bring it to the stage. By the time you've got to the stage, you've got the lights, you won't be as free. It can happen easiest when I play guitar. It's one of my big thrills. Who'd have ever thought I'd still be messing around with electric guitars?

In 1989 the lack of a band name was probably intuitive on McCartney's part. As a collective they were not destined to last more than a couple of years. Paul's policy since then has been to treat recording personnel and touring bands as separate propositions – often overlapping, but seldom identical.

His current stage line-up is the most enduring of his whole career. It took shape in sessions for 2001's *Driving Rain*, and was itself a symptom of his taste for spontaneity:

> It was fated, really. A lot of things in my life have just happened. David Kahne [the producer of *Driving Rain*] asked if I had any thoughts of people I wanted. I said not really, I don't know too many people in LA. He knew some good people and he made some suggestions.

I just wanted to have fun and make a bit of music, I didn't want to be bothered with any heavy breathing. So I didn't show the producer the songs. Just to keep it simple. And I had been doing an interview with you, talking about how I worked with the Beatles. Early Monday mornings, John and I would come in and suddenly realise George and Ringo never even knew the songs.

And I shocked myself, remembering that. So I thought, if it was good enough for them, that's what I'll do. Of course, I'd already *met* George and Ringo. But these guys, I hadn't. But we just got on from the beginning.

His drummer Abe Laboriel, he told me in 2002, 'is a really good drummer who can turn his hand to anything.'

You don't throw him if you say, 'What about electric tablas?' He doesn't go, 'Oh, I'm not into that, man.' He just goes over to his kit and does it. He leaps on ideas, very enthusiastic. And he was cool enough to not mind me drumming on some bits.

Rusty Anderson and I shared the guitar work, again him doing most of it. He's an LA guy who dresses a bit retro, which I like; he reminds me of people I knew. And the funny thing about Rusty is that he went to his doctor for a check-up and the doctor said that the only thing wrong was that he had *too much iron* in his blood.

Then we have Wix from the old tour. Wix is going to play keyboards. He's sort of MD [musical director]. Actually, all the guys are kind of at that level, I think they've all MD'd.

And then we have a guy who I haven't worked with except for at the Super Bowl concert [in 2002, at New Orleans], who is called Brian Ray. I think he's going to be great, but I won't really get to play with him until rehearsals, so he's slightly an unknown element at the moment. He's a guitarist who can also play bass, so that when I go on piano he can double on bass.

Brian Ray duly proved to possess the right stuff and this configuration has supported Paul on stages ever since. But when it came to recording his next album, 2005's *Chaos and Creation in the Backyard*, he met with his new producer Nigel Godrich and there was a difficult conversation to be had:

> At the end of our American tour we were looking forward as a band to making an album. So we started talking about plans for that, assuming automatically that me and the band would go in the studio. We did some recordings with that in mind, but when I met Nigel he had a different take and wanted me to play more of the instruments, rather than take the live band as a given.
>
> So it was awkward, me talking to the guys, saying, 'Look, he wants to do it this way, what do you think?' But they were very cool about it. They all know about making records, it's such an inexact art, so whatever it takes to make an album . . .

From 2002, even as the new band was solidifying into a permanent stage entity, Paul introduced a solo section into his live sets:

> I haven't really sung on my own before. I've always been surrounded by someone or other; John and George in the earliest days and then Wings with Linda. There's always been an element of that. I'll still have my security blanket with the band. But I like the idea of seeing if I can do something solo.
>
> And people say to me, 'It's good to hear just you and a guitar, man'. You're focused. It's a guy and a guitar and that's all. It's like how you write songs, you write it on your own.

Paul, as he says, will normally write songs in seclusion. But sooner or later, unless they're abandoned, he will have to play them to other people. And here begins the rough-and-tumble of collaboration – and perhaps of compromise. Who is usually first to hear a box-fresh McCartney song?

> First, it's whoever's around. Then you take it to the producer, or the band, and that's the next interesting part. Because it might get knocked. Some people say, 'No, I don't want it to be knocked around, this is how it must be.' But I quite like that process, having been in bands, and having been in a band like the Beatles – where we bring in 'Please Please Me', a slow Orbison-esque piece, and George Martin suggests we make it uptempo and jangly.
>
> That happened a lot. John brought in 'Come Together', almost as a copy of 'You Can't Catch Me' – or let's call it an unwitting copy of a Chuck Berry song. It was me, in that case, who had to say, 'There's another way to do this,' and we swamped it out [*does impression of the bass riff and drums*] and all that stuff which became the character of it.
>
> That's the next exciting thing. It doesn't always get changed, but something always happens, because there's now other people on it. Instead of just guitar or piano, there's now drums and bass, singing and backing vocals. All the stuff that makes it into a record rather than just a song.

In the studio, even where he does use other musicians, he might finally re-record their parts himself. Or he may dictate to his fellow players precisely what he wants – a potentially tense method for those unused to working that way. On the other hand, he is often content to give people a free hand to improvise their own parts – an exquisite example being David Gilmour's guitar solo in 'No More Lonely Nights'.

He's not above being dazzled by stellar company. As he recalled of making the 2012 standards collection, *Kisses on the Bottom*:

> We ended up at Capitol A studios, at the base of that very iconic building, where Nat King Cole, Frank Sinatra, Dean Martin, even Gene Vincent recorded. We arrived there one day

> and just started recording. I was thrown in the deep end, because I'm not a jazz player. I didn't have a guitar or a piano to hide behind, so I was just put on what the engineers told me was Nat King Cole's mike – which was pretty intimidating in front of jazz musicians.

But as usual, McCartney overcame his nerves with a pragmatic application of his 'Don't sweat it' philosophy:

> Other than going in to do the vocals, I didn't feel like I had to do much. The players did all the hard work, and I was just in the booth, singing. There was one moment, when we were having a puzzle over some slight problem, and I said, 'I don't mind. I'm in LA. I'm British. I'm a tourist. I'm in Capitol A studios and I'm singing on Nat King Cole's microphone – I'm on holiday!' Whenever we were worried about something I'd go, 'I don't mind, I'm on holiday.'

Paul's belief that such serenity is desirable in the fraught world of recording is probably a legacy of his experiences in the Beatles – at least when George Martin was keeping his calm, avuncular eye on things:

> For years, since George retired from producing, I've been telling people what a fantastic producer he is. For instance, when John brought in 'Tomorrow Never Knows' – suddenly the first Beatle song all on one chord, and its inspiration is Timothy Leary and the *Tibetan Book of the Dead* – and George to his credit didn't even flinch. He just said, 'Ah, that's interesting, John.' I thought, that's George. He could have said, 'Well, I think you could have put more chords in,' or whatever. But he never did. He was a great producer that way.

If Wings were volatile it was perhaps due to some of the band's members, but more especially the problem of working with a leader who knows his own mind and has pop's most staggering track record to back him up. But Paul's solo career has also witnessed some friction. *Press to Play*, in 1986, was not without its tensions and nor, more recently, was *Chaos and Creation in the Backyard* – the latter bringing Paul into conflict with his young producer Nigel Godrich:

> We moved on to Los Angeles and his favourite studio there, Ocean Wave. Because he was producing and engineering I didn't feel it was for me to say 'No, I like such-and-such a studio.' I'm very low-tech anyway. The thing is with someone like Nigel is you've got to get to know him; it's not like George Martin where all the getting to know has been done.

Of the album's track *Riding to Vanity Fair* he adds:

> It was a very different song when I brought it to Nigel and during one moment on the sessions he said, 'I really don't like that song.' It really brought me down.
>
> It was one of our crisis moments. I was about to do what I thought was a great bass part and he says, 'I really don't like that song.' Thanks! It totally did me in. I couldn't do any more work that day. I had to go home. So we had to have a few discussions about that: 'Come on, Nige, what's going on, man?' 'Well, I don't like it too much.'
>
> One day I went into the studio and just changed this and that, we made it a song that we both liked. And because we did that, I think it's a really good song now, with a bit of depth to it.

Though he calls himself low-tech, McCartney is open to any advance in studio science. At the dawn of the 1980s he made *McCartney II* with equipment undreamt of in the Beatles' early days: 'I'd discovered synthesisers and sequencers,' he says. 'Something like "Temporary Secretary" is a sequencer. It was a bit like "Baba O'Riley" [a 1971 track by the Who]. That was probably where I heard the idea.'

Had you been listening to synth-pop pioneers like Kraftwerk?

'No, I was just aware synths were coming in. You'd hear all these stories: Mickie Most had the Dream Machine, the big synth. [The pop producer installed a Yamaha GX-1 at his RAK studio in London; its nickname came from Stevie Wonder.] It cost a fortune – it would cost you what it cost to buy a house, which put a few people off. But it was the big dream synth that you could do anything with.'

The Beatles, in their time, had helped to redefine the very idea of a recording studio. Before them, it was just a room that captured live performances. After them, it grew into a creative medium in its own right. Between the group, who were restlessly inventive, and their producer George Martin, who had the happy combination of traditional know-how and a very open mind, the studio became intrinsic to their art. From the time of *Revolver* onwards – most evident in other-worldly tracks like 'Tomorrow Never Knows' – they used it to construct sounds that could not exist anywhere else. Since then, McCartney has veered between the extremes of space-age electronica and organic earthiness. He seems not to make a fetish of either approach.

He's used studios around the world, but his heart remains at Abbey Road, the former EMI facility and cradle of so many McCartney classics. In late 1978, finding himself unable to book some time there, he had an exact facsimile built beneath his London office: 'In the basement. We had a replica studio, we made a little replica of EMI, had a lot of the same equipment that EMI had. So I obviously needed the support of Abbey Road.'

As a multi-instrumentalist he needs no encouragement to step beyond the bass guitar and piano. He's been bashing away at drum kits nearly all his life. In the famous case of *Band on the Run*, he was obliged to pick up sticks for a whole album:

> I like drumming, and I knew that as long as I kept it simple . . . That's the thing I have in drumming – and I don't have a lot else – but I do have a feel. Often, that's what us guys look for. I remember the rumour that Buddy Rich had made fun of Ringo, cos he wasn't technically good. But much as we admired Buddy Rich, we preferred Ringo's sound and style, cos it was what we were looking for. It was all feel. He obviously couldn't do a thousand paradiddles to the minute, but we didn't want that. So I thought *I'd* be OK.

Still, it's Paul's achievements as a bass guitarist that will always stand out. In his hands, the chunky four-string blossomed from a utilitarian foot-soldier of the rhythm section into a charismatic force in itself. The singularity of his bass lines is all the more impressive when you consider that he often plays them while simultaneously singing melody lines with no immediate connection.

'Which again,' he says, 'is from the Beatles days. If you can do that, then it's something worth valuing because not everyone can. But it's an old skill of mine, because we had to do that in Hamburg.'

> After things like *Revolver*, *Rubber Soul*, it started to be overdubbed, the bass. The problem is, if I'd done something like 'Let It Be' – I'd written that on piano. It was difficult to come in and show John or George the *feel* on piano, when I knew exactly what I wanted. And I know George used to get pissed off with me and I don't blame him, really, thinking about it. But I couldn't see any other way round it. I had to bring the 'feel' instrument, that it was written on, to the live take, and then we can work on it.

> But it did mean we recorded a lot without the bass, which is a bit of a piss-off for a guitar player, it doesn't sound full. Cos you had to imagine the bass, and it meant you don't get a good sound from the off.

When we look at the most uncomfortable footage in the movie *Let It Be*, it suggests a domineering Macca, hectoring his bandmates with the insensitivity of an army drill sergeant. But it's more likely a symptom of his nature. He's the man who wants to get the job done – and then move on to the next one. Arguably, Paul's work ethic would hasten the Beatles' break-up. But it also brought him back from the abyss straight afterwards. Today, in his seventies, that spirit is just as evident.

I asked him more about this. McCartney helps other people to relax in his presence by appearing to be the most laid-back person in the room. But, somewhere deep inside, there seems to be a man who never sleeps.

CHAPTER 27

Do It Now

Can't be done? Oh I think it can, you know

Paul's brother, Mike McCartney, told me that when they were children their house would echo to the command, 'D-I-N.' This was their father's sternest precept. D-I-N . . . Do It Now.

There's no evidence that Paul took it to heart back then. He was not an especially studious schoolboy. Even in the Beatles' early days of struggle, he wasn't averse to skipping a band meeting in favour of a nice lie-in. Yet, at some point in his development, the Do It Now ethos took hold. By the time the Beatles were established, and in every period of his life since then, McCartney has displayed unnerving drive.

It's true that he loves his holidays, and he takes them often. But those vacations are often the times when new songs make their first appearance. Back in the studio, it's clear that he's used his downtime strategically.

McCartney is also confident in his abilities. As well as learning musical instruments he took whatever challenge came along, from swimming and driving to skiing, sailing, horse-riding, animal-rearing, studio-building, filming, painting, poetry, ballet, computer art, symphonies, electronica, calypso or thrash metal. He nearly always succeeds. And when he doesn't? 'At least I had a go.'

He is generally handy. At the height of his fame in 1965, he sawed wood and painted walls for the new Indica gallery in St

James's. Having bought High Park Farm in Scotland, he rocked up with Linda and set about making it a home, pouring concrete floors himself. These are not the acts of a miracle worker, of course, but by the standards of rock stars they are pretty unusual.

He has a song called 'Distractions', on *Flowers in the Dirt*, in which he laments the multiple calls upon his time – the calls of work and business, of problems to resolve. It's time when he could be at home with the woman he loves, blissfully doing nothing. On a similar theme is 'One of These Days', from *McCartney II*, which again speaks wistfully of a time when he will no longer be at duty's call, and his world will start to make sense again. Left to himself, these songs suggest, a sense of wholeness might return. He longs for idleness. But is there a part of him, perhaps, that secretly *craves* all this activity?

'It's a question for me,' he admitted. 'People ask me, "Why d'you do it, man? Why bother with the distractions? You're rich." Everyone's little dream when I was at school was, you'll get a lot of money then go on holiday. *Forever*. Go down the Costa del Crime or whatever it is. "Just go off on a boat, man, it's great." But anyone who's grown up will realise it doesn't work. A year of that, maybe, is funny, and a great groove. But after a year you think, what do I do in life again? Sail around the world in boats? Surely not. I don't mean to put down anyone who does that. But I know that after a year or so I'd start to wonder. I'd pick up a guitar.'

Thinking back to those fractious final days of his first band, he recalls a meeting they held at Apple:

> I said I think it's time we did something. And everybody at that time was very happy to not really work, because they were enjoying the rewards of their success. The guys were all rich, living in nice country homes out in Weybridge and Esher, they

were all married, I wasn't. So I was like, [*snaps fingers impatiently*] 'C'mon guys, we can't sit around, we've gotta do something. We're the Beatles!'

I was very much the motivator. And everyone looked at me, like, *what?* I'd say, 'Maybe we should do a film or something.'

'Why?'

'Well, it'd be great, wouldn't it?'

'What for?' It was like that. I remember John saying, 'I get it, he wants a job.'

I said, 'Yeah, that's it, I do. We ought to work.'

I slightly badgered them into making a film . . . And by that time, I suppose tempers were starting to fray a bit. They weren't all that keen to do it, and I was going, 'Yeah! Yeah!' and without realising that some of the time, they'd be going, 'Who the fuck's he think he is, like? Beethoven?' Bit of that attitude always, about me. But in fact I was just genuinely enthusiastic.

But it's the danger of being very enthusiastic. 'What are you doing, man? Why don't you just go to sleep? Have a holiday.' No, no, we've gotta do it!

Of his writing sessions with Lennon, he remembers how John would get bored when good results did not come straight away. Hating boredom, he was inclined to switch off. To which Paul would be the one to say, 'I know, I know, but we gotta finish it. Can't leave it, it's a good idea.'

While he doesn't dismiss the concept of writer's block, McCartney insists it's never afflicted him:

I've been very lucky about writer's block, touch wood. That's one of those things I don't know about. It occurred to me that me and John sat down on however many occasions, what was it, two hundred and ninety-five songs me and John wrote? And on those two hundred and ninety-five occasions we sat down, we never came away without a song, and that is fucking phenomenal.

The important thing to Paul is that effort should never feel effortful. The phrase he uses, with great distaste, is 'heavy breathing'. If a plan promises too much of that, or 'head banging', he wants the plan changed. If a new song seems to require a struggle, the song will be abandoned. He likes to graft, but he values a creative openness to accident. He is wary of getting intense. 'We don't want to *sweat* this.'

To those who work for him, however, he can appear a tough taskmaster. More than once I've seen people blanching at deadlines that he's given them. But he doesn't like be told that something can't be done. 'Can't be done?' he will say. 'Oh, I think it can, you know . . .' Usually he's proved correct. It's not a brute assertion of his power that wins the day. It's the awareness that he's been here before. He can remember when they told him that guitar groups from Liverpool were plainly without a hope.

Energy is a sort of resilience, and resilience is easier when you're an optimist. Paul McCartney really is the optimist that many of his songs suggest:

> You're right. You look at me, my life, and I'm determined to be optimistic, under whatever circumstances, you know? It's the wartime spirit that my generation grew up with. Even though Hitler was dropping all these bombs, everyone was going, 'Roll out the barrels, we'll have a barrel of fun.' *What?* A barrel of *what?* 'Yeah! We're gonna drink some beer! We're gonna have a laugh, it doesn't matter if they're bombing us.'
>
> I think my parents' generation was very that. I saw a lot of that in Liverpool. So I think that might have leaked into me. Whenever tragedies have occurred in my life, I've thought I'm not gonna let it get me down. Of course I go through a bad period. You can't help it. But there is always this instinct for me

to drag myself out of it – and be, you know, *up*. And keep this optimism going.

Mostly, I would finish our talks by asking what he was up to next. The reply was invariably a torrent of projects.

'A lot of other things,' he said in 1995. 'I've got a painting exhibition in Germany next year. I've been painting for about twelve years, probably been talking to you for about half of those. This guy showed up from Germany. I was always worried about the David Bowie thing: Oh, he's a singer and he thinks he can paint. I'll probably hate the whole experience; it's like showing yer knickers in public.

[Semi-abstract portraits, in oil or acrylic, seem to be a speciality. His subjects have ranged from the Queen to one entitled *Bowie Spewing*.]

'Then I've got this film of the Grateful Dead, at the London Film Festival. It was four rolls of Linda's 35mm stuff that she shot in Haight-Ashbury and in Central Park, and I've made her stills move, that was the trick. It's a nice, late-night head film, nine minutes.'

And there was a radio series, *Oobu Joobu*: 'Me and Linda were driving to Scotland, many years ago, and Viv Stanshall and Keith Moon had a radio show, a nice anarchic programme, and we loved it. So for millions of years I've been planning this thing called *Oobu Joobu* – no particular meaning in the title, it's probably taken off Ubu, the Alfred Jarry stuff that I used to be very into.' (The fifteen shows, broadcast in America, teemed with rarities, soundchecks and out-takes.)

Next year, he added, there'd be an orchestral piece [*Standing Stone*] and probably a new album – and of course some poetry: 'Having been a lyric writer, and doing English Literature at school, I always liked it. Me and John liked Dylan Thomas, Lewis Carroll, and it was a big part of what we ended up doing. Then a friend of mine died [Ivan Vaughan], and I found myself writing a poem about it. It seemed the only way to say it, it didn't seem right in prose, so, I just started getting a little collection together.'

The same question in 2001 produced this: 'I'm carrying on with my multicoloured rainbow life. A chorale for a college in Oxford, a piece of music [*Ecce Cor Meum*] at the Sheldonian. You know me and my fear of being a sort of Renaissance Man, but I do love to do millions of things.

'I was almost not going to tell you that I've been asked to design a set of stamps for the Isle of Man. But it's true! Not only that, I've done 'em. I've got a painting exhibition coming up at the Walker Art Gallery [in Liverpool] next May, which is exciting, cos me and John used to wander around that as kids. I'll probably do some more recording. I'm writing all the time.'

He signed, off, as in nearly every interview, with the words, 'Great, man. Well I'm gonna get back to work.'

Paul McCartney was almost sixty at the time. In the decades ahead he would be even busier. I recall him at the *Off the Ground* cover shoot, doodling suggestions over my sketches for the next tour magazine while simultaneously receiving a pedicure. In the twenty-first century he embarked on something like his own equivalent of Bob Dylan's 'Never Ending Tour', playing global dates incessantly. At the inaugural Q Awards in 1990, we'd made elaborate arrangements for driving Paul to Ronnie Scott's club in Soho, from his office just up the road. In the event he simply walked there, arrived half an hour early and helped us to set the tables.

Not for nothing, I suppose, is the logo of his MPL company a juggling man, keeping three cosmic bodies up in the air.

CHAPTER 28

Fallibility

You just can't win 'em all

In music he might be the closest thing to King Midas, but even McCartney acknowledges that some work has fallen short. He can live with the critics' brickbats, especially when their targets – 'Mull of Kintyre' and 'Ebony and Ivory' spring to mind – were big commercial hits. But he rues the films and the records that were not loved by the public. Much as he likes to experiment, he is a populist to the core, and he intends for his art to be popular.

So it's interesting to hear Paul's own view of the moments when expectations were not quite met. This everyman populist is also a perfectionist. When things don't go to plan, his attitude can vary from contrition to defiance.

In the Beatles' time, their movie *Magical Mystery Tour* was not accepted by the mass of fans in the wholehearted way that the band had come to expect. The psychedelic animation of *Yellow Submarine*, which followed, was better received, yet the band themselves felt a certain lack of ownership. His own film *Give My Regards to Broad Street* was never destined for Oscar glory. And there were solo albums such as *Back to the Egg* and *Flowers in the Dirt* that disappointed his record company's sales force.

But he's quick to add that posterity has a way of coming round, as it has with Wings. By the simple ruse of living long enough, he's had the satisfaction of seeing critical reappraisals and the healthy afterlife of digital reissues. At first it hurts, he shrugs, 'but you just can't win 'em all.'

> I've done so much, there has to be an element that doesn't make it. A TV crew were talking about some guy they'd interviewed. I won't name-drop, but he said, 'If I could write just one of Paul McCartney's two hundred, I'd be happy.' This is a guy who I think writes great stuff.
>
> That's the plus of it all. I don't know how many I *have* actually written. But I've had a fair share of success – he said, shying away modestly – so there's gotta be some stuff that isn't as good. If you're taking the Picasso analogy – which is dead dangerous – I like nearly everything he's done, even the stuff the critics say, 'No, that's a bad period'. I figure it came from the pen of The Man. I'm willing to forgive his lesser stuff. I think it's interesting. I *like* to see him with his pyjamas on. I *like* to see him with that funny little hat he wears. It's maybe not as wonderful as his great *big* outfit, but that's the aspect that I like.

At the same time, he defends his right to veer off in new directions. Recalling a *McCartney II*-era song, 'Secret Friend', he says:

> It's very dismissable: 'A ten-minute track, called "Secret Friend"? Leave it out! It's not "Hey Jude". So shut up.' Well, it isn't 'Hey Jude' but I knew what I was doing. I wasn't trying to write 'Hey Jude'. It's like Picasso – dare I compare myself? Ha! No, you daren't! But whenever he got a groove going, his Blue Period or his Cubist Period, he kicked it over. He never did any more, and the people would go, 'I loved your Blue Period.' 'Yeah, well, I'm fed up with that, I'm doing cubist now.'
>
> That's a bit how I feel. It's difficult to admit, but some of

> those songs, I've written them purposefully avoiding writing hits. Which is very strange. People hear that and go, 'Why did you do that?' It's because I think of myself a bit more as an artist. It's a strange period I went through. I wanted to spew this idea on a tape.

So what of that Christmas 1967 venture, *Magical Mystery Tour*? The songs it contained have always enchanted, but the film's plot-free fantasias were plain baffling on release. Emerging as the world was still absorbing that summer's *Sgt. Pepper* album, there was a new and unfamiliar sense of the Beatles' fallibility.

'I'd always had a feeling,' says Paul, 'I'd love to make a far-out film. I'd tried home movies. So I got interested and *Magical Mystery Tour* came along. It was just a mad idea we had one night: Why don't we do a film?'

> We got a rough idea of what we wanted, then we got *Spotlight*, the actors' directory, choosing actors and actresses who looked about right. We had no idea whether they could act. Ivor Cutler, I liked him. It was a bit like Fellini, just getting faces. But he's a director, that's the difference.
>
> We hired a coach, had it painted with Magical Mystery Tour on the side and said, 'We'll just go down to Devon, film every day, get off and do some set pieces here and there. We'll think it up as we went along.' And I suppose that's what's wrong with it. It hasn't got much structure.
>
> It was cheeky, cos people in film school were dying to make a movie, trained to the hilt, and there was us, the beat boys: 'Hey, we'll have a go! I can do that!'
>
> I somehow ended up as the guy who was gonna get it all together, ring 'em, book 'em. Everyone seemed happy to let me do it, I don't think anyone else wanted the bother.

But as a film, generally . . . if nothing else, just for the 'I Am the Walrus' sequence. I think 'Fool on the Hill' is good too. A couple of the musical sequences make it. It's got an anarchic sway that I like.

What happened is that we totally presented it in the wrong way. We had it on Boxing Day, in the traditional Bruce Forsyth slot – you know – which is everyone sitting there after Christmas, just recovering from the piss-up the night before. 'Uh, what's on there?' It's Brucie: '*Bring me sunshine* . . . Hey! Having a good Boxing Day?' But instead it was '*Maagicalll Mystereee Tooour* . . . Hey maan,' with eggheads and everything.

People were up in arms. 'Beatles' bomb flops!' Terrible. They came round to my house the next day. 'What did you think then, Paul?' 'Oh, I don't know, I thought it was rather good.' Ha! Tried to bluff my way out. I took it in the neck, cos I had kind of directed it. But the credits said 'Directed by the Beatles', cos I didn't want to ego-trip.

The film *Yellow Submarine* arrived in cinemas the following summer, and like its predecessor it presented some fine new Beatles music, with four original songs and a selection of familiar tracks going back to 1965. But the soundtrack album betrays a lack of involvement by the band. Released six months after the film, its second side was given to George Martin's instrumental score, while the sleeve note was actually about the White Album. In 1999 Apple revamped the entire record with a CD called *The Yellow Submarine Songtrack*.

For all the gorgeousness of its animation, *Yellow Submarine* was for the Beatles an awkward compromise. Its origins lay in a US cartoon series *The Beatles*, which was grounded in *A Hard Day's Night* and Beatlemania; the film itself shadowed the aesthetic revolution of *Sgt Pepper*. By the time it was complete, however, the Beatles had moved on:

We weren't too keen. King Features, the Americans who'd done *Popeye*, and we respected that, a guy called Al Brodax, came and said, 'We want a Saturday morning TV series for kids.' We said, 'Sounds all right, let's see what you're doing.' And it was very cutesy. We said, 'Sure.'

They explained it's a traditional thing in America, they show millions of cartoons, the kids'd love it. We thought, no harm in that, for the younger audience, that's fine. But we said we don't want to get too heavily associated. [The Beatles cartoon series duly ran for four years from 1965.]

In other words, we're not going to do the voices, because once that happens it has to be good, our heads are on the line. We wanted to distance ourselves and yet let them do it. So other people were doing the voices, which were fairly disastrous. [*Dopey, parodic Scouse*]: 'Oh, hullo Paul, how are you? Oh, don't be like that John. You're dropping your aitches.' It prototyped us into these terrible stereotypes. We should have stopped it right there.

I got that image of, 'Oh, don't do that, Ringo.' The very sensible one. John was laconic, a satirical wit. Ringo was a right dummy and George was hardly in it.

But that went so well, the *Beatles* cartoon series, that they figured, 'Wait a minute, we've spent a lot of time getting how these guys walk, how they talk, their humour. We've earned a lot of money. Let's do a feature.'

I was excited, because I'm a major Disney fan. I really think it's high art. So they said, 'What kind of ideas, if you were going to do something?' I said, 'We've just got a song, "Yellow Submarine". I've written it for Ringo, very childrensy, but it could be great. "In the land where I was born, lived a man who sailed to sea . . ."'

I thought of it very realistically, this old sea captain who tells the story. There's a land of submarines out there. But of course, what *they* were seeing was where we were up to, which was *Sgt. Pepper* time. Fairly heavily 'sedated'. Ha! Slightly otherworld.

We hoped to keep that for *us*, the art, the creative thing – but let *Yellow Submarine* be a bridge between those kids' things, and yet a really good film. So they got George [actually Erich] Segal to write it, who did *Love Story*, a Harvard professor, Yale, Princeton, those swotty schools.

I said, 'Yeah, great,' to all this. But they saw us getting psychedelic and thought, this is the kind of film we'll make. I was disappointed about that. I thought it would have worked better with a bit of Disney depth. But I've changed my mind since then, because it has a sort of trippiness that looks nice now. You don't see that stuff any more. 'Oh, Humphrey, where are you going? To the Sea of Holes!'

So it's dotty. I don't mind that. But at the time I was disappointed that Segal didn't just go away and write this marvellous, interesting story – about this guy who took people to his land of submarines, where there was a yellow submarine, a red submarine. Some big Disney-type adventure story.

We did the music a bit begrudgingly. If we were involved, we had to do a few songs. They forced us to do one specially, 'Only a Northern Song', which George did with a very big tongue in his cheek, because Northern Songs was the name of the publishing company. And I played trumpet on it. I'm a very bad trumpet player, but it was *Sgt. Pepper* time and I was experimenting with this avant-garde stuff, Cage and Stockhausen. It didn't matter to me, it was sped-up trumpet, sounds like a maniac.

Then we had to actually appear in it, at the end. I'm sure it was 'They gotta be in it. They gotta write an extra song.'

We fought about silly things. A guy came to see us. I said, 'It should be *The Beatles' Yellow Submarine: A Cartoon*'. He said, 'We really don't want to call it a cartoon, Paul. Animated Feature is what we call them these days. Cartoon is sort of little.' 'But we love calling them cartoons where I'm from.' But no, they were the bosses.

So we weren't that involved, and did it begrudgingly. I think it turned out surprisingly all right, considering.

Hindsight is not so kind to Paul's 1984 movie *Give My Regards to Broad Street*. On the upside, just like those earlier films, the music was great. Among the new numbers, its signature song 'No More Lonely Nights' ranks among McCartney's finest moments. There were fresh versions of various Beatle tunes and the lesser-known solo pleasures 'Wanderlust' and 'So Bad'.

But the film was poorly received and has not fared well since then. '*Broad Street*,' Paul explains, 'was originally going to be a TV thing. I thought it would be nice to do an hour. I like TV cos it reaches the most people. Just stay in for an hour, that's the most you're asking. Me and Linda thought it would be great to do some of my better songs, do them really nice and film them. You could have a story with it.'

> So then I got carried away with myself as a writer. It's very tempting with these great dreams. I had a lot of time in the car, going up to London. I took a pad of foolscap paper and started writing, a bit here and a scene there. Got this idea of the tapes get nicked, and the baddies are gonna do everything, unless they can get them back in time. And we'd have these songs.
>
> That was OK to that point. Then what happened was the fatal mistake. We said, 'Well, you know, it's an hour's TV, a film's only an hour and three quarters. Wouldn't be hard to extend it.' That was the mistake, cos a film is a whole other beast. I saw Spielberg say recently, 'Thank God for the fifth draft.' They look at it at least five times until they've honed it all down and they feel it's perfect.
>
> But I basically got with the whole idea. I loved the fact that I'd written it. I started telling people how to write. I got these theories about how you dash it off, then you go back and . . .

you create it. Looking back, should have waited till it was a success before I started telling them all.

A feature film has got to have some dynamics, some strength and depth. We didn't really get round to that, and about halfway I started to realise what I'd written. I'd written *me*, totally as me, which was a mistake. It would have been better if I'd been playing someone else.

Halfway through I started to think, Oh God. But we were stuck with it. We'll have to see it out. But it's one of those things, you can't win 'em all.

I'm not discouraged now, because there's been enough time. There's a couple of redeeming features about it, but it's just not very good. What can you say? I mean, George did *Shanghai Surprise*. You've just got to own up when it's a bit of a bummer.

Where *Yellow Submarine* was outsourced to a talented team of artists, and proved itself worthy of the Beatle brand, the *Mystery Tour* and *Broad Street* projects were stubbornly home-brewed. It's often been levelled at McCartney that he works uneasily with outside help. Given his stature and experience, it takes a brave colleague to push an opposing idea. Musically, no producer since George Martin has held a position of sufficient trust and authority to override him in the studio.

Yet he'll insist he *can* take advice, to good effect. Al Coury was an executive at Capitol, Paul's American label in the 1970s, and made a couple of successful interventions in *Band on the Run*. Despite Paul's misgivings he put the storming single 'Helen Wheels' on the album's US version. He then made a case for two more tracks – 'Jet' and 'Band on the Run' itself – which Paul, surprisingly, did not see as singles material.

'It's always good to have an independent pair of ears

listening to your music,' McCartney now says. 'They can tell you what you've done, whereas you don't always see it. So that was the case. We'd done *Band on the Run* and I said, "Well there it is, I've made an album, you put it out, thank you, end of story."'

> But Al rang and said, 'Hey Paul, I can really make this a more successful album, if you want.' I said, 'Well, of course I want. What would you do?' 'You've got to put "Jet" out as a single.' Then, of course, it was blindingly obvious.
>
> He said, 'If you let me do that then I'd love to follow up with "Band on the Run".' Certainly they *were* obvious choices for singles. So it was great and he was spot-on. I always gave him credit for that.

Nobody, though, could talk Paul into putting 'Mull of Kintyre' on the 1978 LP *London Town*. 'It sometimes happens,' he agrees. 'It didn't seem like it belonged. It was a massive hit and had it been there it would definitely have been a more successful album. There's a wilfulness to those decisions that I quite like. It's kind of nice and anti-commercial.'

Talking in 1989 about his solo years, Paul maintained that 'there's something in all those albums, even if they're my worst ones, like *Back to the Egg*. There's still stuff. I know I did them intending for them to be the greatest things I ever did.' Only McCartney's more rabid fans saw much merit in what turned out to be the final Wings album. But it's an example of how his relative failures may acquire cult status.

After its commercial setback he has come around to *Back to the Egg*. By 1993 he was weaving one of its most oddball numbers, 'The Broadcast', into his ambient work as The Fireman, *Strawberries Oceans Ships Forest*: 'You talk to some young people and they are not wanting to make the charts. It's really cool if you don't, it's got all the cred in the world. It's very alien to my way of thinking. *Are you sure about that?* But there is a lot of that in the underground scene, the club scene: "Kiss of death to get in the charts, that's the establishment."

'So in a way it's cool to have a few albums that didn't make it. Now it's almost like my underground stuff. 'The Broadcast' is quite mix-y. A strange little piece. I'm glad I did that. I didn't *mean* it to be underground and not making the charts, but it's nice to have that.'

Had he released it with the Beatles, 'Waterfalls' would probably sit today among the immortal McCartney ballads. It's a strange and poignant song from 1980, full of that young parental love that can only express itself as tender anxiety. In the event it was somewhat muted by the electronic moods of the album it came with, *McCartney II*. 'A nice song,' he reflects, 'but I could have done more with it. That was me in my laboratory, it was the year of the synth.'

> In the early days you were intrigued by the synth string sounds, you thought they were good. You were later to discover that they weren't. At the time I thought, this is enough, it doesn't need any more. Looking back, it probably would have been a bigger song if it'd had a better production.
>
> I know George Martin would have persuaded me to do a proper orchestra and the backing vocal would have been the Beatles, instead of just me. Or conversely, John would have persuaded me *not* to put strings on and it would have been a tough little song. But that's life, it's what happens.

Sometimes reviewers are kinder than the general public. A later album, 1989's *Flowers in the Dirt*, was widely commended in the press. The presence of Elvis Costello probably helped, as did the general absence of whimsy and overt sentiment. And in its making Paul recruited a strong live band. But the sales were not outstanding. 'It might have done better,' he told me a year later:

> But if I hadn't so much to live up to, I would have said it did brilliant. It's three and a half million or something? For most people that would be a pretty big seller. I dunno, there was a lot of *approval*. The consensus seems to be it was a good album. But we took it to America and they decided it was 'multi-format'. I said, 'Excuse me? What d'you mean?'
>
> 'Well, you've got "My Brave Face" which is kind of MTV/AM, then you've got "That Day is Done", which is heavy-folk-ballad.' In America everything's pigeonholed: you've got to be an Adult Contemporary, which I hate. A contemporary adult? Can you think of anything worse? But then you have 'rock'. And 'heavy metal rock' and 'rap'. You're supposed to fit into one of those categories. "That Day is Done" is a slow waltz, with kind of Irish funereal lyrics. You know *that* doesn't go in any category.
>
> But it was OK, we decided to go on tour. I thought, it's out there, it's our latest album. I'll just keep saying every night, 'And this is from our latest album.' You never know, somebody might go, 'Oh, I'll buy that.' Overall, I'm a bit disappointed, but it certainly didn't put me off my food.
>
> You know, c'mon guys, how disappointed can you be with three and a half million sales? Would *you* be disappointed? I don't think so, when you figure out how much you earn off it. That's a lot of people. But I wouldn't have minded if it had done better, put it that way. Nobody minds a screaming runaway hit.

So he's philosophical. Even songs he was almost inclined to disown, like 'Bip Bop' off Wings' *Wild Life*, might find unexpected admirers:

> I heard it on the radio somewhere and thought, Oh dear me. I happened to mention it to Trevor Horn, and he said, 'Oh I

love that one!' So it's horses for courses. You can't please everyone. There are some people who like the sillier side of what I do, the stop-making-sense side. And there are people who won't accept that.

Like the people who hated 'Within You Without You', on *Pepper*. 'Oh, I don't like that! Is that George? Oh dear, he's all Indian, sounds like a bunch of Indians to me.' So you'd go, 'Well it is, you see. He's into Indian music, it's interesting, it's all on one chord . . .' I like that he dared to develop himself. But you've got to take the critical knocks if you dare to do that.

Like 'Hey Jude'. They're gonna say, 'It's rubbish, seven minutes, just going "Na na na nana-na naa" at the end. It's *obviously* rubbish.' And you go, 'No, it's pretty good. It's long, I'll grant you, but it's kind of interesting.'

I look back on some of the things and think, how did we dare to do that? And some of *this* period [the post-Beatle years], there's a lot of daring stuff. There's a bit of rubbish, too, I'm not saying everything I've done is great. My dad would say, if a girl was revealing a bit too much, 'That'll be a lovely dress when it's finished.' And it's like that with me, 'It'll be a nice song when it's finished.' Some of them are like that, I must admit.

What do you think went wrong in those cases?

What went wrong? I don't know. Stuff that goes wrong. When *you* write a bum article, you don't mean to go wrong. You're always trying to go right. But, you know, Sebastian Coe suddenly couldn't win races. 'What went wrong, Seb?' You tell me. Every dog has his day. I think that's all it is. Whaddya gonna do? Keep justifying yourself? Probably . . .

Just one person can be the saving grace for me. Wings' *Wild Life* wasn't very successful, but we were going down Sunset Strip one day and in one of these trailers, there's this hippy with a *big* beard, and he holds up that album: 'Yeah Paul! All right man!' And really that's your reward. You get the money and stuff, but your *artistic* reward tends to be that one guy who holds it out the window.

It only remains, now, to talk about Paul's longest-serving band member. Her name was Linda.

CHAPTER 29

Linda

One sweet dream came true today

In a world where celebrity relationships seem predestined to brevity, Paul and Linda's romance was an enduring phenomenon. They were married for almost thirty years, had three children together and raised a fourth, her daughter from a previous marriage. In all that time the family were practically inseparable.

Nobody is pretending that Paul and Linda never argued, but by any standards, theirs was a happy marriage. Linda was also her husband's musical partner. Whether as a muse and inspiration, as a co-writer, vocalist or musician, she played a role in his art that is overlooked by commentators. Yet her impact on Paul's life and work was huge.

And it can be traced from the last days of the Beatles. Paul and Linda first met in the early summer of 1967, at the Bag O'Nails nightclub in Soho, just before the launch of *Sgt. Pepper.* It was another year before they really came together as a couple, and their marriage took place a year after that – in London, on 12 March 1969.

Of the many songs Paul wrote about his wife, among the most explicit is 'Magic', which appeared on *Driving Rain*, not long after her death in 1998.

'Very literal,' smiles Paul. 'That's about the night I met her.' In the song he seems to cast their first encounter as a Dante and Beatrice moment – 'There must have been magic' – when a secret electrical understanding passes between two people that will resonate forever:

> I used to say to the kids . . . If I hadn't stood up when she was leaving, sort of said [*with nervous cough*] 'Hello' – cos I never did that, trying to pull birds, I never really did that – I just stood up and said, 'Hi, I'm Paul, what's your name? Er, d'you want to come to another club?' And fortunately for me she said, 'Yeah, OK'. We went on to the Speakeasy, from the Bag O'Nails.
>
> I always told my kids: 'If I hadn't got up and said that, I wonder what would have happened? *You* wouldn't be here, probably.' She may have just disappeared into the night. It was one of those pivotal moments. 'If I hadn't done that . . .' Like if you hadn't met that guy on the corner by the pub you wouldn't have started *MOJO*. Or whatever. There's always those little amazing moments. If I hadn't got the bus with George, he might never have been in the Beatles. If I hadn't known Ivan Vaughan and he hadn't taken me to Woolton Village Fête, I wouldn't have met John. All these things.

The *McCartney* album of 1970 was the first of Paul's records to be rooted in their relationship. As well as Linda's sleeve photos, and her wispy harmonies on 'Teddy Boy' and 'Kreen-Akrore', she's the evident subject of several songs – 'The Lovely Linda', of course, and doubtless 'Momma Miss America', but also, implicitly, 'Maybe I'm Amazed', 'Every Night' and 'Man We Was Lonely'.

Even earlier, it's likely that Linda's spirit informed Paul's last masterpiece for the Beatles, 'You Never Give Me Your Money'. The song's three sections paint an emotional triptych – from the painful stasis of Apple's legal dispute, back to some youthful reminiscence of fugitive escape, through to a rapturous fulfilment: 'One sweet dream came true today.'

In that song – like 'Band on the Run' a few years after, which was a similar suite of perfect pop moments – Paul's optimistic spirit discovers the key to liberation. As in *Let It Be*'s 'Two of Us', the literal catalyst was Linda's simple strategy of driving with her lover into the countryside, far away from city stress and its grim handmaiden, the 'business meeting'.

Shortly after, on *Ram*, Paul was still hymning his infatuation, 'Long Haired Lady' and 'The Back Seat of My Car' being two examples. As for 'Dear Boy', in which Paul seems to mock a man who has carelessly let a prized lover slip from his hands, the song was heard as a dig at John Lennon. But Paul explains it was about Linda's previous husband, Joseph Melville See. 'I never told him that, which was lucky, because he's since committed suicide. "Dear Boy" was a comment: "Guess you never knew what you have missed." Cos I did think, Gosh, she's so amazing and I suppose he didn't get it.'

Many of Paul's subsequent songs took life with Linda as his starting point. Probably the best-known was 'My Love', off 1973's *Red Rose Speedway*. Less celebrated instances are 'It's Not True', off the *Press to Play* CD in 1993, which sounds sweetly loyal; and 'I Owe it All to You' from 1993's *Off the Ground*, which is touchingly direct. And when we turn to his collection of poetry, *Blackbird Singing*, we find the nature-worshipping 'City Park' (written during her final illness), 'Her Spirit' and 'Black Jacket', where Paul looks deep into his grief – and detects the first stirrings of hope for tomorrow.

Linda slipped into the Beatles' circle with rather more ease than Yoko had. But the McCartneys' marriage was a bitter pill for some of Paul's more besotted fans to swallow. Even among the wider British public she was, at first, an object of suspicion. Rather like Edward VIII and Mrs Simpson before them, here was the nation's most eligible bachelor, supposedly snared by a scheming American gold-digger. The idea was founded on nothing more than envy and perhaps some wounded national pride, but it gained traction a few years later, when Linda popped up on public stages with her husband, and even achieved co-billing on his songwriting credits.

Not content with bagging a national treasure – the same supposition ran – she now insisted on sharing the artistic limelight.

While such hostility faded in time, and the sincerity of their attachment was gradually accepted, it was never understood how reluctant Linda was to perform with Paul. Nor was it widely known how great an emotional toll the sniping took on them.

Discussing Linda in 1989, while she rehearsed with his new band in the next room, Paul expressed resentment of his biographers:

> They just dismiss Linda. Everyone dismisses Linda. Which is interesting, cos she's not that dismissable. She's a very talented girl. She's a good photographer, for one. Everyone dismisses her singing: 'Oh, she's out of tune, isn't she?' In actual fact, because of that, I had a period when I started listening to them: 'Well, maybe they're right? I know she's not the world's greatest singer, she's not a front singer.' But I'd always liked it when we sang together, we always seemed to blend – it's the missus.
>
> On 'Let It Be' there was a very high note I couldn't get. So Linda and I went in late at night to Abbey Road and I said, 'Can *you* sing that high note?' And though she wasn't a pro she *could* hit that note. So she's the high note on the 'Let It Be' Beatles recording.

Before the formation of Wings, in which she played and sang for its whole existence, she'd accompanied Paul to New York for the making of *Ram*.

God, I tell you, I worked her on that album. She hadn't done an awful lot, so it was a little out of tune. I was not too pleasant to live with, I suppose. She was all right, she took it. She understood that it had to be good and you couldn't let any shit through. I gave her a hard time, I must say. But we were pleased with the results.

It meant we really forced it, worked on all the harmonies, even if they were hard. Just stuck at it. Elton John said it was the best harmonies he'd heard in a long while.

So it paid off for us. It was very much the two of us against the world at that point. We had two kids. We were going around booking our own hotels. It wasn't like Apple or the Beatles where everything was done for you. It was just us on a groove.

At the time, we were totally paranoid. With Wings, I had Linda in the band, that people were slagging me off for. I knew that she wasn't a great professional musician, but there was something there, some sort of innocence. She brought something to the band, and she brought companionship for me, which was important at that time. So there were two very strong reasons.

There's some good harmonies on there, but they said she was no good. So I started to use more session people, very well-respected people that the top people use. And I just didn't like it. I didn't get off on it. It sounded like session singers. So I've come back to Linda. I think there's some interesting things to be discovered about that period.

When I worked with Michael Jackson, he said, 'How'd you do those harmonies, man?' I said, 'Well, it's me and Linda.' 'Can we ask Linda to . . .?' So she sang harmonies on those sessions too. And he was right, there was a quality that first started in the harmonies of the Beatles' 'Let It Be'.

A few years after she died, Paul revisited those early years to compile *Wingspan: Hits and History*, a CD anthology with a TV documentary:

It's good to see the Wings story. Particularly as it also vindicates Lin. With all the slagging off she got during it, that tended to stick, even with us. We sort of remembered, 'Oh, they caught me being out of tune, that famous tape at Knebworth.'

[This was a widely circulated bootleg of Linda at the 1990 Knebworth rock festival, singing some off-key backup on 'Hey Jude'.]

The truth, the trouble was, she was doing this [*he stands, claps hands above his head*]. She was doing, 'C'mon', being the big cheerleader, 'Hey Jude, naah-naah-na.' You don't see the visual, you just hear this out-of-tune voice, and I know she always wanted the record put straight. And this [the documentary] does. You see her playing. You hear her singing beautifully. And you see what she was to the group. You see why she had to be in the group. She becomes the ballsiest member of it.

In Liverpool in late 1979, Wings began what turned out to be their final tour. I was sent along by the *NME* to cover the concert, attend Paul's press conference and conduct one of Linda's rare solo interviews with the dreaded British rock press.

'She's not the kind of person people think she is at all,' Paul said to me a few years later. 'Her image is very different from how she is. Quite a ballsy person, really. She comes off a bit stiff in interviews because she gets nervous.'

She certainly seemed uneasy on this occasion; leaving aside the *NME*'s intimidating reputation, it was only an hour before the opening gig of a new tour, and for Paul, a homecoming show to boot. Linda's American accent was softened by a gentle Liverpool lilt, learned in the course of ten years' companionship. But when she grew tense her voice acquired a hard New York edge.

To begin, I asked her how the latest line-up of Wings compared with earlier versions:

> It's changed a lot from the beginning to now. It's totally different to play in a band where everyone seems to *like* each other, and this is the first one. I'm more confident nowadays . . . I don't sing quite as out of tune. [*She laughs, drily.*]

You used to come in for some stick, didn't you?

> I still do.

Was that a surprise?

> Yes. I didn't realise. Because I led a pretty free spirit kind of life. It was just me and my cameras, and I wasn't noticed to be criticised. I'd have a loon with people. Getting criticised is like being back at school. But I'm nervous on and off through life. Don't *you* get nervous? I'm not a natural talent, so obviously I'm gonna get nervous.

So why did you join the group?

> I loved music, I was a rock-and-roll kid, though I never sang or played keyboards or anything. It was Paul. We were up in Scotland after the Beatles had split and he had nobody to play with, friendship-wise. So he said, 'Let's get a group together.' I said, 'Yeah.' Cos I'm always jumping in the deep end.

How did the criticism affect you?

> I suppose subconsciously it affected me a lot. It probably made me sing *more* out of tune, because everyone was saying I was out of tune. It made me more nervous about what I was doing. [*The NYC voice comes in.*] I always want to get the people who

said it, go kick them in the teeth. I never *met* any of them, y'know? That was the biggest joke. They were all telling people what I'm like and I never even met them. So obviously I got a bit vicious.

So why carry on?

It was wanting to be with Paul that kept me in it. It's not the sort of thing I'd normally do, because it's not where my talents really lie. Not that I have any talents anyway . . . [*She paused, and looked at me in a challenging way.*] There's a lot I'd like to say to *NME*.

Please go ahead.

But I can never think of it at the time.

That's a shame.

I don't think it's as serious as all the word people say it is. It's all a bit phoney, even talking to you. I could tell you my philosophies, but what do I matter? I believe in not killing people, if you're interested in that. We have a lot of sheep and we don't kill any of them and we don't cut their balls off either – so we got a lot of sheep. We don't need to kill them for money, so we don't. To me, taking money for a dead body, I wouldn't get off on that. I'm total vegetarian, no fish, no friendly little chickens. The earth is very important to me – earth things, roots – much more than concrete and space age and all that. For me personally, all that 'progress', that's regress really.

I turn the interview back to Wings. Although unaware that this would be their final tour, she already betrays a sense that Paul is better off without a fixed band:

I don't think we've gotten our potential on record yet. Maybe 'C Moon' or 'Band on the Run', where Paul played drums and things, and could get what he wanted. This group is the closest we've gotten so far and it'll grow, musically. The trick is to get a few laughs out of it. But if everybody's saying you're rubbish, you don't laugh.

Paul's a funky musician, and he can get that feeling over when he doesn't have to get hung up, telling everybody what to play. The Beatles were four funky people who loved rock and roll and playing together. When you have something like that, and it breaks up, it takes time to get it back again.

People are always digging, digging away. It's like being at school, when the teacher tells you you're no good. Half of you wants to please the teacher, cos we have a totally false society; achievement and competition to win is what everybody pats you on the back for. Which is totally rubbish.

How did you react to punk rock, a couple of years ago?

I liked a lot of the music. I thought the attitude was a bit 'posey'. What is anarchy when you think about it? I mean, it sounds good, but it would be quite a world if we had it, wouldn't it? When you get down to it, we've all got hearts. We all want the world to be right.

If I had one correct instinct that evening, it was that she wished she wasn't on the road, let alone doing a promotional interview with the *NME*.

Are you happy to be touring again?

I'd like to just play Britain on and off for the rest of my career. I don't like the travelling. So it's a bit selfish. But there's so many places in Britain to play, I don't really think you need to do the big American tour or the Far East tour. We'll probably do it, but I'd like just to do it here and not on a huge level. If there's a gig in Sheffield, just go and do that one. If there's something in Glasgow, go play that one a month later.

We've had a lot of pressure on us and music isn't like you'd like it to be when there's pressure. It's gonna get better. I was pleased with the last album [*Back to the Egg*] but I would have liked to be a bit less 'trying'. I don't think we're trying to please as much now. We were a new group and we'd never played together.

Do you miss America?

I really like Britain a lot. I don't miss America at all – maybe the pizzas, but that's about it.

In the event, Wings were doomed; but Linda's 1979 dream of limited live dates was equally destined for disappointment. She would live to travel the world in her husband's band a few times more. I asked *him* about this in 1990, amid two more of those global jaunts.

Linda will go out on tour, but she's more of a homebody than I am. She can sit around all day and be happy. I'm a bit fidgety. A lot of fellas are like that. I don't mean to be sexist, but I think women can just sort of dig it, enjoy being happy, whereas a guy's got to go and put a fence up or chop a tree down.

So Linda, before the tour, I had to say to her, 'Look, y'know, we're really either going right through this tour or we're not. If you don't want to do it, let's just call it off.' And she said, 'No, I want to do it.' I said, 'OK, you're really gonna have to commit. We're going on tour, it'll be a long time. We'll make the best of it, and try and make it into a holiday.'

As Paul defended Linda, so she fought his corner also. In my 1979 interview she hit back at accusations of his 'schmaltzy' inclinations. Her New York self was now in the driving seat:

> He likes so many kinds of music that he does a bit of everything. He's not schmaltzy, let me tell you. Have you ever heard him play? He's such a good musician. Even his 'nice' music, it's good. He doesn't take it as seriously as everyone else does, meaning journalists. He's a really good guitar player, a really heavy drummer. Like Jimi Hendrix was a great musician, Paul is a great musician. So to make fun of him because he writes schmaltz, it really doesn't matter, does it? In fact, I don't think he's schmaltzy at all.
>
> I mean, 'Yesterday', you can say that's schmaltzy, but it's a nice piece of music. You could say '[All I Have to Do Is] Dream' by the Everly Brothers was schmaltzy, but it gets *me* every time.
>
> But I mean, what else are you going to say about Paul? That he's cute? Or . . . It's all bullshit. It's *really* bullshit. But then there's a lot of bullshit in the world, if you'll excuse me.

After the show, that evening in Liverpool, she was much more relaxed. I spent many hours with her in the years ahead, normally while waiting for a break in Paul's rehearsals. Watching them together, the couple looked calmly affectionate; they'd stroll across those gigantic studio hangars, hand in hand.

Linda's American way of greeting people, with a hug, was at first quite alien to me. Paul would look on and laugh, explaining to her that it wasn't what Liverpool men were raised to do.

Still, this Venus and Mars were less intense than, say, the Ono-Lennons. 'It's what went on in the Sixties,' Paul told me. 'You thought, if I'm gonna go with this person for the rest of my life, like John and Yoko or me and Linda, I really ought to look them in the eye all the time. John and Yoko did spend a lot of time [*unblinking, close-up eye contact*] and it got fairly mad. After a couple of hours you get worn out: Dear me, can't we have some *fun* around here?'

Linda never professed great musical talent, but her love of pop music ran deep: 'I was a typical high school rock-and-roll freak,' she told me. 'I was there with the radio in the Fifties. You know Alan Freed? I heard his first show. He played all the good stuff, Moonglows and the Dells, Penguins' "Earth Angel". I love R&B, really love it.'

Her own musical legacy, leaving aside the part she played in Paul's catalogue, was collected up in a posthumous CD, *Wide Prairie*. Paul is ever-present on the record, whether as co-writer, producer or performer. But the dominant voice – and personality – is unambiguously Linda's. 'Seaside Woman', a jolly reggae effort she wrote for the 1973 line-up of Wings, shows how pleasing her voice could be in the right setting, when the mood is light and the pressure is off.

Elsewhere she delves into her teenage record collection with covers of 'Poison Ivy', 'Mister Sandman' and 'Sugartime' – the latter made with reggae's great maverick Lee Perry at his studio in Jamaica. There are homages to her beloved Arizona, and the horses she delighted in riding there, and expressions of her animal activism. There are two fine ballads, 'Love's Full Glory' and 'Endless Days', and Paul's 1976 composition 'Cook of the House', which Wings had included on their *Speed of Sound* album.

The sixteen tracks on *Wide Prairie* were gathered from sessions right up to the closing months of her life. Overall they present a woman with enormous heart, shrewd good humour, flashes of anger, and a strongly defined outlook on life that celebrated love, family and nature.

Linda McCartney left other memorials too. It's in the photography that her openness to life was most evident. The camera was her constant companion. She'd amassed an impressive body of work even before she became Mrs McCartney, and once their lives were joined together she documented each step of the way. Since her death her marvellous archive has been curated by the couple's first daughter together, Mary McCartney – owner of that tiny face to be seen snuggling in Dad's jacket on the cover of his debut solo album.

Linda was, in addition, one of the world's most famous vegetarians. In the hours of downtime that I passed in her company it was her favourite topic of conversation and she was nothing if not persuasive. Passionate rather than strident, she talked me into trying the meat-free life and presented my family with a copy of her *Home Cooking* book, on which she scrawled 'Go veggie'. I made a diligent effort and have certainly modified my diet under her influence, but she was delighted to learn she made a complete convert of my wife.

After she passed away, in Tucson, Arizona on 17 April 1998, there were many reappraisals of this remarkable and often misunderstood woman. Paul himself has lent force to the process in retrospective exercises like his DVD collection *The McCartney Years*, which was not always an easy experience for him:

> There is that feeling of drowning, just seeing all these images from your life flashing by. And some of it is very emotional, obviously, seeing Linda in a lot of the work. In a way it's lovely, very happy memories, but the fact she's no longer here is very sad.
>
> That was always going to happen if we put together a collection of videos. She was in them and I knew that would be one of the factors I would have to deal with. The emotional side. But it actually was kind of pleasant, like going through old snapshots. It's sad but it's great, because you're thinking, we *did* this.

Linda made a rare attempt to defend herself in a song to be found on *Wide Prairie*. A beguiling kind of punk-hippy hybrid, 'The Light Comes from Within' was recorded just four weeks before the end of her life. Her son James can be heard playing guitar. And Paul, in his sleeve note to the track, wrote these words:

'It was her answer to all the people who had ever put her down and that whole dumb male chauvinist attitude that to her had caused so much harm in our society. God bless her . . . my little baby literally had the last word.'

CHAPTER 30

Love

I don't think there's ever going to be a time when there's no one in love

McCartney acknowledged one of his perennial stereotypes with a 1976 single called 'Silly Love Songs'. As a mission statement it was both defensive and defiant. Love is the default subject of his songs. While it has made him a target for criticism and even mockery, romantic love is what he articulates best. And his professional regard for other masters of that craft is undiminished.

'Silly Love Songs' seemed to be a blast at those detractors (including John Lennon) who had pegged him as the Prince of Syrup. In 1976 it fell upon a sceptical music scene in London, where people like me were gathering behind tough new acts like Dr Feelgood and Eddie and the Hot Rods. We shared a mood of unsentimental impatience that would shortly erupt as punk rock.

Yet here was Paul, unabashed by a reputation for over-sugared romance. He was asking what was wrong with singing love songs. He declared that those songs – like love itself – were not so silly at all. The message of the record arrived inside the light and airy trappings of Seventies 'soft rock', a genre that Britain's hip young gunslingers were militating against.

It was a phase of Wings' sound that I only came to appreciate later, when it occurred to me that another song of that period, 'With a Little Luck', was up there with McCartney's greatest work, and that any sensible listener should find space in his heart for optimism and tenderness as well as fire and brimstone. Soon, even 'Silly Love Songs' would strike me as entirely reasonable. A few years after that, I met Paul and we discussed love songs. He really did believe in their moral value.

It was a topic we often talked about. I realised that, for Paul, 'Silly Love Songs' was a straight personal statement. We know the 'soppy' songs that pre-dated Elvis Presley were central to his musical education. As time went by his sensibilities broadened – became broader, I think, than those of any comparable songwriter. But he never repudiated that first instinct. 'Try love,' he suggests to aspirant songwriters who are stuck for a starting point.

In their early years as writers Paul and John liked the 'personal pronoun' love song. Every title had an 'I', or a 'you', a 'me' or a 'she', and the lyrics allowed young fans to project themselves on these scenarios of teen romance. You think you lost your love, last night I said these words to my girl, with love from me to you, love me do, you know I love you, this boy wants you back again.

The Beatles' personal pronoun songs of 1962–4, though world-beating in their success and still endlessly fresh, are easily dismissed as formulaic. The boy who wants to hold your hand can seem a mere cypher compared with later characters like 'Dr Robert', 'The Fool on the Hill', or the man who blew his mind out in a car.

Perhaps. But I remember as a child how I heard those simple stories and took them as important glimpses of the world I would eventually join. The older boys – teenagers! – with their girlfriends, promenading around Liverpool, going to dances, canoodling in bus shelters, arguing, falling in and out of love. Before I had the faintest conception of what a real relationship might comprise, I had memorised the words to 'And I Love Her' or 'Things We Said Today', and wondered if all this was in store for me.

You could say those songs were lyrically unambitious, for all they fizzed with musical inventiveness. And the group moved rapidly on to new and hypnotically complex ideas, redefining forever the possibilities of pop's subject matter. But all those personal pronouns were rooted in something real and true. The early songs might not depict specific incidents or people. But they arose from the actual life experiences of the writers and their friends and the young people who watched them from the dance-hall floor.

They are not the stuff of Jacobean drama. But in these simple songs are all the hopes and fears of first love, the pain of rejection, the speculations of lust, the niggles of jealousy, gossip and insecurity, and – this being the Beatles, after all – an overwhelming *joy*, the belief that magic happens. They ride on that remarkable tide that flows in those days of our lives, when even naïve entanglements are of stupendous significance.

So, I've never discounted songs like 'P.S. I Love You' or 'Thank You Girl' or 'All My Loving'. They were in my head when I looked from the school bus and watched the big kids, with clothes and hairstyles they could choose for themselves, and I tried to imagine what their lives were like. For me, those silly love songs have a powerful reality that I will never get from enigmatic numbers such as 'Fixing a Hole' or 'Lucy in the Sky with Diamonds' . . . much as I love them also.

Think of 'I Saw Her Standing There', the first track of the Beatles' first LP. After that urgent count-in – 1-2-3-4*!* – it describes the object of Paul's desire. She is 'just seventeen'. His favourite novelist Charles Dickens would have understood; Dickens populated his novels with feminine ingénues of seventeen, probably because of his beloved sister-in-law's death at that age. For Paul, it was no more than a matter of lyrical metre and an appreciation of his core audience in 1963. But we can see how his understanding of love would deepen with every year that passed, from teenage kicks to young marrieds, to fuller maturity and eventually – inevitably – to the quiet ache of bereavement.

Talking to Paul in 1989, after receiving my promo copy of his new album *Flowers in the Dirt*, I mentioned that a track called 'We Got Married' was the one that had grabbed me the quickest.

I said that it probably helped that I was married.

'I think it does,' he replied. 'Our drummer didn't like it. It nearly didn't get on the album, we had to overrule him. He's not married, you see. And he's, "I don't really like it, you know?" *What?* Come on man, it says something, this one! And we had to persuade him. But I think it does help if you're married. It's a subject you normally shy away from.'

It seems to me the basic sentiment of 'We Got Married' is nice – we're together and it's great. But the song itself is not very sweet, it's really quite tense:

> I don't think marriage *is* sweet. That's why I did it. I'd taken this idea of celebrating marriage, because I don't want to shy away from it. I think millions of people are well into it, and I think it's something, if you're lucky, to be celebrated. But there's also this slightly cynical edge, because it isn't all that sweet.
>
> To me it's very much what happened in the Sixties when we were all in Liverpool. The first verse is very John and Cyn [Cynthia Lennon, his first wife]: 'Going fast, coming soon, we made love in the afternoon.' Cos they were art students, and it was the first time I'd heard of anyone making love in the

afternoon. What was I, sixteen or something? '*What?* In the *afternoon*? Great! It's like a French film, isn't it?' I was fairly naïve.

As a teenager in Liverpool, I'd been to art school parties in the very flat that Brian Epstein had loaned to the newlywed Lennons a decade earlier. 'We Got Married' has continued to chime for me.

In 2001 and again in 2005, I asked Paul to choose love songs he had admired by other artists. 'Oh shit,' he said. This was the very territory that traditionally lost him cool *kudos*. 'The game is up.'

The King and I. Damned good record, man. Yul Brynner. Rodgers and Hammerstein, their writing is great. I mean, talk about men and women's relationships. [*He sings a few lines from* 'Something Wonderful'.] I go for that.

I've always loved 'Stardust', it was one of my all-time favourites, by Hoagy Carmichael. A great melody.

A song that's become one of my particular favourites is 'The Very Thought of You', which interestingly was written by Ray Noble, a British guy. It's not often that you get these classics that Sinatra and Nat King Cole and Tony Bennett would sing as part of their regular repertoire, written by a British guy. So, well done *our* team.

I love 'When I Fall in Love', particularly Nat King Cole's version, which I remember as a kid. Though I always liked Nat King Cole, I never really listened to a lot of Sinatra, and now I have, and see what people were on about. It's nice to have come to him later, actually. There's a lot of stuff he sings that I like. [*He offers a section of* 'A Lovely Way to Spend an Evening'.] When you've got the candles going, and you're having dinner with your bird, a glass of wine, there's no finer record.

What else? 'The Way You Look Tonight' . . . *Are the stars out tonight?* No! that's not 'The Way You Look Tonight', that's 'I Only Have Eyes for You.'

Well, that's a great song as well . . .

Yeah, that's another good one. I love 'Julia', of John's, that's a particularly beautiful song and that's very special to me because I knew John's mum Julia, and I knew how fond of her he was, and the tragic circumstances in which she died. So years later, when John recorded that, it was very special. I love his finger-picking style that he used, a very gentle song and obviously very meaningful to John. And me, too, cos she was a great lady. And also just a real good tune.

Do songwriters, specifically you, like writing love songs because they're about love? Or is it just because love songs are what go over with people? Everybody loves a love song.

There's a kind of timelessness, because people are always falling in love. There's people now who aren't even dreaming of it, who tomorrow will be in love, and there's people in school who in five years' time might be in love. There's people now whose hearts are broken, who might find love. So they're very useful things on a practical level, love songs.

But more importantly, they touch you. All the corny old phrases, 'they pull at your heartstrings'. That's what I was getting at with 'Silly Love Songs'. It was daring to allow those emotions, cos I think from time to time it's a bit unfashionable to be soppy: 'Aw, come off it.' Sometimes you've got to be positive.

I remember Bruce Springsteen coming up to me at one of those Rock and Roll Hall of Fame awards and saying, 'Hey man, you know that song of yours, "Silly Love Songs"? When it came out I thought it was a bit soppy,' or whatever the word he used was. He said, 'I didn't get it, but I really get it now, man.' And it's something that happens. He's fallen in love, he's had kids, and he's more able to accept that thought, which bothered a lot of people at the time.

So that basically sums it up to me, love songs are eternal. I don't think there's ever going to be a time when there's no one in love. I certainly hope not.

Finale

Fifty Favourites

They say you should never meet your heroes. But I must have been quite fortunate. The Liverpool footballers we harassed for autographs in the 1960s were perfect gents. Later I interviewed David Bowie, Dusty Springfield, Ray Davies, Smokey Robinson, Bruce Springsteen, and many others I'd hugely admired. They were all fine, for which I'm grateful, because there were some exceptions (whom I shan't name), and I could never enjoy their music as much again.

It's the ones you idolised in childhood that mean the most, so I'm especially relieved that Paul McCartney turned out to be good company. Ringo Starr was a treat, too. In 1963 the Beatles' first hits were playground chants at my school. Their mysterious mid-period masterpieces were exactly what a solemn adolescent was looking for. And then the moral complexities of those troubled last albums had the tang of impending adulthood.

I never expected I'd come close to their actual earthly selves, but the post-Beatle Liverpool I grew up in was full of odd connections, such as the parish priest who thought he was mentioned in 'Eleanor Rigby', the mother and child that people whispered were on Brian Epstein's payroll ('to avoid the *scandal*, like, yer know wharrimean?'), the man who said he'd got his broken nose in a fight with John Lennon, the nutter on the last bus home who claimed he'd written 'She Loves You' and given it to them in a pub for ten bob.

Then I started knocking around with a beautiful Irish girl who lived near the Liverpool docks. She was just seventeen. Her family sort of knew the big McCartney clan and that's how she ended up at a Christmas party, on the night she turned eighteen, where Paul McCartney sang 'Happy Birthday' just for her. When she told me this the next day, I thought it was the coolest thing I had ever heard of. (*Reader, I married her.*)

During his solo years I admit my attention wavered occasionally, but in the last few years I've come to love nearly everything he has recorded. Matters reached a point where I would seek out everything I'd once disliked. In reassessing my own most sceptical responses, I took perverse delight in welcoming new favourites. But the human mind is like fine underwear; all the better for being changed occasionally.

Let me sign off with a personal choice of Paul McCartney tracks that have kept me company while I was writing this book. The list is not a league table, and is alphabetical rather than chronological. I've left out Lennon and McCartney songs that seem to have had an equal or majority input from John. And I've confined myself to tracks that are easily available. But I have also mixed the well-known songs, a few of them by no means fashionable, with some relative obscurities. It's in discovering the latter that much of the pleasure lies.

I know that my own favourites tend to change all the while. But will any generation to come be unmoved by 'Things We Said Today' or 'My Love'? And those McCartney creations are by no means untypical. They were only two of the great songs that fell into our hands like a cascade of golden apples:

AND I LOVE HER (1964)

A Hard Day's Night number of subtle simplicity, laced together by that indestructible eight-note riff. The first time I heard it, I thought it must have existed since time began.

ANOTHER GIRL (1965)

It's the Beatles at their sunniest and least assuming, but listen out for Paul's country-and-western guitar, playing over chord changes that delight the heart and mind.

ARROW THROUGH ME (1979)

I'd forgotten this jazzy *Back to the Egg* song until I randomly rediscovered it through YouTube. Now it's lodged in my head forever.

THE BACK SEAT OF MY CAR (1971)

A widescreen road movie of a song, starring Linda and Paul as defiant teenage runaways. And the big, bad parent figures they were escaping? Probably the Beatles.

BLACKBIRD (1968)

The musical inspiration, says Paul, came from Bach; the guitar style came from Donovan, who stayed with the Beatles in Rishikesh ('Donovan learned it, I think, off Gypsy Dave'). The underlying sentiment is pure McCartney: hope of deliverance.

CAN'T BUY ME LOVE (1964)

In the film of *A Hard Day's Night* it marks a moment of pure release, when the four boys push through a fire escape to swap the claustrophobic corridors of fame for a mad romp across some sunlit suburban playing field.

CELEBRATION (1997)

'Love is the oldest secret of the universe.' Designed by Paul to be *Standing Stone*'s 'scarf-waving finale', it obeys the gravest showbiz rule of all: send 'em home happy.

DEAR FRIEND (1971)

Intended as an olive branch to Lennon in the depths of their estrangement. Didn't do the trick. Lovely all the same.

FOLLOW ME (2005)

Paul: 'I was thinking of 'Let It Be', and that was almost a religious anthem. I was getting a great vibe about many people; I could mention God, my parents, my best friends. They'd all be, "You lift up my spirits, you shine on my soul." All the people who really can do that thing, starting with God onwards.'

GET BACK (1969)

Its chugging, back-to-basics feel was emblematic of 1969 and the twilight of pop's imperial phase; constant novelty would now give way to recovery of roots.

GOLDEN SLUMBERS (1969)

McCartney is reckoned to have a tenor voice that dips into baritone without losing its shape. More interesting, here, is his dynamic range – from a murmuring start to that rasping roar. It becomes the loudest lullaby you ever heard.

GOODNIGHT PRINCESS (1984)

A Northern tea-dance pastiche that sweetly completes the album of *Give My Regards to Broad Street*. Rock and roll made McCartney a star but he would have been successful fifty years earlier.

GOT TO GET YOU INTO MY LIFE (1966)

The 'you' of the title is said to be pot – which, given Paul's remarks in Chapter Five, seems entirely likely.

HERE THERE AND EVERYWHERE (1966)

The Beatles' *Revolver* probably packs more McCartney classics into its track list than any other album. And this is his favourite.

HERE TODAY (1982)

Written not long after John's death in 1980, *Here Today* has really come into its own years later – as an emotional pivot of Paul's live shows.

HEY JUDE (1968)

It was the Beatles' most successful single, and their least eager to please. The length looked problematic, the pace is slow, the chorus repetitive and the lyric opaque. But it worked and Paul always knew it would.

HONEY HUSH (1999)

A vintage Big Joe Turner number covered on *Run Devil Run*. McCartney attacks it with all the excitement of somebody making his first record.

HOSANNA (2013)

Though it's from his 'mainstream' album *New*, there is a ragged-edged psychedelia here that could have come from a Fireman record.

HOUSE OF WAX (2007)

A darkly gothic drama, played in a sonic thunderstorm. Should McCartney publish a second volume of verse, these lyrics surely merit inclusion.

'HUMAN' THEME (1997)

'Maestoso', or majestic, is the musical instruction for this passage of *Standing Stone*. The London Symphony Chorus are wordless, wraith-like and, yes, extremely *maestoso*.

I SAW HER STANDING THERE (1963)

There had been a handful of great rock records made in Britain before the Beatles, but they were essentially imitations of an American art. Here, though, is the moment when authentically British rock and roll was born.

I'LL FOLLOW THE SUN (1964)

Short and sweet, for sure, but notice how naturally Lennon and McCartney share the lead vocal line, with occasional space for Paul to float away on his own melodious zephyr.

I WILL (1968)

There is a demo-like intimacy to Paul's vocal here, as if he's singing purely for himself. Apparently, though, such insouciance took sixty-seven takes to perfect.

JUNIOR'S FARM (1974)

Insofar as its lyrics mean anything, there is Paul's usual enthusiasm for getting out of town. Most of all, though, the guitar parts are a monument to Jimmy McCulloch's brief tenure in Wings.

LET 'EM IN (1976)

Door chimes introduce a trance-like litany that draws on memories of his family – 'Sister Susie' was his Auntie Milly, her husband was Uncle Albert – and characters whose whimsical diversity recalls the *Sgt. Pepper* sleeve.

LET ME ROLL IT (1973)

This distinctly Lennon-ish affair has always sounded like an affectionate reaching-out. Was it? Paul has remarked that it's actually about the construction of a spliff.

LIVE AND LET DIE (1973)

Commissioned to write and perform a James Bond movie theme, McCartney enjoyed the made-to-order songcraft it required. And, typically for this period of his music, he delivered about three songs in one.

LONDON TOWN (1976)

The tune, as always, speaks for itself. The question posed by these lyrics is not so much 'What do they mean?' as 'What was he on?' Handily, McCartney himself will explain it as surrealism.

THE LONG AND WINDING ROAD (1970)

'When I wrote "Long and Winding Road", I thought I was Ray Charles singing it,' Paul told me. 'I wasn't, patently I wasn't.' Maybe so, but his real regret was Phil Spector's additions, finally edited out in 2003.

LONG TALL SALLY (1964)
The very essence of rock and roll and maybe the nearest we'll get to the ecstatic magic of those sweaty cellar nights in Germany and Liverpool.

MAXWELL'S SILVER HAMMER (1969)
I was always inclined to skip this track until I watched Paul recite its lyric at a poetry reading. All of a sudden it sounded 100 per cent less jaunty.

MAYBE I'M AMAZED (1970)
The whole *McCartney* LP stands up well, after all these years, but this remains the towering achievement. Features one of the great McCartney lead guitar solos, too.

OB-LA-DI OB-LA-DA (1968)
It comes in for snobbish derision, but this is pop music that dares to be popular. It took Scottish band Marmalade to number 1 just after the White Album came out. What I hear is a sunny celebration of the new multiracial London. Demonic Lennon piano, too.

OLD SIAM, SIR (1979)
Although its cod-orientalism never really gets further east than Walthamstow, the song's sheer oddness is another case for the rehabilitation of *Back to the Egg*.

ON MY WAY TO WORK (2013)
Just as in Paul's middle section of 'A Day in the Life', we're taken back to those big green tins of cigarette smoke that served as Liverpool buses in the 1950s. 'How far away the future seemed.'

ONLY OUR HEARTS (2012)

Stevie Wonder adds his beautifully sad harmonica to one of the two new songs written for *Kisses on the Bottom*; the vocal is lower and slower than we're used to from Paul, but the effect is movingly personal.

P.S. I LOVE YOU (1963)

In hindsight, McCartney's melodic magic was evident as early as the Beatles' first B-side. Soon he would show the world there was plenty more where that came from.

ROCKY RACOON (1968)

Even Mozart made time for the odd 'musical joke' and we should cut Macca the same slack. The source here might be the cowboy ditties of Lancashire-born Robert W. Service: 'The Shooting of Dan McGrew' and so on were front-parlour favourites in old Liverpool homes.

SHE'S A WOMAN (1964)

Another counterweight to Paul's Beatle image as the polite balladeer, it's the sensuous swing of this song that carries it through. And, with all the insolence of their talent, they merely parked it on a B-side.

SHE'S LEAVING HOME (1967)

Rely on McCartney to write a song of the generation war and show such empathy with the 'enemy' side. From his youngest days he wrote with an awareness of travelling that age continuum himself.

SING THE CHANGES (2008)

For a song from his supposed 'side-project', The Fireman's *Electric Arguments*, this is one of the sturdiest stadium-pleasers he has ever penned.

SOMEDAYS (1997)
Paul invited George Martin to orchestrate this heartfelt song – perhaps he sensed that he'd written a track to rival his best Beatle work, but with the added maturity of his middle years.

SPIRAL (1999)
From *Working Classical*, and the most eerily beautiful of all his compositions in that genre.

THINGS WE SAID TODAY (1964)
McCartney can write lines that float outside of time, whether past or future ('Can you take back where I came from?'). And this, like 'When I'm 64', is one of the latter sort. He was twenty-two at the time.

THROUGH OUR LOVE (1983)
Pipes of Peace was not an outstanding album and this poignant track has rather fallen through the cracks of memory. Ripe for rediscovery.

TREAT HER GENTLY/LONELY OLD PEOPLE (1975)
Somewhere on the other side of London, punk rock was brewing. McCartney, meanwhile, was writing with simple tenderness of isolation and dementia in the old folks' home.

WARM AND BEAUTIFUL (1976)
Like a lot of his post-Beatle ballads, this one never acquired the 'standard' status it deserved. It's only right that 'Warm and Beautiful' was one of the catalogue songs that Paul found worthy of a second life on *Working Classical*.

WE ALL STAND TOGETHER (1984)
Maybe it's the faint echo of 'The Eton Boating Song' that riles, but the infamous 'Frog Song' has never warmed hipsters' hearts. I am perversely fond of it. It is a children's song, and contempt for childhood is an adolescent attitude, not an adult one.

WINEDARK OPEN SEA (1993)

The title sounds straight out of Homer. No classical scholars, however, have leapt to this track's defence. It's probably one of those love-or-loathe songs Paul comes up with occasionally.

YESTERDAY (1965)

Familiarity may dull the edge of any music, but the power of this song is refreshed whenever I see its effect on a McCartney audience. Paul was four days shy of his twenty-third birthday when he wrote his bleakly beautiful description of nostalgia's soulful ache. And I write this two days after he turned seventy-three, when he can still sing rock and roll like a juvenile delinquent. Nice one, la'.

Acknowledgements

Firstly I thank Paul himself, for his time, his words and his personal go-ahead to write this book.

Many people at his company, MPL, have helped to bring the book about, but especially Lisa Power. My thanks as well to their photographic coordinator Eithne Staunton.

Along the way I was given great assistance by Geoff Baker, Stuart Bell, Tony Brainsby, Bernard Doherty, Caroline Grimshaw, John Hammel, Roger Huggett, Lilian Marshall, Barry Miles, Richard Ogden, Scott Rodger and Phil Sutcliffe. The same goes for all of Paul's band members down the years – not least Linda McCartney. Several interviews were organised by these magazines: *NME*, *Q*, *MOJO* and *The Word*. Various editors deserve thanks, including Mark Ellen, David Hepworth and Phil Alexander.

To that distinguished list let me add the photographer Brassaï, from whose book *Conversations with Picasso* I pinched the title; Stephen Bayley for suggesting Pete Hamill's *Why Sinatra Matters* as my starting point; and the late Robert Sandall, who said, 'You must write this'.

Finally, for all their encouragement and guidance: my wife Una; my agent Ros Edwards at Edwards Fuglewicz; and, at Hodder & Stoughton, my editors Hannah Black and Briony Gowlett.

The books I found most useful in my research were these: Mark Lewisohn: *The Beatles, All These Years, Vol. 1, Tune In*, Little, Brown, 2013; Ian MacDonald: *Revolution in the Head*, Fourth

Estate, 1994; Paul McCartney: *Each One Believing*, Chronicle, 2004; Barry Miles: *Many Years From Now*, Secker & Warburg, 1997; Ian Peel: *The Unknown Paul McCartney*, Reynolds & Hearn, 2002; Luca Perasi: *Paul McCartney Recording Sessions* 1969–2013, L.I.L.Y., 2013.

Index

Abbey Road (Beatles) xi, 73, 81, 207
Abbey Road studio 25, 58, 114, 283
All Things Must Pass (Harrison) 98–9
'And I Love Her' (McCartney/Beatles) 327
Anders, Allison 244
Anderson, Rusty 257, 278
animal rights 244, 316
'Another Day' (McCartney) 93, 211
'Another Girl' (McCartney/Beatles) 328
Anthology (Beatles) 6–7, 39, 130, 171, 174–81
  film 171–2, 174
Antonioni, Michelangelo 65
'Anyway' (McCartney) 207–8
Apple Corps 73, 76, 85–6, 87, 173, 183, 189, 306
Applejacks 188
Armstrong, Louis 216
'Arrow Through Me' (McCartney) 121, 328
Asher, Jane 62–3, 188
Asher, Peter 62, 188
Aspinall, Neil 20, 171, 172, 173
Astaire, Fred 211
'At the Mercy' (McCartney) 208–9
avant-guarde 62, 63–6, 70, 132, 225, 297

'Baby's Request' (McCartney) 190–91
'Back Seat of My Car, The' (McCartney) 96, 98, 307, 328
Back to the Egg (McCartney/Wings) 100, 121–2, 123, 132, 191, 292, 300, 314
Badfinger 189
Baker, Geoff 215
'Ballad of John and Yoko' (Lennon/McCartney) 74, 159
Band on the Run (McCartney/Wings) 98, 108–14, 206, 207, 299–300
Barrow, Tony 20
BBC 40–41
Beatles
  accents 8
  in America 42, 53–5, 92
  and art 57–8, 61–2, 63
  Beatlemania 43, 49–50, 115, 295
  commercial instinct 206
  and democracy 120
  disbanding 5, 73–83, 86–8
  dress 229, 230–34
  fame 21, 43, 49–50, 92, 115, 162, 227
  haircuts 20, 35, 139, 234
  invention of the pop video 138–45
  lifestyle 45–9, 63–4
  Liverpool and the birth of *see* Liverpool
  McCartney's badgering 287–8
  move to London 24
  pop perfection xii–xiii
  and the press 41, 71–2, 87–8
  and rock culture xiii, 57–8, 61–2
  start of 26–42
  success in early Sixties 188

Beatles, The (US cartoon series) 295–7
Beatles For Sale 56
Berio, Luciano 66
Berry, Chuck 131, 149
Best, Pete 29, 35, 39
'Big Boys Bickering' (McCartney) 244
Bill Hayley & His Comets 18
'Bip Bop' (McCartney/Wings) xv, 102, 302
'Bison' (McCartney/Youth) 132
Black, Cilla 188–9
Black Dyke Mills Band 189
'Black Jacket' (McCartney) 307
'Blackbird' (McCartney) 209, 328
Blackbird Singing (McCartney) 160, 307
Blake, Peter 69, 133
Bonzo Dog Doo-Dah Band 189–90
Boone, Pat 14
Bowie, David 104, 190, 224, 249
Boyd, Patti 39
Brambell, Wilfrid 141
Bramwell, Tony 20
Brando, Marlon 67, 68
Bream, Julian 149
Britton, Geoff 114, 115
'Broadcast, The' (McCartney/Wings) 121–2, 300–301
Brodax, Al 296
Brown, Peter 20
Burroughs, William 63

'Can't Buy Me Love' (McCartney/ Beatles) 74, 328
Cardew, Cornelius 65
'Carnival of Light' (McCartney) 64
Cash, Johnny 190
Cassidy, Eva 215
'Catcall' (McCartney) 191
Cavendish, Leslie 235
'Celebration' (McCartney) 328
Chamberlain, Dean 234
Chaos and Creation in the Backyard (McCartney) 135, 207–10, 279, 282
Chaplin, Charlie 210–11
charity 222
Charles, Ray 19, 215
'Cheek to Cheek' (Berlin/Astaire) 213
Choba B CCCP (McCartney) 129
'City Park' (McCartney) 307
Clarke, Stanley 128
Cliff Bennett and the Rebel Rousers 188
'Close Your Eyes' (Petkere) 27
Cole, Nat 'King' 215–16, 280–81, 323
'Come Together' (Lennon) 183–4, 280
'Coming Up' (McCartney) 124, 126, 145, 146, 163–4, 259
'Cook of the House' (McCartney/ Wings) 316
Cooper, Alice 251
Cooper, Tommy 44
Cornell, Joseph 155
Costello, Elvis 129–30, 174, 185, 186–8, 301
Coury, Al 299–300
Cox, Maureen 39
'Cracking Up' (Diddley) 32

Dale, Jim 28
Daumier's Law (film) 156
Davis, Carl 151, 152
'Day in the Life, A' (Lennon/ McCartney) 68, 159, 207
'Day Tripper' (Lennon/McCartney) 74
'Daytime Nighttime Suffering' (McCartney) 244
de Kooning, Willem 203
'Dear Boy' (McCartney) 97, 307
'Dear Friend' (McCartney) 103, 160, 328
Delaney, Paddy 37
Dickens, Charles 321–2
'Distractions' (McCartney) 287
Dodd, Ken 44, 139
Domino, Fats 29, 30
Donegan, Lonnie 19, 27

Donovan 59–60
Doran, Terry 20
Double Fantasy (Lennon) 163–4
dress 229, 230–34, 235
'Drive My Car' (McCartney/Beatles) 199–200
Driving Rain (McCartney) 134, 256–7, 277–8
drugs 59, 60
Dudgeon, Gus 190
Durband, Alan 23
Dylan, Bob 58, 59, 61–2, 91, 103–4, 259

Each One Believing: On Stage, Off Stage, and Backstage 134
'Early Days' (McCartney) 136, 161
Eastman, Lee 74
Eastman, Linda *see* McCartney, Linda, née Eastman
Eavis, Michael 240
'Ebony and Ivory' (McCartney/Wonder) 128, 145, 193, 292
Ecce Cor Meum (McCartney) 136, 155, 291
Edmunds, Dave 129
'Eleanor Rigby' (McCartney/Beatles) 59, 61, 150, 211
Electric Arguments (McCartney/Youth) 133
Electronic Sound (Harrison) 64
Elizabeth II xii, 6
Ellington, Duke 216
Emerick, Geoff 110, 128, 131
EMI 25, 68, 79, 108, 154
Parlophone 26, 39
Eminem 245
'End of the End, The' (McCartney) 135
English, Joe 115, 117
'English Tea' (McCartney) 209
Eno, Brian 201
Epstein, Brian 20, 26, 38, 51–2, 72, 141, 188, 206, 230–31, 323
Epworth, Paul 136
Evans, Mal 20
'Ever Present Past' (McCartney) 135
'Every Night' (McCartney) 83, 84, 306
'Excerpt from a Teenage Opera' (West) 207
Exi's 35

Family Way, The (soundtrack) 22, 150–51
'Feet in the Clouds' (McCartney) 135
feminism 244
'Fields of Gold' (Sting) 215
Fireman 130, 131–3, 136, 300
'First Stone, The' (McCartney) 243
'Fixing a Hole' (McCartney/Beatles) 270
Flaming Pie (McCartney) 130–31
Flowers in the Dirt (McCartney) 130, 186, 256, 292, 301–2, 322
'Fluid' (McCartney/Youth) 132
'Follow Me' (McCartney) 329
food 47
'Footprints' (McCartney) 211
Frame, Peter 175
Fraser, Robert 63, 65, 66, 69–70
'Free as a Bird' (Beatles) 171, 176, 179
Freed, Alan 316
'Freedom' (McCartney) 245–7
Freeman, Robert 235–6
'From Me to You' (Lennon/McCartney) 41

Gallagher, Noel 175
Garcia, Jerry 253
Gaye, Marvin 215
Geldof, Bob 273
Gershwin, George and Ira 214
'Get Back' (McCartney/Beatles) 10, 261, 329
Gilmour, David 280
Ginsberg, Alan 65, 190
'Girl is Mine, The' (McCartney/Jackson) 128, 192
'Girlfriend' (McCartney) 118, 191
'Give Ireland Back to the Irish' (McCartney/Wings) 22, 100, 106, 237

Give My Regards to Broad Street (McCartney) 128–9, 138
film 292, 298–9
'Glass Onion' (Lennon/McCartney) 162
Glastonbury 239, 240
Glover, Martin (Youth) 131–3
Godrich, Nigel 135, 279
'Golden Slumbers' (McCartney/Beatles) 329
Goldmann, Peter 144
'Good Day Sunshine' (McCartney/Beatles) 55
Goodman, Benny 184
'Goodnight Princess' (McCartney) 129, 329
Gorcey, Leo 68
Gorman, John 63
'Got to Get You into my Life' (McCartney/Beatles) 188, 329
Grateful Dead 253, 290
Guercio, Jim 96
Gustafson, Johnny 37

Haley, Bill 18
Hall, Huntz 68
Hamburg 34–6, 39, 284
Hammel, John 144, 267
Hard Day's Night, A (Beatles album) 56
Hard Day's Night, A (film) 39, 45, 139–43
'Hard Day's Night, A' (Lennon/McCartney) 159
Harrison, George 24, 29, 35, 38, 39, 64, 79–80, 98–9, 173–4, 177, 179, 217, 225, 248, 284, 303
death 181
memorial concert 257
'Havana Moon' (Berry) 32
'Helen Wheels' (McCartney/Wings) 110
'Hello, Goodbye' (McCartney/Beatles) 73–4, 145, 259
Help! (Beatles) 56, 144
'Helter Skelter' (McCartney) 187, 250
Henderson, Dickie 44
Hendrix, Jimi 66–7
Henri, Adrian 63
'Her Spirit' (McCartney) 307
'Here, There and Everywhere' (McCartney/Beatles) 212, 213, 329
'Here Today' (McCartney) 160, 329
'Hey Jude' (McCartney/Beatles) xv, 62, 78, 145, 162, 224, 303, 330
High Park Farm, Scotland 287
'Highway' (McCartney/Youth) 133
'Hiroshima Sky Is Always Blue' (McCartney/Ono) 190
Hoffman, Dustin 271
Holley, Steve 121
Holly, Buddy 33
'Home (When Shadows Fall)' (McCartney) 26
'Honey Hush' (McCartney) 330
'Hope for the Future' (McCartney) 156
Hopkin, Mary 189
Horn, Trevor 302–3
'Hosanna' (McCartney) 330
'How Do You Sleep?' (Lennon) 93, 159
Howerd, Frankie 44
'Human' theme' (McCartney) 330
Hurrell, George 129
Hurt, John 269
Hussey, Olivia 138, 139, 181–2

'I Am the Walrus' (Lennon/Beatles) 9, 64, 151, 162, 224, 295
'I Feel Fine' (Lennon/Beatles) 74
'I Owe it All to You' (McCartney) 307
'I Saw Her Standing There' (McCartney/Beatles) 39–40, 166, 321–2, 330
'I Wanna Be Your Man' (Beatles/Rolling Stones) 188
'I Want to Hold Your Hand' (Lennon/McCartney) 41, 62
'I Will' (McCartney/Beatles) 331
'If You Gotta Make a Fool of Somebody' (Ray) 32

'I'll Be Back' (Beatles) 178
'I'll be Home' (Boone) 14
'I'll Follow the Sun' (McCartney/ Beatles) 261, 330
'I'm Down' (McCartney) 64, 250, 264–5
Innes, Neil 190
International Times 63
Iolas, Alexandre 66
'It's Not True' (McCartney) 307
'I've Had Enough' (McCartney) 243

Jackson, Michael 118, 128, 146, 185, 191–2, 210, 249, 253, 309
Jagger, Mick 247
Japanese Jailbird 125
jazz 15, 16, 17, 27, 36–7, 216
Jelly Babies 48–9
'Jenny Wren' (McCartney) 198, 209
'Jerk of All Jerks' (McCartney) 160
Jimmy Mac's Jazz Band 15, 16, 17
John, Elton 166, 190, 245, 309
Johns, Ethan 136
Jones, Brian 61, 65
Jones, Quincey 118
Juber, Laurence 121
'Julia' (Lennon) 324

Kahne, David 134, 135, 277
Kerr, Roy 133
King and I, The 323
Kinks 45
Kirchherr, Astrid 35
Kisses on the Bottom (McCartney) 17, 135–6, 191, 212–13, 226, 280–81
Klein, Allen 73, 74, 76, 82, 88–9, 93
'Kreen-Akrore' (McCartney) 85, 306
Kuti, Fela 112

Laboriel, Abe Jnr 257, 278
'Lady Madonna' (McCartney/Beatles) 74
Lagos 108–9, 112–13
Laine, Denny 100, 101–2
Leary, Timothy 281
Led Zeppelin 104
Lee, Peggy 32
Lennon, Cynthia 39, 322
Lennon, John 23, 35, 38, 50–51, 63, 67, 221–2, 249, 315, 322
 abrasiveness 5
 avant-guarde 63, 66
 'bigger than Jesus' quip 92, 162
 marriage 39
 move to New York 92
 murder 5, 128, 165
 partnership with McCartney 10, 61, 64, 80–81, 158–68, 204, 206–7, 288
 post-Beatles 92–3, 96, 118
 and the Quarrymen 29
Lennon, Julia 324
Lennon, Julian 39
Lester, Dick 140, 141
'Let 'Em In' (McCartney) 331
Let It Be . . . Naked (Beatles) 181–2
Let It Be (album) 74, 78, 81, 83, 85, 252
Let It Be (film) 36, 74, 78–81, 252, 285
'Let It Be'(McCartney) 50–51, 204, 243, 260, 274
'Let Me Roll It' (McCartney) 331
'Letting Go' (Wings) 115
Lewis, Jerry Lee 29, 32, 33
Lewisohn, Mark 10
'The Light Comes from Within' (Linda McCartney) 317–18
Lindsay-Hogg, Michael 78, 144
LIPA (Liverpool Institute for Performing Arts) 23–4
'Listen to what the Man Said' (McCartney/Wings) 114
Litchfield, David 114
'With a Little Luck' (McCartney/ Wings) 211, 320
Little Richard 29, 30, 250
'Little White Lies' (Donaldson) 27
'Little Willow' (McCartney) 131
Live Aid 204, 237, 248, 272–4
'Live and Let Die' (McCartney) 100, 107, 113–14, 133, 207, 331

Liverpool 13–25, 29, 39, 123, 152, 165–6, 225, 230, 256, 310, 315, 326–7
 avant-guarde 63
 Cavern club 24, 36–8, 256
 LIPA 23–4
 Walker Art Gallery 291
Liverpool Oratorio (McCartney) 130, 151–4
Liverpool Sound Collage (McCartney) 22, 133
Lockwood, Sir Joseph 68
'London Town' (McCartney) 146, 331
London Town (McCartney/Wings) 118, 191, 300
London Undersound (Sawhney/McCartney) 219
'Lonely Road' (McCartney) 134, 202
'Long and Winding Road' (McCartney/Beatles) 331–2
'Long Haired Lady' (McCartney) 97, 98, 133, 307
'Long Tall Sally' (McCartney/Beatles) 332
'Looking for Changes' (McCartney) 244
'Love Me Do' (Lennon/McCartney) 41
'Love Me Tender' (Presley) 30, 214
'Lovely Linda, The' (McCartney) 154, 306
'From a Lover to a Friend' (McCartney) 134, 200–202
Lynch, Kenny 113
Lynne, Jeff 131, 178

MacMillan, Keith 145–6, 193
Madonna 227, 254
'Maggie Mae' (Beatles) 51, 83
'Magic' (McCartney) 134, 305–6
Magic Christian, The (film) 189
Magical Mystery Tour (film) 72, 138, 189, 224, 292, 294–5, 299
Magritte, René 63, 65, 66, 199
Maharishi Mahesh Yogi 72
'Man, The' (McCartney/Jackson) 128, 192
'Man We Was Lonely' (McCartney) 84, 306
Margary, Harold and Dierdre 121–2
Martin, George 39, 128, 129, 131, 135, 150, 172, 206, 217–18, 280, 281, 283
Martin, Giles 136
Marvin, Hank 122
'Mary Had Lamb' (McCartney/Wings) 100, 106
Matthew, Brian 41
'Maxwell's Silver Hammer' (McCartney/Beatles) 209–10, 332
'Maybe I'm Amazed' (McCartney) 85, 90, 154, 260, 306, 332
Mayles, Albert 78
Mayles, David 78
McCartney, Beatrice (daughter) 7
McCartney, Heather (daughter) 84, 250
McCartney, Jack (uncle) 16
McCartney, James (son) 117, 131, 318
McCartney, Jim (father) 13, 15–16, 17, 20, 276
McCartney, Linda, née Eastman 73, 83, 84, 85, 92, 128, 131, 203–4, 256, 269, 290, 305–18
 in America 93–5, 308–9
 death 155
 and The Fireman 132
 in Nigeria 108–13
 photos 4–5
 and Wings *see* Wings
McCartney, Mary (daughter) 84, 317
McCartney, Mary (mother) 13, 238–9
McCartney, Mike (brother) 8, 13, 16, 24, 31, 63, 189, 286
McCartney, Paul
 accent 8
 in America 42, 53–5, 92–5, 115, 179–80, 245–7, 264, 302, 308–9
 and the audience 267–8, 271
 avant-guarde 62, 63–6, 70, 132, 225, 297

as bass player 4, 34–6, 37, 183–4, 217, 239–40, 270, 284
beliefs and ideals 237–9, 240–48
birth xiii, 13
and British light music 148–57
as a businessman 228
and charity 222
childhood and upbringing xiii, 13–17, 148–9, 152, 213, 225, 286
children's education 222–3
commercial instinct 254, 258
diplomatic skills 5
Do It Now ethos 286–91
education 148
fallibility 292–304
fatalism 219–20
and feminism 244
in The Fireman 130, 131–3, 136, 300
at High Park Farm, Scotland 287
interview tolerance, control, characteristics and accuracy 7–11
'Japanese episode' 124–5, 256
love of touring 255–65
on making music 275–8, 279–85
marriage to Linda Eastman 73, 305–18 *see also* McCartney, Linda, née Eastman
marriage to Heather Mills 134
marriage to Nancy Shevell 134, 136
and money 18, 28, 35, 104, 106, 179–80, 221–2
musical instruments and equipment 31–2, 34, 35–6, 284
natural musical ability 31
nerves 52, 269, 281
in Nigeria 108–13, 206
and 9/11 terrorist attack 245–7
as optimist 289–90
and the ordinary 222–4, 228–9
painting 290, 291
and paparazzi 219
partnership with Lennon 10, 61, 64, 80–81, 158–68, 204, 206–7, 288
as 'Paul Ramon' 77, 249
popularly seen only as a Beatle xiv–xv
the 'real' McCartney 217–29
response to Lennon's murder 5, 128
rural life 91
songs that influenced 214–16
on songwriting 196–205, 206–12, 288–9
style and fashion 231–6
vegetarianism 244
versatility 212
and Wings *see* Wings
world tours 130, 218, 227, 252, 256, 261–4, 266–8
McCartney, Stella (daughter) 84
McCartney (album) 81–2, 83–4, 86, 87, 90, 125, 194, 275, 306
McCartney II 125, 275–6, 282–3, 301
McCartney Years, The 317
McCracken, Hugh 94, 101
McCullough, Henry 104, 107, 109, 119, 120
McCullough, Jimmy 114, 117, 119–20
McFall, Ray 37
McGough, Roger 63
McIntosh, Robbie 256
Melville, Joseph 307
Memory Almost Full (McCartney) 135
Mighty Like a Rose (Costello) 187
Miles, Barry 62–3, 65, 204
Milk and Honey (Lennon) 164
Mill (Hog Hill) 5
Miller, Steve 77, 131
Millings, Dougie 231, 233
Mills, Heather 134
Mitchell, Adrian 156
MOJO 158
'Momma Miss America' (McCartney) 83, 306
money 18, 28, 35, 104, 106, 179–80, 221–2

'Monkberry Moon Delight' (McCartney) 97
Montery Pop Festival 66–7
Moon, Keith 250, 251, 290
Morrison, George Ivan ('Van) 91
'Motor of Love' (McCartney) 238
MPL 4–5, 10, 155, 228, 291
'Mr Bellamy' (McCartney) 211
'Mull of Kintyre' (McCartney/ Denny) xiv, 117–18, 250, 252, 292, 300
'Mumbo' (McCartney/Wings) 133, 201
'My Carnival' (McCartney/Wings) 114–15
'My Love' (McCartney) 107, 154, 252, 307
'My Valentine' (McCartney) 136
'On My Way to Work' (McCartney) 332

'New' (McCartney) 136–7
New (McCartney) 136–7, 161
Newson, Richard 252
Nigeria 108–13, 206
NME (*New Musical Express*) 5, 121, 122
  first poll-winners' concert 52
'No More Lonely Nights' (McCartney) 129, 280, 298
'Nothing Too Much Just Out of Sight' (McCartney/Youth) 133
Nowhere Boy (film) 27
Nutter, Tommy 231

'Ob-La-Di Ob-La-Da' (McCartney/ Beatles) 332
Ocean's Kingdom (McCartney) 155, 157
Off the Ground (McCartney) 130, 132, 187, 291
Off the Wall (Jackson) 118, 191
'Old Siam, Sir' (McCartney) 121, 332
One Hand Clapping (film) 114
'One of These Days' (McCartney) 287
'Only Our Hearts' (McCartney) 333
Ono, Yoko 63, 73, 96, 171, 176, 181–2, 190, 249, 315
'Oo You' (McCartney) 133
Oobu Joobu (radio series) 130, 290
  Owen, Alun 140

Padgham, Hugh 129
Page, Jimmy 115
'Palo Verde' (McCartney/Youth) 132
paparazzi 219
'Paperback Writer' (McCartney/ Beatles) 58, 60, 78
Parkinson, Michael 113
Parlophone 26, 39
Paul McCartney in Red Square 218
'Penina' (McCartney) 191
'Penny Lane' (McCartney/Beatles) xv, 22, 58, 61, 144, 159
Perkins, Carl 128
Perry, Lee 190, 316
Phillips, John 67
Picasso, Pablo xii, xiii, 293
Pipes of Peace (McCartney) 128, 145, 192
'Please Please Me' (Lennon/ McCartney) 41, 74, 219, 280
Porter, Cole 214
Postcard (McCartney/Hopkins) 189
Presley, Elvis 11, 29, 30, 33, 131, 182–3, 187, 212, 214, 215, 245
Press to Play (McCartney) 129, 186, 282
Preston, Billy 74
'Pretty Vacant' (Sex Pistols) 251
'Promise to You Girl', (McCartney) 248
'P.S. I Love You' (McCartney/Beatles) 333
punk 49, 117, 121, 243, 249–52, 313, 319, 334
'Put It There' (McCartney) 20, 199

Q magazine 175
Quarrymen xii, 28–9

'Rain' (Lennon/Beatles) 60, 78
Ram (McCartney) 95–8, 159, 207, 307, 308–9
Ramone, Phil 129
Ramones 249
Ray, Brian 257, 278–9
'Real Love' (Beatles) 171, 177–8, 180–81
Red Rose Speedway (McCartney/Wings) 106–7
religion 237–9, 241
Return to Pepperland 129
'Revolution 9' (Lennon/Beatles) 64, 78
Revolver (Beatles) 58, 60, 188
Rich, Buddy 284
Richard, Cliff 212
Richards, Keith 65
'Riding to Vanity Fair' (McCartney) 210, 282
Rihanna 191
Rimmer, Freddy 15
Riviera, Jake 231
rock and roll
  American 27, 29–30
  and art 57–8, 61–2
  Beatles and rock culture xiii, 57–8
  early development 212
  movies saved by the Beatles 138–45
  punk rock *see* punk
  and rock culture 61–2
Rock and Roll Hall of Fame 172–4
'Rock and Roll Music' (Berry) 149
'Rock Around the Clock' (Bill Hayley & His Comets) 18
'Rock Island Line' (Donegan) 27
'Rock Show' (McCartney/Wings) 115
'Rockestra Theme' (McCartney/Wings) 122
'Rocky Racoon' (McCartney/Beatles) 333
Rolling Stones 103–4, 188, 253, 258
Ronson, Mark 136
Royal Command Performance, Prince of Wales Theatre 52–3
Royal Court Theatre, Liverpool 123
Rubber Soul (Beatles) 56, 58
Run Devil Run (McCartney) 131, 155, 256
Rupert and the Frog Song (film) 127–8
Rushes (McCartney/Youth) 131–3
Russell, Bertrand 61
Rutles 190

Saturday Club 40–41
Sawhney, Nitin 219
'Say Say Say' (McCartney/Jackson) 128, 146, 191–2
Scaffold 63, 189
'Scared' (McCartney) 136
Schlesinger, John 105
Scotch 46, 59, 62
Scott, Terry 45
'Seaside Woman' (Linda McCartney) 316
'Secret Friend' (McCartney) 293
Seiwell, Denny 93, 101, 109
Sellers, Peter 8, 106, 140
sex 39
Sexton, Edward 231
Sgt. Pepper's Lonely Hearts Club Band (Beatles) 58, 60, 61, 66, 67–72, 224
Shadows 118–19
'Shallow Grave' (Costello) 187
'She Loves You' (Lennon/McCartney) 41
Shea Stadium 53–5
'She's a Woman' (McCartney/Beatles) 333
'She's Leaving Home' (McCartney/Beatles) 333
Shevell, Nancy 134, 136
'Silly Love Songs' (McCartney) 319–20, 324–5
Simons, Judith 71
Sinatra, Frank 185, 194–5, 215, 280, 323–4
'Sing the Changes' (McCartney/Youth) 133, 333
skiffle 27, 28, 29

Small Faces 117
Smash Hits 91
'Smile' (Chaplin) 210–11
Smith, Walter 230
smoking 46–7
'Somedays' (McCartney) 130, 334
'Something' (Harrison/Beatles) 74
'Something' (McCartney) 257
'Somewhere Over the Rainbow' (Cassidy) 215
'Song We Were Singing, The' (McCartney) 130
Spector, Phil 74, 77–8, 249
Spies Like Us (film) 156
Spike (Costello) 187
Spinetti, Victor 146
Spinozza, Dave 93, 94
'Spiral' (McCartney) 154, 334
Springsteen, Bruce 324–5
Standing Stone symphony (McCartney) 22, 154, 157
Stanshall, Viv 190, 290
'Stardust' (Carmichael) 323
Starr, Ringo 11, 24, 39, 45–7, 98, 99, 128, 129, 131, 176–7, 258, 326
acting 140–41, 144
Steele, Tommy 212
'Step Inside Love' (McCartney/Black) 189
Stewart, Eric 128, 129, 186
Stewart, Rod 135
Strawberries Oceans Ships Forest (McCartney/Youth) 132, 300
'Strawberry Fields Forever' (Lennon/Beatles) 22, 61, 144, 159, 166, 231
Stuart, Hamish 243, 256, 277
'Sugar Time' (Linda McCartney) 316
'Suicide' (McCartney) 194–5
Super Furry Animals 132–3
Sutcliffe, Stuart 29, 34–5, 217

tailors 230–31
Taylor, Alistair 20
Taylor, Derek 20, 172
'Teddy Boy' (McCartney) 85, 211, 306
'Temporary Secretary' (McCartney) 226, 283
10cc 186
terrorist attack, 9/11 245–7
'That Day is Done' (McCartney) 302
'That Was Me' (McCartney) 135, 227
'That'll Be The Day' (Holly) 33
'Things We Said Today' (McCartney/Beatles) 334
'Thingummybob' (McCartney) 189
'This One' (video) 234
'Those Were the Days' (McCartney/Hopkins) 189
Thriller (Jackson) 128, 192
Thrillington (McCartney) 252
'Through Our Love' (McCartney) 334
Thunderclap Newman 114
'Ticket to Ride' (Lennon/Beatles) 74
'Till There Was You' (Lee) 32
Tokyo, McCartney's 'Japanese episode' 124–5, 256
'Tomorrow Never Knows' (Beatles) 64, 281, 283
'Too Much Rain' (McCartney) 210
Townshend, Pete 122, 247
Traffic 91
'Treat Her Gently / Lonely Old People' (McCartney) 211, 334
Troggs 81, 119
'Try Not to Cry' (McCartney) 131
Tug of War (McCartney) 127–8, 160, 192
'Twenty Flight Rock' (Cochran, McCartney rendition) 29, 31
Twickenham Studios 79
Twin Freaks (McCartney/Kerr) 133
'Twist and Shout' (Lennon) 53
'Two of Us' (McCartney/Beatles) 307
Two Virgins (Lennon) 64

'Uncle Albert/Admiral Halsey' (McCartney) 97

United States of America 42, 53–5, 92–5, 115, 264, 302, 308–9
9/11 terrorist attack 245–7
cartoon series, *The Beatles* 295–7

Vaughan, Ivan 28, 290–91
Venus and Mars (McCartney/Wings) 114–15, 204, 211
'Very Thought of You, The' (Noble) 323
Vincent, Gene 29, 280
'Vintage Clothes' (McCartney) 135
Vollmer, Jürgen 35

Warhol, Andy 65
'Warm and Beautiful' (McCartney) 334
'Watercolour Guitars' (McCartney/Youth) 132
'Waterfalls' (McCartney) 301
'We All Stand Together' (McCartney) 127–8, 334
'We Got Married' (McCartney) 322–3
Weller, Paul 175
West, Kanye 92, 191
West, Keith 207
Weston-super-Mare 44–5
'What'd I Say' (Charles) 19
'What's That You're Doing?' (McCartney/Wonder) 128
'When I Fall in Love' (Cole) 323
'White Album, The' (*The Beatles*) 73
Whitten, Chris 256
'Whole Lotta Shakin' (Lewis) 32
Wickens, Paul 'Wix' 256, 257, 278
Wide Prairie (Linda and Paul McCartney) 316, 317–18
Wild Life (McCartney/Wings) 102–3, 302–4
Williams, Allan 123
Williams, Robbie 135
Wilson, Brian 190
'Winedark Open Sea' (McCartney) 335
Wings 100–103, 104–7, 108–16, 117–26, 128, 253–4, 255–6, 259, 281–2, 310–15, 316, 319–20
Wings at the Speed of Sound 115, 117
Wings Over America 115
Wingspan: Hits and History (McCartney) 309–10
Wonder, Stevie 128, 185, 192–3, 283
'Wonderful Christmastime' (McCartney) 123
Wonderwall Music (Harrison) 64
Wooler, Bob 37
Working Classical (McCartney) 154–5, 157
With the Beatles 56

Yellow Submarine (film) 292, 295–7
'Yellow Submarine'(Starr) 60–61
'Yesterday' (McCartney/Beatles) 64, 150, 200, 212, 215, 241, 261, 335
'You Never Give Me your Money' (McCartney/Beatles) 203, 306–7
'You Win Again' (Lewis) 32
'Within You Without You' (Harrison/Beatles) 224, 303
Youth (Martin Glover) 131–3
'You've Got to Hide Your Love Away' (Lennon) 62

Zec, Donald 6
Zeffirelli, Franco 138–9

List of Illustrations

Page 1
© Keystone Pictures USA / Alamy
© Trinity Mirror / Mirrorpix / Alamy

Page 2
© Pierluigi Praturlon/Rex

Page 3
© Mirrorpix
© PA / PA Archive/Press Association Images

Page 4
© AP/Press Association Images
© akg-images / picture-alliance

Page 5
© Keystone Pictures USA / Alamy
© Ted West & Roger Jackson/Central Press/Getty Images

Page 6
© 1967 Paul McCartney/Photographer: Linda McCartney
© Bridgeman Images

Page 7
© AF archive / Alamy
© 1968 Paul McCartney/Photographer: Linda McCartney

Page 8
© Trinity Mirror / Mirrorpix / Alamy
© 1968 Paul McCartney/Photographer: Linda McCartney

Page 9
© 1970 Paul McCartney/Photographer: Linda McCartney
© 1972 MPL Communications Ltd

Page 10
© akg-images / Album
© AP/Press Association Images

Page 11
© 1976 MPL Communications Ltd/Photographer: Robert Ellis

Page 12
© 1976 MPL Communications Ltd/Photographer: Clive Arrowsmith

Page 13
© Richard Young/Rex
© Kevin Mazur/WireImage for Rock and Roll Hall of Fame/Getty Images

Page 14
© 1995 Paul McCartney/Photographer: Linda McCartney

Page 15
© 2007 MPL Communications Ltd/Photographer: Bill Bernstein
© 2008 MPL Communications Ltd/Photographer: Ruth Ward

Page 16
© 2014 MPL Communications Ltd/Photographer: MJ Kim
© 2014 MPL Communications Ltd/Photographer: MJ Kim